Sexual Offending in Ireland

Laws, Procedures and Punishment

SEXUAL OFFENDING IN IRELAND

LAWS, PROCEDURES AND PUNISHMENT

Dr SUSAN LEAHY

and

Dr MARGARET FITZGERALD O'REILLY

CLARUS
PRESS

Published by
Clarus Press Ltd,
Griffith Campus,
South Circular Road,
Dublin 8.
www.claruspress.ie

Typeset by
Gough Typesetting Services
Dublin

Printed by
SprintPrint Ltd
Dublin

ISBN
978-1-905536-93-1

A catalogue record for this book is available from the British Library

FOREWORD

It is very welcome to have a book that sets out the substantive legislation on sexual offences in Ireland in a very clear, cohesive, accessible manner while at the same time staying true to an academic rigour that is flawless.

From the first chapter entitled *Rape*, through to the last chapter entitled *Post-Release Provisions*, Leahy and Fitzgerald O'Reilly take us on a journey that is filled with the relevant procedural rules relating to sexual offences and the laws and processes which apply to the punishment of sex offenders in Ireland. While each chapter can be read as a stand alone in its own right, there is a thread that runs through the book, which bring it all together in an engaging and seamless manner. They comprehensively map the changes that pertain to each element of the sexual offences legislation over the years and present very interesting observations and thorough analyses throughout.

This book will hold great interest for those working in the Criminal Justice System, including An Garda Síochána, the Prosecution Services, Defence Lawyers, the Judiciary and the Court Services. It will also be of great support to those working with victims of crime. It will be an excellent teaching tool and should be included on all the reading lists for lawyers, barristers, social workers, psychologists and guardian ad litems.

I commend this book to anyone interested in the law on sexual offences in Ireland. You won't be disappointed!

Ellen O'Malley Dunlop.
Adjunct Professor of Law UL

PREFACE

This book provides an account of the laws, procedures and processes which govern the trial and punishment of sexual offences in Ireland. It is published at a significant juncture in the development of the law in this area. Until the recent enactment of the Criminal Law (Sexual Offences) Act 2017, the substantive and evidentiary rules relating to sexual offences had lain largely untouched since they were first legislated for in the Criminal Law (Rape) Act 1981 and the Criminal Law (Rape) (Amendment) Act 1990. Any reforms which were enacted emerged in a piecemeal or often reactionary way, for example, the enactment of the Criminal Law (Sexual Offences) Act 2006 to fill the lacuna created when Irish statutory rape laws were struck down as unconstitutional by the Supreme Court in *CC v Ireland*.[1] Reforms such as legislating for the protection of individuals with limited decision-making capacity from sexual abuse (Criminal Law (Sexual Offences) Act 1993) or the introduction of post-release supervision of sex offenders (Sex Offenders Act 2001) emerged on an individual basis, without significant consideration of their fit within the pre-existing rules prevailing in the area. Thus, the 2017 legislation, which touches upon all aspects of the law in this area, is a very welcome development.

The 2017 Act includes some important additions to the law, perhaps most notably, the introduction of a statutory definition of consent, a reform which was long-awaited and had been repeatedly called for by both legal commentators and victims' representatives groups such as Dublin Rape Crisis Centre and the Rape Crisis Network of Ireland. The inclusion of this definition brings Ireland in line with other common law jurisdictions such as England and Wales, Canada and Australian states such as New South Wales and Victoria, all of which have long-since introduced statutory definitions of consent. Other significant reforms in the legislation include: the regulation of the use of counselling records in sexual offence trials; a more modern regime for the protection of individuals with limited decision-making capacity from sexual abuse and exploitation; prohibiting self-representing defendant from personally cross-examining complainants, and; permitting the use of screens for victims when giving evidence.

However, although the legislation contains many long-awaited reforms, there are some significant omissions. For example, although a statutory definition of consent has been introduced, the honest belief in consent defence which

---

1 [2006] 4 IR 1.

exculpates a defendant who held an honest, even if unreasonable belief, in consent, remains unchanged. The government have referred this issue to the Law Reform Commission for consideration but it is regrettable that this defence was not reformed in tandem with the introduction of a definition of consent as this would have allowed for a more meaningful assessment of the interplay between these two aspects of the law. Moreover, given the pace of the legislative process, it is likely that the reform of honest belief defence will take some time and thus has the potential to detract from the benefits offered by the new definition of consent. The new legislation also fails to reconsider rules of evidence such as the regulation of the use of sexual history evidence and the corroboration warning, both of which are worthy of review. Throughout this book, omissions from the most recent reform effort are highlighted and options for future reform are discussed.

Given its publication so close to the enactment of the 2017 Act, the authors were in a position to offer a timely consideration of the recent reforms. However, an inevitable drawback of such an early overview is that the new laws are as yet untested and thus one can only theorise on the how they will be implemented or the effect which they will have. A full review of the effectiveness or otherwise of the new provisions must be reserved for future editions. However, although the authors cannot offer a definitive account of the impact of the new law, comparative research and reference to relevant academic viewpoints are relied upon throughout the discussion here to provide meaningful analysis of the recent changes and highlight avenues for further reform.

Another significant development which coincides with the publication of this text is the enactment of the Criminal Justice (Victims of Crime) Act 2017, which seeks to honour Ireland's commitments under the EU Victims' Directive (Directive 2012/29/EU). This legislation gives victims statutory rights to effective services such as information at all key stages of the criminal justice process and access to support measures such as accompaniment during Garda interviews and medical examinations. The availability of these services will help to ensure that victims of sexual violence do not suffer secondary victimisation at the hands of the criminal justice system. As the focus of this book is on legal rules, a full consideration of the impact of the victims of crime legislation is outside the scope of discussion here. However, the impact of the Act on extending the availability of the special measures available in the Criminal Evidence Act 1992 (e.g. the use of TV link) will be discussed in chapter 4. The victims of crime legislation provides that all victims must be assessed to ascertain whether they have 'special protection needs'. If they are found to have such needs, special measures may be made available to them. This extension of protection is very significant for sexual offence victims who typically find the process of testifying in court extremely traumatic. Indeed, many victims report that their experience in court was as damaging as the experience of sexual violence itself. Hopefully, the additional support measures available as a result of the Directive will lead to a significant improvement of sexual offence victims' experiences within the criminal justice system.

As a final note, it is worth mentioning that while this book focuses predominantly on legal rules, the authors have sought to remain true to the socio-legal orientation of their research. Where appropriate, the realities of sexual violence in Ireland (e.g. the impact of societal attitudes on the operation of the law and the statistics regarding the type of sexual crime which occurs) are highlighted to demonstrate that there is much more to the investigation, trial and punishment of these crimes than the 'law on the books'. The authors have at all times sought to ensure that the discussion here is both comprehensive and reflective. It is hoped that the text will be beneficial to all those criminal justice stakeholders who work in this area, as well as students seeking to learn more about this challenging and ever-evolving area of criminal offending.

Susan Leahy
Margaret Fitzgerald O'Reilly
12th February 2018

ACKNOWLEDGEMENTS

We would like to express our gratitude to a number of individuals who have contributed to the completion of this work.

We wish to thank our friends and colleagues in the School of Law and Centre for Crime, Justice & Victim Studies in the University of Limerick for their collegiality during the completion of this project. Working with such a vibrant group of researchers is a constant source of inspiration and motivation.

We particularly wish to acknowledge our Head of School, Professor Shane Kilcommins, who has mentored both of us since the beginning of our research careers as PhD candidates. His continued guidance, encouragement and friendship has been invaluable in the development of our research throughout our careers. We could not have asked for a better mentor.

We are grateful to Ellen O'Malley Dunlop, Adjunct Professor at the School of Law, for contributing the foreword for this text and for her friendship and willingness to share her depth of knowledge of this area with us.

Our thanks are also owed to Clarus Press, in particular to David McCartney for commissioning this work and for his patience and assistance in the completion of the manuscript and its preparation for publication.

Susan wishes to thank Professor Mary Donnelly, University College Cork, who co-supervised the PhD research which was used in some of the chapters in this book, and for her continued friendship and encouragement. Susan is also grateful to Noeline Blackwell, Shirley Scott and their colleagues at Dublin Rape Crisis Centre for sharing their knowledge and expertise and always supporting her research in this area. Finally, on a personal level, she wishes to thank her parents, Denis and Rita Leahy, for their consistent support and encouragement in this project and, indeed, all endeavours.

Margaret would like to thank her husband Seamas for all his love, support and encouragement, not just in the completion of this book but from the moment they met. She would also like to thank her mom Eileen, whose patience, love and guidance provide an eternal source of inspiration.

TABLE OF CONTENTS

PART THREE: SENTENCING AND PUNISHMENT

TABLES OF CASES

TABLES OF LEGISLATION

Rules of Court

European Legislation

Australia

Canada

England and Wales

Scotland

INTRODUCTION

Introduction

[0–01] This book offers a discussion and critique of the substantive and procedural rules relating to sexual offences and the laws and processes which apply to the punishment of sex offenders in Ireland. The need for a text which concentrates solely on sexual offences owes to the inherently complex nature of these crimes and the unique challenges posed in their effective investigation, trial and punishment. These difficulties are evidenced in the high rate of attrition and low conviction rates associated with this category of crime. There are a number of factors, legal and social, which contribute to the "justice gap" which is said to exist between reports of sexual offences and successful convictions.[1]

[0–02] There are three key stages at which attrition occurs in sexual offence cases. First, complainants themselves may withdraw from the process because they want to move on and forget the incident, are concerned about the trial process, or are dealing with the incident in another way such as counselling. In a study of files on 597 reported rapes received by the Director of Public Prosecutions from 2000 to 2004, Hanly et al found that 27 percent of complainants withdrew their complaint.[2] The second key point of attrition is when a decision to prosecute is being taken. The DPP may decide not to prosecute because, given the private context in which such offending occurs, there is often insufficient evidence to ground a conviction. Indeed, in Hanly et al's study of DPP files, it was found that the most common explanation given by the DPP for the decision not to prosecute was "lack

---

1 Of course, it must also be remembered that sexual offences have a significant "dark figure". The "dark figure" of crime is the true figure of crime, the amount of crime we would know about, if all the genuine crime was properly reported, properly recorded and properly counted: O'Mahony, *Crime and Punishment in Ireland* (Round Hall Press, Dublin, 1993), p 10. The *SAVI* Report found that 47 percent of those who disclosed sexual violence in the study reported that they had never previously discussed the abuse with others: McGee et al, *The SAVI Report: Sexual Abuse and Victimization in Ireland* (The Liffey Press, Dublin, 2002), p 121.

2 When cases in which no reason were excluded, the most frequent reason given for withdrawal was that the complainant wanted to "move on" or forget about the incident. 28.5 percent were concerned about the court appearance or the trial and nearly 6 percent claimed to be dealing with the rape in some other way, such as through counselling: Hanly, et al, *Rape & Justice in Ireland: A National Study of Survivor, Prosecutor and Court Responses to Rape* (The Liffey Press, Dublin, 2009), pp 243–248.

of evidence".[3] Decisions not to prosecute based on "lack of evidence" are also likely in cases involving historic sexual abuse where delay means that evidence may have been lost. Finally, even if the case gets to trial, the fact that many cases amount to a "swearing contest" between the complainant and the defendant may make it difficult for the prosecution to convince the jury beyond reasonable doubt that the defendant is guilty. This problem is particularly pronounced in rape trials. For example, in Hanly et al's study of rape files received by the Central Criminal Court from 2000 to 2005, the researchers found a "striking reluctance on the part of juries to convict on rape charges".[4] When not guilty verdicts and directed not guilty verdicts were combined, "almost two-thirds of juries acquitted the defendant".[5] Interestingly, Hanly et al found that "[j]uries that considered lesser and non-sexual offences were far more willing to convict; excluding cases in which verdicts were either not given or were unrecorded on the files, the conviction rate was 49 per cent".[6]

[0–03] Given the specific nature of sexual offences, it is unsurprising that special laws and procedures apply to these cases. This book emerges at an important stage in the development of Irish sexual offences law, with the recent passage of the Criminal Law (Sexual Offences) Act 2017, which is the first significant reform of the law in this area since the original legislation on this topic was enacted (i.e. the Criminal Law (Rape) Act 1981 and the Criminal Law (Rape)(Amendment) Act 1990). The Act includes a number of notable and long-awaited developments including the introduction of a statutory definition of consent, regulation of the disclosure of counselling records in sexual offence trials and the extension of special measures to aid complainants in giving evidence at trial (e.g. the introduction of the possibility of giving evidence from behind a screen). On a broader general level, the recent implementation of the Victims' Directive on 16 November 2015 has given rise to a number of specific protections and rights for victims of crime more generally which will, of course, also yield positive practical benefits for victims of sexual crime. The Directive and the Irish legislation which implements it (i.e. the Criminal Justice (Victims of Crime) Act 2017) will considerably expand victims' entitlements to protection, support and information during the criminal process, providing them with legally enforceable rights to aids such as court accompaniment, separate waiting areas in courtrooms and extending the availability of special

3 This explanation was relevant on its own or in combination with other factors in 42.6 percent of all cases. In 37 percent of cases, the complainant was deemed "not credible" or unreliable and in 27.8 percent of cases not pursued, there were inconsistencies in the complainant's statement: *ibid*, p 243.

4 *ibid*, 294. Hanly et al reviewed 173 rape case files which were received by the Central Criminal Court between 2000 and 2005.

5 *ibid*.

6 *ibid*, 295.

measures such as the giving of evidence by television link. Such protections will undoubtedly ease the passage of sexual offence victims through the criminal justice system. However, as will be seen here, while there have been significant advancements in this area in recent times, there are still a number of deficiencies in the current laws and procedures which will be highlighted in the discussion in this book.

Of course, effective responses to sexual offending require much more than legal solutions. The attrition rates and difficulties of proof in sexual offence trials are caused not just by legal deficiencies but also societal factors. Some such factors are incidental to the factual scenarios that surround this type of offending which typically occurs in private, with no witnesses, thus amounting to an "oath against oath" contest between the complainant and the defendant. Since the dictates of due process demand that any doubt must be resolved in favour of the defendant, it is inevitable that there will be a significant number of cases which result in acquittal. However, a more troublesome aspect of the social context in which sexual offending occurs is the impact of negative societal attitudes about sexual offences which inform societal, and necessarily the criminal justice system's, responses to allegations of sexual violence. The persistence of "rape myths" in society first identified by feminist theorists[7] in the latter decades of the 20th century is now a generally accepted aspect of the investigation and trial of sexual offences. Such myths include stereotypes regarding what constitutes a "real rape" (i.e. an attack by a stranger in a public place with significant attendant injury) or a "real victim" (i.e. an individual who has a "respectable lifestyle",[8] is not promiscuous and does not drink alcohol to excess or otherwise engage in "risky" behaviour[9]). **[0–04]**

Although these stereotypes are at odds with the realities of sexual offending, there is evidence of rape-myth acceptance within the Irish population. For example, in the *SAVI* study,[10] 37.9 percent of women and 42.3 percent of men thought that allegations of rape are often false.[11] Further, 18.3 percent of **[0–05]**

---

7 See: Brownmiller, *Against Our Will: Men, Women and Rape* (Fawcett Books, New York, 1975); Estrich, *Real Rape: How the Legal System Victimizes Women Who Say No* (Harvard University Press, Cambridge, Massachusetts, 1987); Lees, *Carnal Knowledge: Rape on Trial* (2nd ed, The Women's Press, London, 2002).

8 Adler, *Rape on Trial* (Routledge, London, 1987), pp 119–120.

9 Larcombe, "Falling Rape Conviction Rates: (Some) Feminist Aims and Measures for Rape Law" (2011) 19(1) *Feminist Legal Studies* 27, 37.

10 The objective of this report was to estimate the prevalence of various forms of sexual violence among Irish women and men across a lifespan from childhood through to adulthood. There was also some assessment of public perceptions and beliefs about sexual violence. The survey was conducted via anonymous telephone interviews with 3,000 randomly selected adults from the general population in Ireland.

11 McGee et al, *The SAVI Report: Sexual Abuse and Victimization in Ireland* (The Liffey Press, Dublin, 2002), p 158.

women and 23.8 percent of men believed that sexually experienced people are less traumatised by rape.[12] More recently, a 2008 attitude survey conducted by *The Irish Examiner* revealed notable levels of rape-myth acceptance in Irish society.[13] For instance, 23 percent of respondents believed woman was partially or totally responsible for rape if she previously had many sexual partners.[14] Thirty-three percent felt that a woman who had consumed alcohol and/or illegal drugs is partially responsible for rape, while 8 percent said she is totally at fault in such circumstances.[15] The persistence of these attitudes in society raise particular problems for victims of sexual violence whose complaints may be met with incredulity if they fail to conform to societal stereotypes of rape or if they fall short of the idealised victim. Indeed, mock jury studies in England and Wales have repeatedly shown that prejudicial attitudes about sexual offences negatively influence jurors' deliberations in rape trials. For example, a study conducted by Temkin & Krahé showed that jurors were more convinced that a defendant should be held liable and blamed the complainant less in stranger rapes than in rapes by acquaintances, and in particular, rapes by ex-partners.[16] A study carried out by Ellison and Munro also strongly suggested that claims of non-consensual sex that are not accompanied by evidence of physical force and attendant resistance are significantly less likely to be accredited as rape by jurors.[17] Jurors have also been found to be critical of complainants who were intoxicated at the time of an alleged incident of non-consensual sexual activity. A study by Finch and Munro found that women who consume alcohol in the presence of a male drinker will be perceived to be more sexually available than a non-drinking counterpart. Even in situations in which the complainant's intoxication was not wholly voluntary (i.e. where her drink was spiked with additional alcohol or the defendant coerced her into drinking greater quantities than she intended) the complainant was frequently viewed as being partially responsible.[18] Thus, though the emphasis in this book is on the legal, procedural and policy responses to sexual violence, it must be remembered that in the area of sexual offences, the law is only part of the

---

12 *ibid.*

13 In this study, 1002 adults were questioned about their attitudes and beliefs about rape: Ryan, "Belief: Our Blame Culture", *Irish Examiner*, 26 March 2008.

14 *ibid.*

15 *ibid.*

16 Temkin and Krahé, *Sexual Assault and the Justice Gap: A Question of Attitude?* (Hart Publishing, Oxford, 2008), p 120.

17 Ellison and Munro, "Reacting to Rape: Exploring Mock Jurors' Assessments of Complainant Credibility" (2009) 49(2) *British Journal of Criminology* 202, 206.

18 Finch and Munro, "The Demon Drink and the Demonized Woman: Socio-Sexual Stereotypes and Responsibility Attribution in Rape Trials Involving Intoxicants" (2007) 16(4) *Social & Legal Studies* 591, 599. These results mirror the findings of an earlier pilot study by the same researchers: Finch and Munro, "Juror Stereotypes and Blame Attribution in Rape Cases Involving Intoxicants: The Findings of a Pilot Study" (2005) 45(1) *British Journal of Criminology* 25.

story, and thus only a partial solution to sexual offending. Societal change and extra-legal initiatives which tackle negative and erroneous attitudes about sexual offences and appropriate socio-sexual behaviour are a vital component of the programme for change.

Societal attitudes towards sex offenders are also an important part of the conversation in considering legal policy and developments in this area. Considering the abhorrent nature of sexual offending and the harm it can inflict, those convicted of committing such crimes are detested and intensely reviled by society. The prism through which sex offenders are often viewed reveals a stereotype of the "typical" sex offender. The predatory, anonymous, paedophilic offender is the common public image of who the sex offender is. Evidence counters this stereotypical image. It is well established that most sex offenders are known to their victim, rather than being an anonymous stranger and not all those who perpetrate a sex offence against a child are paedophiles, a term which carries an altogether different meaning.[19] Another common perception is that sex offenders are prone to reoffending, while research demonstrates a lower rate of recidivism amongst this group when compared with other categories of offenders.[20] **[0–06]**

Nonetheless, those who perpetrate a sexual crime are unlikely to elicit much sympathy from the public. While some laws and policies reflect a need for rehabilitation of such offenders, the overwhelming focus is upon punishment, regulation and public safety.[21] Expectation for harsh and durable sentences against those convicted of a sex offence dictates strategies that affect the individual long after they have served their punishment within the formal legal system. Post-release provisions under the Sex Offenders Act 2001 (as amended) are intended to provide for public safety through regulation and monitoring of released sex offenders in the community. Provisions which compel signing on at Garda stations and restrict the movements of the individual, have now become part of the norm in how we deal with convicted sex offenders. Such restrictions are welcomed unquestioningly, often without ascertaining their true value or necessity. Although the intention is to target high-risk offenders, the laws can often sweep violent, high risk offenders and non-violent, low-risk offenders into **[0–07]**

[19] See Richards, "Misconceptions about child sex offenders" (2011) *Trends and issues in crime and criminal justice*, No. 429.

[20] O'Donnell, Baumer and Hughes, "Recidivism in the Republic of Ireland" (2008) *Criminology and Criminal Justice* 123; Probation Service. *Recidivism Study 2007 – 2011* (The Probation Service, Dublin, 2012); Irish Prison Service. *Recidivism Study* (Irish Prison Service, Dublin, 2013).

[21] McAlinden, "Managing risk: From regulation to the reintegration of sexual offenders" (2006) 6(2) *Criminology and Criminal Justice* 197.

the same category, raising questions as to their proportionality as well as their effectiveness.[22]

[0–08] Post release monitoring can also impact upon rehabilitation processes in ways seldom considered or anticipated. Thus the paradox created by public demand for protection is that the net product of such demand—harsher laws—do not necessarily always provide for such safety, and may even prove counterproductive by inhibiting opportunities for offenders to reform and become law-abiding members of society.[23] The struggle for the law and indeed for society is finding a way of providing justice for victims of sexual violence and protecting the public, while at the same time ensuring that punishment is proportionate and that the collateral consequences of a conviction do not unduly interfere with the ability of offenders to rehabilitate. These should not be opposing forces, and providing for one should not mean cancelling out the other. Since future developments in this area seem likely to augment rather than diffuse the intensity of sex offender laws, the feat for policy makers will be in finding a balance, wherein high-risk offenders are justifiably monitored post-release in the interests of public safety, while at the same time preventing a trail of collateral damage being levied at low-risk offenders. It is clear then that societal response to sexual offences and offenders cannot be ignored in any discussion of the law in this area. Consequently, although this text concentrates on the law relating to sexual offences and offenders, the societal context which shapes the operation of these laws must be acknowledged and provides a significant backdrop throughout the discussion of the legal rules.

[0–09] For accessibility, the book is divided into three parts, reflecting the three main issues which must be considered in any discussion of this area, that is, laws, procedures and punishments. The overview of the substantive law offered in Part I is divided into three chapters which reflect three key areas of sexual offending: rape (chapter one); sexual assault-based offences (chapter two); and capacity-related offences (i.e. offences against children and those with limited decision-making capacity) (chapter three). Part II divides the discussion of the relevant rules of evidence and procedures into a further three chapters which focus on: the special procedures which apply in sexual offence trials (chapter four); the admissibility of character evidence (chapter five); and the doctrine of recent complaint and the use

[22] See further Vess, Day, Powell and Graffam, "International sex offender registration laws: research and evaluation based on a review of current scientific literature" (2014) 15(4) *Police Practice and Research* 322.

[23] See further on the desistance from sexual offending: Farmer, McAlinden, Maruna, "Understanding desistance from sexual offending: A thematic review of research findings" (2015) 62(4) *Probation Journal* 320; Cooley, Moore and Sample, "The role of formal social control mechanisms in deterring sex offenders as part of the desistance process" 2017 30(2) *Criminal Justice Studies* 136.

of corroboration warnings (chapter six). Finally, Part III focuses on the punishment of sex offenders, discussing sentencing (chapter seven) and post-release provisions (chapter 8).

In conclusion, it is necessary to mention one point of nomenclature in relation to the discussion in this text. The authors have adopted the use of the feminine gender when referring to complainants and the use of the masculine gender when referring to defendants. This is not done to suggest sexual offences are only committed by men upon women, thereby denying the experiences of male victims or the fact that women may commit sexual offences. Rather, this approach to terminology has been chosen largely to simplify discussion of complex legal rules. **[0–10]**

PART ONE

THE SUBSTANTIVE LAW ON SEXUAL OFFENCES

CHAPTER ONE

Rape

Introduction

This chapter will focus on the law relating to what is colloquially referred to as "common law" rape. Although this is something of a misnomer as the offence is now statutorily defined,[1] the legislative definition of rape reflects the traditional common law definition, that is, non-consensual vaginal penetration of a woman by a man.[2] This chapter discusses the Irish law on rape, in particular, recent reforms of the offence in the Criminal Law (Sexual Offences) Act 2017, as well as proposals for further reform. **[1–01]**

Rape

Section 2(1) of the Criminal Law (Rape) Act 1981, states that a man commits rape if: **[1–02]**

> "(a) he has sexual intercourse with a woman who at the time of the intercourse does not consent to it, and
> (b) at that time he knows that she does not consent to the intercourse or he is reckless as to whether she does or does not consent to it".

Section 2(1) encapsulated in statutory form the common law gender-specific definition of rape whereby the offence can only be perpetrated by a man against a woman. The section neatly sets out the *actus reus* and the *mens rea*. Section 2(1)(a) refers to the *actus reus* (i.e. sexual intercourse with a woman who does not consent to it). Section 2(1) (b) defines the *mens rea* (i.e. knowledge that the woman was consenting or recklessness regarding the presence or absence of consent). Section 48 of the Offences against the Person Act 1861 provides for a penalty of up to life imprisonment for those convicted of rape.[3] **[1–03]**

---

1 O'Malley, *Sexual Offences* (2nd, Round Hall, Dublin, 2013), p 35.

2 A gender-neutral offence of "rape under section 4" which covers other forms of non-consensual penetrative sexual activity also exists. This will be discussed in chapter two, where arguments for the amalgamation of rape and rape under s 4 to form one gender-neutral offence are canvassed.

3 Sentencing for rape and other sexual offences is discussed in chapter seven.

The *Actus Reus* of Rape

[1–04] As already stated, the *actus reus* of rape is sexual intercourse with a woman who does not consent to it.

Sexual Intercourse

[1–05] Rape as defined in s 2(1) only refers to vaginal sexual intercourse. Section 1(2) of the 1981 Act states that references to sexual intercourse within the Act should be construed as references to carnal knowledge as defined in s 63 of the Offences against the Person Act 1861. Section 63 provides that it is unnecessary to prove emission to establish that natural intercourse occurred. Penetration is all that must be proven and any degree thereof is sufficient. In *The People (AG) v Dermody*,[4] the complainant gave evidence that the defendant had put his private part "a wee bit" into hers but the evidence showed that the hymen had not been ruptured. Maguire CJ held that once penetration is proven, natural sexual intercourse sufficient to ground a charge of rape has occurred.[5]

[1–06] In *Kaitamaki v R*,[6] the New Zealand Court of Appeal held that sexual intercourse is a continuing act which only ends with withdrawal. An accused who fails to withdraw once he realises that the woman is no longer consenting can be found guilty of rape. Historically, there was a presumption that a boy under the age of 14 years could not perform a penetrative act. This presumption was abolished by s 6 of the Criminal Law (Rape) (Amendment) Act 1990, and the general rules regarding the age of criminal responsibility now apply equally to sexual offences. Although the age of criminal responsibility is generally 12,[7] rape is one of five offences where an individual can be held be responsible from the age of 10.[8]

---

4 [1956] IR. 307.

5 Maguire CJ stated that:

> "It should hardly be necessary to say that in law if the male organ is proved to have entered the opening of the vagina this amounts to penetration even if there is no emission … If penetration is proved, though not of sufficient depth to penetrate the hymen, still this was sufficient to constitute the offence of rape."; *ibid*, 312.

6 [1985] AC 147; [1984] 2 All ER 435.

7 The Children Act 2001, s 25(1) (as substituted by s 129 of the Criminal Justice Act 2006).

8 A child aged 10 or 11 years may be charged with murder, manslaughter, rape, rape under s 4 of the Criminal Law (Rape) (Amendment) Act 1990 or aggravated sexual assault: s 52(2) of the Children Act 2001 (as substituted by s 129 of the Criminal Justice Act 2006). Where a child under 14 years of age is charged with an offence, no further proceedings in the matter (other than any remand in custody or on bail) shall be taken except by or with the consent of the Director of Public Prosecutions: s 52(4) of the Children Act 2001 (as substituted by s 129 of the Criminal Justice Act 2006).

The gender-specific formulation of the definition of rape creates uncertainties regarding transgender individuals. It is unclear whether an individual who has undergone male-to-female sex reassignment surgery and has a surgically constructed vagina would be legally recognised as a woman for the purposes of being a victim of s 2 rape. Likewise, it is not clear whether an individual who has undergone female-to-male sex reassignment surgery would be recognised as a man for the purposes of being a perpetrator of s 2 rape.[9] Campbell et al note that although rape perpetrated by or on a transgender individual has not yet come before the Irish courts,[10] current Irish law would seem to suggest that a transgender person would continue to be legally identified by the sex on his/her birth certificate and thus be so classified for the purposes of rape law.[11] The Gender Recognition Act 2015 helps to offset some of this uncertainty. The legislation permits transgender individuals to apply for a gender recognition certificate which, once granted, would give formal legal recognition to his/her chosen gender. The State would thus recognise that individual as his/her chosen gender for all purposes, including criminal law.[12] This is a welcome development, but in the context of sexual offences, it should be bolstered by legislative clarification that surgically constructed sexual organs are recognised for the purposes of rape offences. This would protect individuals who have undergone surgery but have not yet obtained a gender recognition certificate. In this respect, Irish legislation should follow the example of the English Sexual Offences Act 2003, and provide that "[r]eferences to a part of the body include references to a part surgically constructed (in particular, through gender reassignment surgery)".[13] **[1–07]**

The current gender-specific formulation of rape is also open to criticism for not including male victims whose experiences of non-consensual penetrative sexual activity are punished by the separate offence of rape under s 4 of **[1–08]**

---

9 Of course, as O'Malley notes, even if the courts were to refuse to recognise surgically constructed genitalia for the purposes of rape without statutory intervention, "a person alleged to have sexually assaulted another in circumstances which would amount to rape were it not for the victim's gender assignment could still be held guilty of sexual assault or aggravated sexual assault".: O'Malley, *supra* note 1, p 58.

10 For a discussion of some of the cases involving transgender defendants in England and Scotland, see: Sharpe, "Criminalising Sexual Intimacy: Transgender Defendants and the Legal Construction of Non-Consent" (2014) 3 *Criminal Law Review* 207.

11 Campbell, et al, *Criminal Law in Ireland: Cases and Commentaries* (Clarus Press, Dublin, 2010), p 552.

12 Gender Recognition Act 2015, s 18(1), provides that:

> "Where a gender recognition certificate is issued to a person the person's gender shall from the date of that issue become for all purposes the preferred gender so that if the preferred gender is the male gender the person's sex becomes that of a man, and if it is the female gender the person's sex becomes that of a woman."

13 The Sexual Offences Act 2003, s 79.

the Criminal Law (Rape) (Amendment) Act 1990. The appropriateness or otherwise of this approach is considered in the discussion of rape under s 4 in chapter two.

The Absence of Consent

[1–09] Until the enactment of the Criminal Law (Sexual Offences Act) 2017, consent was not statutorily defined in Irish sexual offences law. The Law Reform Commission (LRC) recommended the introduction of a definition of consent prior to the enactment of the Criminal Law (Rape) (Act) 1990.[14] However, addressing the Seanad prior to the introduction of the Act, the then Minister for Justice noted that as far as he was aware the fact that consent was not statutorily defined had not given rise to any problems in rape trials.[15] On that basis alone, the Minister stated that he saw no justification for including a definition of consent and that any attempt to do so could give rise to considerable difficulties. Consequently, until 2017, the guidance on what precisely constitutes a legally valid consent had to be gleaned from common law rules. As will become clear in the following discussion, the common law guidance which exists is dated, with some rules deriving from cases that were decided as far back as the late 19th century, and there is a heavy reliance on English case-law. The legislative definition of consent in the 2017 Act is heavily based upon the pre-existing common law, and thus common law guidance will necessarily inform the interpretation of the new definition. For this reason, and to provide context for the introduction of the legislative definition of consent, the common law guidance is discussed here prior to a consideration of the new definition of consent in the 2017 Act.

Common Law Guidance on Consent

[1–10] Consent is a mental state. In *R v Olugboja*,[16] it was held that "consent" "covers a wide range of states of mind … ranging from actual desire on the one hand to reluctant acquiescence on the other".[17] Consent does not

---

[14] It was recommended that legislation should provide as follows:

> "1. 'Consent' means a consent freely and voluntarily given and, without in any way affecting or limiting the meaning otherwise attributable to those words, a consent is not freely and voluntarily given if it is obtained by force, threat, intimidation, deception or fraudulent means.
>
> 2. A failure to offer physical resistance to a sexual assault does not of itself constitute consent to a sexual assault.": Law Reform Commission, *Rape and Allied Offences* (Law Reform Commission, Dublin, 1988), para 17.

[15] Minister for Justice (Deputy Collins), *Dáil Debates*, 1 February 1989, (Vol 121), col 1919. The Minister pointed out that the LRC had made a similar point in their Report. However, the LRC had conceded that the lack of a definition was capable of causing difficulty: *ibid*, para 16.

[16] [1982] QB 320.

[17] *ibid*, 331.

have to be performed or affirmatively expressed to be valid. There does not have to be any observable conduct which signifies that the complainant is consenting. Of course, in practice, the absence of an outward expression or indication of consent may be seen as contraindicative of the complainant's willingness to consent.

An early definition of consent may be found in *R v Dee*,[18] where Palles CB described consent thus: **[1–11]**

> "Consent is the act of man [*sic*], in his character of a rational and intelligent being, not in that of an animal. It must proceed from the will, not when such will is acting without the control of reason, as in idiocy or drunkenness, but from the will sufficiently enlightened by the intellect to make such consent the act of a reasoning being."[19]

More recently, in *The People (DPP) v C*,[20] Murray J. described consent as: **[1–12]**

> "… voluntary agreement or acquiescence to sexual intercourse by a person of the age of consent with the requisite mental capacity. Knowledge or understanding of facts material to the act being consented to is necessary for the consent to be voluntary or constitute acquiescence."[21]

These two definitions illustrate that for consent to sex to be legally valid it must have been given by an individual with requisite capacity, who acts voluntarily (i.e. not as a result of threats or fear), and who possesses sufficient knowledge of the material facts (i.e. the consent must not have been obtained by fraud). As will be seen below, the common law offers guidance on each of these prerequisites. **[1–13]**

Capacity

To provide a legally valid consent to sexual intercourse, an individual must have attained the legal age of consent (i.e. 17 years[22]) and must have the requisite capacity to legally consent. The rules relating to sexual offences against children and those with limited decision-making capacity are explored in chapter three. The discussion of capacity which is offered here will focus on what may be termed transient states of incapacity, that is, where an individual who normally possesses the legal capacity to exercise sexual choice has been rendered temporarily unable to do so. This may occur **[1–14]**

---

18 (1884) 15 Cox 579.
19 *ibid*, 593.
20 [2001] 3 IR 345.
21 *ibid*, 360.
22 As was explained above, sexual activity with individuals who are under the age of consent is regulated by the Criminal Law (Sexual Offences) Act 2006.

where the complainant was asleep[23] or unconscious when the intercourse took place. If a complainant is intoxicated to such a degree that she cannot offer a valid consent to sexual activity, an apparent consent will also be vitiated. However, deciphering whether an individual was intoxicated to this degree is often a difficult task for a jury. In *R v Lang*,[24] the Court of Appeal held that there is no special rule which is applicable to alcohol and rape. Scarman LJ held that the critical question is whether the woman understood her situation and was capable of making up her mind.[25] In *R v Lang*, the complainant's testimony consisted of a detailed account of "seduction, struggle, submission to force and intercourse".[26] Because of her ability to provide such a detailed account, it was held that her drinking had not impaired her understanding or capacity to exercise judgment to the extent that she was incapable of giving consent.[27] There is no bright-line rule which applies to intoxication and consent. Indeed, given the varying reactions of different individuals to alcohol, it would be impossible to devise a strict test that could apply in these situations. Consequently, proving that consent was absent where the complainant was intoxicated is a difficult task.

[1–15] As Leahy notes, complainant intoxication is a feature of a large number of rape trials.[28] In 2009, a case-tracking exercise which examined 100 rape cases found that 78 per cent of complainants were intoxicated at the time of the attack.[29] A similar study of 173 rape case files which was conducted for the attrition study, *Rape & Justice in Ireland*, revealed that nearly two-thirds of the complainants in those cases had engaged in what is officially classified as "binge-drinking" prior to the incident in question.[30] Thus, the difficulties posed in proving an absence of consent where intoxication arises are likely to affect a large number of trials.

---

23 *R v Mayers* (1872) 12 Cox CC 311; *R v Larter & Castleton* [1995] *Criminal Law Review*, p 75.

24 (1976) 62 Cr App R 50.

25 *ibid*, 52.

26 *ibid*.

27 Scarman LJ noted that it would have been difficult to infer from her evidence that she lacked understanding of her position or capacity to exercise judgement. "Indeed, if she was to be believed, she very sensibly submitted when she saw further struggle would be of no avail": *ibid*.

28 Leahy, "Reform of Irish Rape Law: The Need for a Legislative Definition of Consent" (2014) 43(3) *Common Law World Review* 231, 236.

29 Corr, et al, *Different Systems, Similar Outcomes?: Tracking Attrition in Reported Rape Cases in Eleven Countries, Country Briefing: Ireland*, (Child and Woman Abuse Studies Unit, London, 2009), p 4.

30 Hanly, et al, *Rape & Justice in Ireland: A National Study of Survivor, Prosecutor and Court Responses to Rape* (The Liffey Press, Dublin, 2009), p 272

Voluntariness

Consent to sexual activity must be freely given.[31] Where the complainant's participation in sexual intercourse is secured by violence or the threat of violence, any apparent consent will be vitiated. Prior to the 2017 Act, s 9 of the Criminal law (Rape) (Amendment) Act 1990 made clear that the prosecution does not need to prove that the complainant resisted the efforts of her attacker, stating that: [1–16]

> "... in relation to an offence that consists of or includes the doing of an act to a person without the consent of that person any failure or omission on the part of that person to offer resistance to the act does not of itself constitute consent to the act."[32]

Section 9 was enacted to offset the last vestiges of the resistance requirement which traditionally formed part of the common law definition of rape, and required that carnal knowledge had to be obtained forcibly and against the will of the woman in order for the offence of rape to be established. While the resistance requirement had long fallen out of usage in the common law by 1990,[33] s 9 was seen to be necessary as a declaratory provision. In practice, of course, as Hanly notes, notwithstanding s 9, a failure to offer resistance is likely to be taken into account by a jury as evidence from which consent may be inferred.[34] [1–17]

An apparent consent to sexual intercourse may also be vitiated by fear of adverse consequences other than physical violence. This was made clear in *R v Olugboja.*[35] In that case, the defendant and his friend had offered to drive two teenage girls, J and K, home from a disco. However, instead of bringing them home, the men brought the girls to a bungalow. The girls refused to go into the house and began walking away. The defendant's friend followed them in the car and after an argument during which the girls tried to escape, the friend got both girls back to the bungalow, raping J on the [1–18]

---

31 It must, however, be noted that the fact that sexual activity was voluntary does not automatically mean that it will be legally acceptable. There are certain circumstances where voluntary sexual activity may be found to be criminal for the protection of the public interest. For example, in the case of *R v Brown* [1993] 2 All ER 75, it was held that consent could not be a defence to sadomasochistic sexual activity which resulted in actual bodily harm.

32 As will be seen below, s 9 is repealed by the 2017 Act and substituted with a full statutory definition of consent.

33 Fennell notes that by the mid-19th century, the test for rape was not whether sexual intercourse had been obtained "against the victim's will" but rather whether it was "without her consent": Fennell, "Annotation of the Criminal Law (Rape) (Amendment) Act 1990", *Irish Current Law Statutes Annotated,* 32–01 at 32–20.

34 Hanly, *An Introduction to Irish Criminal Law* (3rd ed, Gill and MacMillan, Dublin, 2015), p 323.

35 [1982] QB 320.

way. Once inside the bungalow, the defendant told J that he intended to rape her and insisted that she remove her trousers. She complied out of fear and as the defendant raped her she did not struggle, resist or cry for help. The defendant's conviction for rape was upheld. The Court of Appeal noted that J had been tricked into going to the bungalow in the first place. When the defendant raped her, she had already been raped by the defendant's friend; she was crying and frightened and the defendant was determined to have sex with her. In those circumstances, the Court held that the jury was fully justified in concluding that J had not consented to sexual intercourse with the defendant, even though the defendants had not made a direct threat of physical violence towards her.

[1–19] Although fear of an adverse consequence has been held to vitiate consent to sex, it is unclear precisely what types of threats other than those of physical violence will suffice to vitiate an apparent consent. In *R v Olugboja*, the Court of Appeal held that, in cases such as these, the jury should be directed to concentrate on the state of the mind of the complainant immediately prior to the act of intercourse. In doing this, the jury should have regard to all the relevant circumstances and the complainant's reaction to them. This would help the jury to assess the impact of the situation on the individual complainant's state of mind.[36] In addition to this general direction, the Court of Appeal recommended that the jury should be reminded that, where violence or the threat thereof is absent, the dividing line between real consent on the one hand and mere submission on the other may not be easy to draw.[37] Deciding where to draw the line is the task of the jury, and they should reach this decision by "applying their combined good sense, experience and knowledge of human nature and modern behaviour to all the relevant facts of the case".[38] This approach provides juries with significant discretion to decide for themselves whether, on the basis of the facts in an individual case, the complainant was subjected to a threat which was sufficient to prevent the genuine exercise of sexual choice.

[1–20] However, while the decision in *R v Olugboja* suggests that fear induced by any circumstances could be sufficient to vitiate an apparent consent, Leahy notes that, in practice, this is unlikely to happen within the common law because of the vague directions which the decision provides regarding the types of adverse consequences which might be capable of producing fear which is enough to invalidate consent.[39] Temkin argues that the net effect of this failure to spell out or provide any criteria by which lack of consent can

---

[36] *ibid*, 332.
[37] *ibid.*
[38] *ibid.*
[39] Leahy, *supra* note 28, 235.

be judged is that "much oppressive behaviour is likely to go *unpunished*",[40] that is, that it will not be categorised as impeding consent. This is because neither prosecutors nor juries can be expected to stray far from common understandings of rape as forcible compulsion.[41] Temkin makes a valid point. Without express legislative or judicial direction, it is likely that prosecuting counsel will face significant difficulty in convincing jurors that a threat of adverse consequences other than violence is incompatible with a valid and meaningful consent to sexual activity. As will be seen in the discussion below, the reforms in the 2017 Act continue to limit the guidance on threats to those of force. Thus, the issues identified with the common law on this issue continue to persist.

Knowledge

For consent to sexual intercourse to be valid, it must be fully informed. If an individual has been deceived about the nature of the act or the identity of her partner, then any apparent consent will be vitiated. A complainant will be deceived about the nature of the act where as a result of the defendant's fraud, she believes that the act she is engaging in is something other than sexual intercourse. An example of this form of fraud may be seen in *R v Flattery*.[42] The defendant was convicted of rape where he had sexual intercourse with a girl on the pretence that it was a surgical procedure. The complainant had believed that what was taking place was a surgical operation and thought that penetration was being effected with the defendant's hand or with an instrument. A similar incident took place in *R v Williams*.[43] The defendant was convicted of rape where he deceived the complainant into believing that sexual intercourse was a procedure which would improve her singing voice by making an air passage. **[1–21]**

The victims in these cases had no idea that the act performed on them was sexual intercourse. Although the facts of these cases appear difficult to believe in the context of the 21st century, such deceptions may have been possible when these cases occurred in the late 19th and early 20th century when many women were not fully aware of sexual matters. As Feinberg notes, it is almost impossible to imagine similar frauds occurring today. He does, however, point out that an analogue to these cases may exist today in the context of psychiatrist/patient relationships: **[1–22]**

> "While few persons are so naive these days as to believe, even on the immense

40 Temkin, *Rape and the Legal Process* (2nd ed, Oxford University Press, Oxford, 2002), p 93.
41 *ibid.*
42 (1877) 2 QBD 410.
43 (1923) 1 KB 340.

authority of a doctor, that sexual intercourse (with him) will cure or prevent cancer, even the sophisticated (especially when desperately neurotic) will accept a similar opinion on the authority of their psychoanalyst."[44]

[1–23] Whilst it is possible that frauds such as these could occur in modern times, such deceptions are better described as fraud as to the purpose of the act, rather than its nature. Contrary to the sexual naivety of the complainants in *Williams* and *Flattery*, individuals are unlikely now to be tricked into believing sexual intercourse is another act such as a surgical intervention. They may, however, be deceived into believing that sexual activity will aid recovery or in some other way benefit them. Such deceits are more correctly conceptualised as fraud regarding the purpose of the act. Under common law, it is unclear whether such fraud is sufficient to vitiate consent to sexual activity. However, as will be discussed in the next section, the 2017 Act extends the definition of sexual fraud to include fraud as to purpose.

[1–24] Aside from fraud relating to the sexual act itself, consent will also be vitiated where the complainant is deceived about the identity of her partner. However, where the complainant is deceived as to her partner's attributes (e.g. his wealth or marital status), the validity of her consent is unaffected. This was first made clear in *R v Clarence.*[45] In that case, it was held that a husband's failure to inform his wife that he was suffering from a sexually transmitted disease would not vitiate her consent to sexual intercourse.[46] Similarly, in *R v Papadimitropoulos*,[47] the High Court of Australia held that a man who induced a woman to have sexual intercourse with him by fraudulently leading her to believe they were married[48] was not guilty of rape.

[1–25] Once the complainant is aware of the nature of the act and the identity of her partner, it appears that any other deception will not invalidate her consent.

---

44 Feinberg, "Victim's Excuses: The Case of Fraudulently Procured Consent" (1986) 96 *Ethics* 330, 336.

45 (1889) 22 QBD 23.

46 *ibid*, 44. A defendant who fails to disclose to a sexual partner that he has a sexually transmitted disease might be guilty of an offence under s 4 of the Non-Fatal Offences against the Person Act 1997 which makes it an offence to deliberately cause another serious harm (see Charleton, McDermott and Bolger, *Criminal Law* (Butterworth, Dublin, 1999), p 633). For a discussion of the issues surrounding the criminalisation of the intentional or reckless transmission of sexually transmitted disease see Ormerord, "Criminalising HIV Transmission—Still No Effective Solutions" [2001] *Common Law World Review* 135; Spencer, "Liability for Reckless Infection" (2004) 154 *New Law Journal* 384–385 (Pt 1) and 448–471 (Pt 2).

47 (1956) 98 CLR 249.

48 The victim was a young migrant who was unable to speak English. The defendant told her that the notice of intention to marry which they had signed at a registry office was an actual marriage ceremony.

This was confirmed in *R v Linekar.*[49] The complainant, who was working as a prostitute, agreed to have sexual intercourse with the defendant for the sum of £25. After the intercourse had taken place, the defendant left without paying. The defendant's conviction for rape was quashed by the Court of Appeal, the Court holding that the complainant's consent to sexual intercourse was not vitiated by its having been induced by the defendant's false pretence that he would pay her. The Court of Appeal suggested that the appropriate charge in a case such as this would be a charge of procuring sexual intercourse by false pretences under s 3 of the Criminal Law (Amendment) Act 1885.[50] This offence had a maximum penalty of two years' imprisonment and so provided a good option for punishing fraudulent behaviour which was not considered by a jury to be sufficiently grave to justify a conviction for rape.

There is significant potential for fraud as to purpose to arise in medical contexts or other similar settings where touching which would otherwise be sexual is rendered permissible as it is necessary for a legitimate purpose such as examination. These frauds are more likely to arise in sexual assault cases. Leahy cites the example of a healthcare worker who carries out a procedure such as a breast check or a vaginal examination on the basis that this is necessary for diagnostic or therapeutic purposes when in fact it is carried out purely for the healthcare professional's sexual gratification.[51] Similar concerns arise where an individual poses as a medical professional in order to deceive individuals into consenting to an examination.[52] A situation analogous to this arose in *R v Tabassum.*[53] In this English case, the defendant posed as a breast cancer specialist. Believing him to be a qualified medical professional, a number of women permitted him to examine their breasts. They all later testified that they would not have consented to the examinations if they had known that he was not so qualified. The defendant was convicted of sexual assault. There has been no similar case in Ireland so it cannot be stated with certainty that the Irish courts would extend the current understanding of fraud to encompass this sort of fraud as to purpose. However, fraud as to purpose is included in the new definition of consent in the 2017 Act. **[1–26]**

---

49 (1995) 2 WLR 237.

50 Criminal Law (Amendment) Act 1885, s 3 also provides for the offences of procuring sexual intercourse with a woman through threats or intimidation. Both of these offences were subject to the same maximum penalty of two years' imprisonment. Originally, s 3 also provided for the offence of administering an intoxicating substance with the intent to procure sexual intercourse but this offence was repealed by s 31 of the Non-Fatal Offences against the Person Act 1997.

51 Leahy, *supra* 28, 237.

52 *ibid.*

53 [2000] 2 Cr App R 328.

Reform: Legislatively Defining Consent

[1–27] The discussion here has illustrated the lack of clarity surrounding the precise meaning of consent at common law. The common law defines consent negatively, with reference to factors which vitiate consent, and these vitiating factors are themselves quite vaguely defined. A better approach is a positive definition of consent which sets out clearly what is required for a legally valid agreement to engage in sexual activity. Certainly, the vagueness at common law allows for expansive interpretation of the factors which may vitiate consent to sexual activity (e.g. by interpreting the guidance in *Olugboja* to include threats of harm to a third party or revelation of a damaging secret as threats of adverse consequences sufficient to vitiate consent). Appropriate directions by a trial judge may encourage jurors to take an enlightened approach to interpreting the current guidance on consent. However, without legislative prompting, it seems unlikely that this will happen, particularly in light of research which indicates the prevalence of stereotypical attitudes about rape which persist in Irish society and consequently in the minds of jurors.[54] Judicial inertia in the development of the common law guidance on consent is evidenced in the dearth of reported judgments which consider the meaning of consent in this area.

[1–28] Given the challenges posed by relying on common law, negative definitions of consent in this area, it is perhaps unsurprising that, in general, common law jurisdictions have opted to introduce positive legislative definitions. This approach has been adopted in England and Wales,[55] Canada[56] and Australian jurisdictions such as Victoria[57] and New South Wales.[58] Irish legal commentators and victim support groups have, over the years, repeatedly called for the introduction of a similar approach in Irish sexual offences law. As noted above, the LRC recommended the introduction of a definition of consent prior to the enactment of the Criminal Law (Rape) (Act) 1990.[59] The Rape Crisis Network of Ireland (RCNI) has also repeatedly called for statutory clarification of the meaning of consent,[60] and the Dublin Rape Crisis Centre lobbied extensively for the definition of consent which was

54 For discussion see: Leahy, "Bad Laws or Bad Attitudes? Assessing the Impact of Societal Attitudes upon the Conviction Rate for Rape in Ireland" (2014) 14(1) *Irish Journal of Applied Social Studies*, article 3. Available at: http://arrow.dit.ie/ijass/vol14/iss1/3 (last accessed: 23 May 2017).

55 Sexual Offences Act 2003, ss 74, 75 and 76.

56 The Canadian Criminal Code, ss 265(3) and 273.1.

57 Crimes Act 1958, s 36.

58 Crimes Act 1900, s 61HA (as amended by the Crimes Amendment (Consent-Sexual Assault Offences) Act 2007).

59 Law Reform Commission, *supra* note 14, para 16.

60 Rape Crisis Network of Ireland, *Agenda for Justice I: Towards Ending Injustice for Survivors of Sexual Violence*, (Rape Crisis Network of Ireland, Galway, 2005), p 4; *Consent on Sexual Contact: RCNI Discussion Document*, (Rape Crisis Network of

ultimately included the Criminal Law (Sexual Offences) Act 2017.[61] Section 48 of the Act substitutes the following for s 9 of the Criminal Law (Rape) (Amendment) Act 1990:

> "(1) A person consents to a sexual act if he or she freely and voluntarily agrees to engage in that act.
>
> (2) A person does not consent to a sexual act if-
>
> (a) he or she permits the act to take place or submits to it because of the application of force to him or her or to some other person, or because of the threat of the application of force to him or her or to some other person, or because of a well-founded fear that force may be applied to him or her or to some other person,
>
> (b) he or she is asleep or unconscious,
>
> (c) he or she in incapable of consenting because of the effect of alcohol or some other drug,
>
> (d) he or she is suffering from a physical disability which prevents him or her from communicating whether he or she agrees to the act,[62]
>
> (e) he or she is mistaken as to the nature and purpose of the act,
>
> (f) he or she is mistaken as to the identity of any other person involved in the act,
>
> (g) he or she is being unlawfully detained at the time at which the act takes place,
>
> (h) the only expression or indication of consent or agreement to the act comes from somebody other than the person himself or herself."

The new definition provides a positive statement of what consent means (thus marking a break with the negative approach to definition found in the common law), followed by a non-exhaustive[63] list of situations where consent will be deemed to be absent. The latter largely replicates the situations where consent would be deemed to be absent under the common law, but there are some significant extensions to the current understandings **[1–29]**

Ireland, Galway, 2008), p 2; *RCNI Agenda for Justice Discussion Document*, (Rape Crisis Network of Ireland, Galway, 2009), p. 12.

61 The efforts of the Dublin Rape Crisis Centre in this regard were acknowledged by An Tánaiste Frances Fitzgerald during the Dáil Debates on the definition of consent: See comments of An Tánaiste and Minister for Justice (Deputy Fitzgerald), *Dáil Debates*, 1 February 2017, (Vol 937, No 1), col 944.

62 Examples of individuals who might be affected by this provision are those suffering from cerebral palsy or the effects of a stroke and thus may not be able to express themselves fully: Leahy, *supra* note 28, p 256. This provision only applies to individuals with physical disabilities. Complainants with limited decision-making capacity who consequently may not be able to exercise free sexual choice are protected under capacity-related offences: see chapter three.

63 Criminal Law (Rape)(Amendment) Act 1990, s 9(3), provides that "[t]his section does not limit the circumstances in which it may be established that a person did not consent to a sexual act".

of the factors which may vitiate an apparent consent to sexual activity under common law.

[1–30] In relation to "force", there is now a clear statement that submission in the face of the application or threatened application of force towards the individual "or some other person" is inconsistent with a legally valid consent. Consequently, the provision applies where the force is directed towards the complainant or a third party such as a family member or friend. Further, it seems that the force or threat thereof does not have to emanate from the defendant. Although the clarification in this area is welcome, it is questionable whether the legislature could have gone further and provided that threats of adverse consequences other than force would result in consent being deemed to be absent. As Leahy highlights, there are a number of threats other than those of force that are sufficiently serious to preclude freedom to exercise sexual choice. She cites as examples, "threats to: abduct or detain the complainant or a third party[64] (e.g. the complainant's child); expose a secret that would be highly damaging to the complainant's interests,[65] or; withdraw financial support where the complainant is wholly dependent upon the defendant for survival".[66] Thus, Leahy suggests that the list of situations where consent would be deemed to be absent should include the circumstance where "the complainant submits to sexual activity as a result of threats of serious harm or serious detriment of any type to the complainant or a third party".[67] Of course, cases involving such threats could still be dealt with by reference to the general definition of consent but expressly providing that such threats are contraindicative of consent would be a welcome extension of the law.

[1–31] The list of situations where consent will be deemed to be absent also offers an expanded understanding of sexual fraud to include fraud regarding the purpose of a sexual act. As noted above, under common law, it is not clear whether fraud as to the purpose would vitiate consent to sexual activity. When the meaning of sexual fraud was statutorily clarified in English law in s 76 of the Sexual Offences Act 2003, it created space for greater protection of complainants. For example, in *R v Jheeta*,[68] it was confirmed that fraud as to purpose would apply where a complainant consents to an act believing it to be for medical purposes when really it is merely for the sexual gratification of the defendant.[69] Further, in *R v Piper*,[70] fraud as to

64 Temkin, *supra* note 40, p 101.
65 *ibid*.
66 Leahy, *supra* note 28, 254.
67 *ibid*, 261.
68 [2007] EWCA 1699.
69 *ibid*, para 26.
70 [2007] EWCA Crim 2131.

purpose was found where the complainant agreed to be measured for a bikini by the defendant on the understanding that this was necessary to determine her modelling potential when it was actually done for the sexual gratification of the defendant. Similarly, in *R v Matt*,[71] an individual who posed as a filmmaker and induced the complainant to engage in sexual acts with him as part of a casting process was found to have deceived her as to the purpose of the act because the individual's "ostensible purpose was not sexual pleasure but simulated sexual pleasure for commercial purposes".[72] The extension of the understanding of sexual fraud to cover fraud as to purpose and thus to increase the likelihood that cases such as these would be recognised as sexual violation in Ireland is a welcome clarification.

As with threats, there is a question as to whether the definition of sexual fraud should have been extended even further than fraud as to nature, identity and purpose, to include any deception which caused a complainant to agree to sexual activity. Herring suggests that the law should specifically provide that *any* deception which causes an individual to consent to sexual activity where she otherwise would not have done so should be recognised as a criminal offence.[73] He suggests the formulation of a legal rule which provides that: **[1–32]**

> "If at the time of the sexual activity a person:
> (i) is mistaken as to a fact; and
> (ii) had s/he known the truth about that fact would not have consented to it,
>
> then s/he did not consent to the sexual activity. If the defendant knows (or ought to know) that s/he did not consent (in the sense just described) then s/he is guilty of an offence."[74]

A provision like this would deem consent to be absent whenever a complainant was mistaken about any fact relating to sexual activity if her understanding of that fact influenced her decision to engage in sexual activity. Thus, it would include the situation where the complainant consented to sexual activity because she believed that the defendant loved her or intended to marry her. Herring posits that such a rule is justified because restricting the information on which one makes a choice can be as inhibiting of a free choice as making an option unattractive through a threat.[75] Indeed, he suggests that "in one sense deception can be regarded as worse than a threat because the deception uses the victim's own decision- **[1–33]**

---

[71] [2015] EWCA Crim 162.

[72] Rook and Ward, *Rook and Ward on Sexual Offences: Law & Practice* (5th ed, Sweet & Maxwell, London), p 142.

[73] Herring, "Mistaken Sex" [2005] *Criminal Law Review* 511, 517.

[74] *ibid.*

[75] *ibid*, 515.

making powers against her, thereby rendering her an instrument of harm against herself".[76] However, while morally it may be felt that such activity is unacceptable, Leahy suggests that including lesser frauds such as this within the remit of sexual offences is unacceptable for a number of reasons.

[1–34] First, as Leahy notes, "deceptions other than those as to the nature and purpose of the act or the identity of one's partner are generally not serious enough to warrant the imposition of liability for rape".[77] As Temkin comments:

> "... where a man perpetrates a fraud as to identity or as to the nature of the act, he deprives a woman of her right to choose whether and with whom to have sexual intercourse. The same is not true of the man who falsely assures a woman that he will love, marry, promote or house her if she has sexual intercourse with him. However reprehensible his conduct, it is sexual intercourse with him that he offers her. He has not deprived her of the right to choose whether to have intercourse with him or not."[78]

[1–35] Thus, whilst it is justifiable to impose criminal liability for rape in the case of fraud as to the nature or purpose of the act or the identity of one's partner, other lesser deceptions do not warrant the same penal consequences.[79]

[1–36] Secondly, Leahy highlights that frauds other than fraud as to the nature or purpose of an act, or the identity of one's partner, are difficult to prove, particularly where they relate to false declarations of love or fabricated promises of future benefits such as marriage or job promotion.[80] For example, it is difficult to show that the defendant's declaration of love or promise is untruthful. He may have meant it at the time and subsequently changed his mind.[81] In addition, measuring the causal impact of the deception is challenging. It is inherently difficult to prove that lesser deceptions such as declarations of love or intentions of marriage were the reason or at least a significant motivating factor in the complainant's decision to consent.[82] Even where the complainant believed the defendant's

---

76 *ibid.*

77 Leahy, *supra* note 28, 252

78 Temkin, "Towards a Modern Law of Rape" (1982) 45(4) *Modern Law Review* 399, 405.

79 Leahy, *supra* note 28, 252.

80 *ibid.*

81 Schulhofer notes that it is difficult to distinguish between a false promise and a genuine change of heart: Schulhofer, "Taking Sexual Autonomy Seriously: Rape Law and Beyond" (1992) 11 *Law and Philosophy* 35, 90.

82 Wertheimer, *Consent to Sexual Relations* (Cambridge University Press, Cambridge, 2003), p 201.

statements and was induced to consent as a result, it will be hard to prove this fact.[83] As Schulhofer notes:

> "What a date or sexual partner says about his feelings of attraction, future plans, or commitment to the relationship may be disbelieved, half believed, or believed but not relied upon. Perhaps more complicated, the parties sometimes may believe and not believe all at the same time."[84]

Consequently, Schulhofer suggests that "[l]egal evaluation of these questions after the fact can be heavy-handed, and it may be preferable to leave to the individual the decision whether to believe, whether to rely, and whether to assume the risk of deception by trusting the other party".[85] These concerns about proof are both sensible and valid. As Leahy notes, "the most likely result of such difficulties of proof is that a rule regarding lesser deceptions would be rarely (if ever) used".[86] For all of these reasons, it would seem prudent to limit the definition of fraud in this context to fraud as to the nature or purpose of the act and fraud as to the identity of one's partner. This would not, of course, prohibit the creation of a lesser offence of obtaining sexual intercourse by fraudulent means. A rather antiquated version of this offence exists in s 3 of the Criminal Law Amendment Act 1885, which is discussed above in the context of the decision in *R v Linekar*. This offence imposes criminal liability where a woman or girl "not being a common prostitute or of known immoral character" is procured by false pretences or false representations to have unlawful sexual intercourse anywhere in the world. This is an outdated provision and there is no evidence of its use in recent times. However, the creation of a more modernised version of this offence might provide a suitable means of dealing with sexual frauds which are not seen as serious enough to warrant a conviction for rape but still are worthy of criminal liability.[87] **[1–37]**

Importantly, s 9(5) retains the message provided for in the original incarnation of s 9, stating that "[a]ny failure or omission on the part of a person to offer resistance to an act does not of itself constitute consent to that act". Further, s 9(4) makes clear that "[c]onsent to a sexual act may be withdrawn at any time before the act begins, or in the case of a continuing **[1–38]**

83 Wertheimer notes that women often have sexual relations with men who do not say that they love them or intend to marry them: *ibid*. Thus, it does not follow that because these statements were made, that they induced the complainant to consent.

84 Schulhofer, *Unwanted Sex: The Culture of Intimidation and the Failure of the Law* (Harvard University Press, Cambridge, Massachusetts, 1998), p 158.

85 *ibid*.

86 Leahy, *supra* note 28, 252.

87 A reformed version of the 1885 offence has also been recommended by O'Malley: O'Malley, *supra* note 1, p 74.

act, while the act is taking place".[88] Notably, the new definition has been expressly declared to apply to all the non-consensual offences against adults. This is a welcome clarification as the common law considerations of the meaning of consent generally have arisen in the context of rape cases, generating some confusion as to whether the jurisprudence applies equally to sexual assault offences. For the purposes of the new definition of consent, "sexual act" means: (a) an act consisting sexual intercourse or buggery; (b) an act described in s 3(1) or s 4(1) of the 1990 Act (i.e. aggravated sexual assault or rape under s 4), or; (c) an act which if done without consent would constitute a sexual assault.[89]

The *Mens Rea* of Rape

[1–39] The *mens rea* of rape is set out in s 2(1)(b) of the 1981 Act which provides that a man has the necessary mental element for rape if at the time the sexual intercourse occurred, he knew that the woman did not consent or he was reckless as to whether she did or did not consent. Intention is the most straightforward form of *mens rea*. Here the defendant has as his conscious object sex with an individual whom he knows is not consenting.

[1–40] According to Campbell et al, "[a] person is said to act recklessly where he does not intend to cause a harmful result but takes an unjustifiable risk of causing it".[90] As noted by Walsh J in *DPP v Murray*,[91] recklessness may be defined subjectively or objectively:

> "Recklessness may be found either by applying a subjective test as where there has been conscious taking of an unjustified risk of which the accused actually knew, which imports foresight, or by applying an objective test as where there has been a conscious taking of an unjustified risk of which the accused did not actually know of but which he ought to have been aware."[92]

[1–41] In *Murray*, the subjective approach to recklessness was preferred. Griffin J held that "there must be advertence on the part of the accused—recklessness involves foresight of the possibility and the taking of a risk".[93] In the aftermath of *Murray*, there was some uncertainty regarding whether the interpretation of recklessness espoused there applied across Irish criminal law or merely to the offence considered in that case (capital murder).[94]

---

88 This gives statutory expression to the rule in *Kaitamaki v R* [1985] 1 AC 147.
89 s 9(6).
90 Campbell et al, *supra* note 11, p 131.
91 [1977] IR 360.
92 *ibid*, 386.
93 *ibid*, 415.
94 Campbell et al, *supra* note 11, p 144.

The Supreme Court dispelled this uncertainty in *DPP v Cagney; DPP v McGrath.*[95] Geoghegan J approved the approach to recklessness in *Murray* and further approved the definition of recklessness contained in the Model Penal Code,[96] endorsed by Henchy J in that case, as representing the Irish law:

> "A person acts recklessly with respect to a material element of an offence when he consciously disregards a substantial and unjustifiable risk that the material element exists or will result from his conduct. The risk must be of such a nature and degree that, considering the nature and purpose of the actor's conduct and the circumstances known to him, its disregard involves culpability of high degree."[97]

Most recently, the subjective interpretation of recklessness was endorsed in *Clifford v DPP*,[98] where Charleton J stated that: **[1–42]**

> "Recklessness consists of an accused subjectively taking a serious risk, involving high moral culpability, that his conduct will bring about the wrong defined by the charge. ... For an accused to be reckless, it must occur to the mind of the accused that his conduct will bring about the consequence impugned but, nonetheless, he proceeds to act."[99]

Applying the general rules on recklessness to rape in *DPP v O'R*,[100] Charleton J noted that in this context: **[1–43]**

> "... recklessness means that the possibility that a woman was not consenting actually occurred in the mind of the accused. Where an accused decides to proceed with or continue with intercourse in spite of adverting to that risk; that is recklessness".[101]

The difference between the knowing rapist and the reckless rapist is well-articulated by Burgess-Jackson who notes that the knowing actor, but not the reckless actor, is aware of the other party's non-consent. According to Burgess-Jackson, "the knowing rapist says, in effect: 'I know you're not consenting, but it doesn't matter'". On the other hand, "the reckless rapist says: 'You're giving every indication of not consenting, and if I knew you

---

95 [2008] 2 IR 111. This was a combined judgment relating to two separate appeals in relation to convictions for the offence of endangerment as defined in s 13 of the Non-Fatal Offences against the Person Act 1997.

96 Model Penal Code, s 2.02(2)(c).

97 [2008] 2 IR 111, 138.

98 [2008] IEHC 322. This case concerned an interpretation of s 6 of the Criminal Justice (Public Order) Act 1994.

99 *ibid*, para 14.

100 [2016] IESC 64.

101 *ibid*, para 45.

weren't, I'd desist; but maybe, in spite of appearances, you are consenting, so I'll proceed'".[102] Thus, the reckless rapist may be seen by some as being less morally culpable than the intentional rapist.[103] If this is the case, the difference in culpability may be reflected at sentencing stage. These general rules relating to the *mens rea* of rape are unremarkable and reflect the *mens rea* for other crimes. The more contentious aspect of the rules relating to *mens rea* is the honest belief defence.

The Honest Belief in Consent Defence

[1–44] The honest belief defence operates to exculpate a defendant who, at the time of the impugned sexual encounter, honestly believed that the complainant was consenting. A defence like this can be defined objectively or subjectively. In the former instance, the defendant could only rely on the defence if his belief was reasonable (i.e. was one that the average person would have formed). Conversely, where the defence is defined subjectively, a belief honestly held (no matter how unreasonable) would exculpate. The appropriate construction of the honest belief defence was first considered in *R v Morgan.*[104] Morgan was an officer with the Royal Air Force. He invited three junior officers to come to his house and have sexual intercourse with his wife, telling them that any apparent resistance on her part would be feigned. The men accompanied Morgan to his house where they found his wife asleep. Each of the men had sexual intercourse with her. Immediately after the incident, Morgan's wife presented herself at hospital and reported having been raped. The three men were charged with rape and Morgan was charged with aiding and abetting rape.[105] At trial, the judge directed the jury that the prosecution had to prove that the appellants had intended to have intercourse with Mrs Morgan without her consent. If the defendants had believed that she was a willing party they could not be found guilty provided that their belief was a reasonable one. All four defendants were convicted. They appealed, arguing that the trial judge had misdirected the jury. The House of Lords upheld their appeal, ruling that a belief in consent did not have to be reasonable to exculpate and thereby endorsing a subjective construction of the honest belief defence. Lord Hailsham stated that "since honest belief clearly negatives intent, the reasonableness or otherwise of

---

[102] Burgess-Jackson, *Rape: A Philosophical Investigation* (Dartmouth Publishing Company, Aldershot, 1996), p 139.

[103] Burgess-Jackson notes that the difference in culpability between knowledge and recklessness presumably resides in the lack of certainty on the part of the actor, with the knowing actor being (practically) certain of non-consent and the reckless actor not being certain but being aware of a substantial risk that consent is absent: *ibid.*

[104] [1976] AC 182.

[105] Morgan could not be charged with rape because the common law marital exemption (i.e. the rule whereby a man could not be charged with the rape of his wife) was still a part of English law at the time.

that belief can only be evidence for or against the view that the belief [and therefore the intent] was actually held".[106]

[1–45] The decision in *Morgan* was much criticised, with the judgment dubbed a "Rapists Charter".[107] However, a committee established to consider the law concluded that the judgment was correct and recommended statutory clarification of the position.[108] Section 1(1) of the Sexual Offences (Amendment) Act 1976 placed the subjective construction of the honest belief defence on a statutory footing:

> "It is hereby declared that if at a trial for a rape offence the jury has to consider whether a man believed that a woman was consenting to sexual intercourse, the presence or absence of reasonable grounds for such a belief is a matter to which the jury is to have regard, in conjunction with any other relevant matters, in considering whether he so believed."

[1–46] Following the English authorities, the subjective approach was transcribed into the Irish law in s 2(2) of the Criminal Law (Rape) Act 1981, which copied verbatim the wording of the English legislation.[109] Although the English rules on honest belief have been reformed and now reflect a more objective construction of the honest belief defence,[110] the subjective construction still represents the law in Ireland. It is necessary to consider how the defence has been applied in case law, as well as proposals for reform.

Section 2(2) in Practice

[1–47] Section 2(2) offers no guidance on how it should be applied. Consequently, in the 1990s a series of cases arose which questioned when s 2(2) should be drawn to the attention of the jury and the extent to which it must be explained

106 [1976] AC 182, 214. Although their appeal was upheld, the conviction of the appellants was not quashed. The House of Lords held that, on the facts, even if the jury had been properly directed, they would still have found the appellants guilty.

107 Nottelmann, *Blameworthy Belief: A Study in Epistemic Deontologism*, (Springer, The Netherlands, 2007), p 4.

108 The Helibron Committee, *Report of the Advisory Group on the Law of Rape*, (1975, Cmnd 6352).

109 s 2(2) provides that:

> "It is hereby declared that if at a trial for a rape offence the jury has to consider whether a man believed that a woman was consenting to sexual intercourse, the presence or absence of reasonable grounds for such a belief is a matter to which the jury is to have regard, in conjunction with any other relevant matters, in considering whether he so believed."

110 The new provisions on honest belief in the Sexual Offences Act 2003 are discussed below.

by the trial judge. In *The People (DPP) v Gaffey*,[111] the defendant and the complainant were acquaintances. The complainant stated that she had not consented to sexual intercourse but was forced into it by the defendant. The defendant contended that the complainant had consented and had never raised any objection or made any protest. The trial judge did not draw the jury's attention to s 2(2) when directing them. The Court of Criminal Appeal held that there were two issues which had to be tried by the jury in this case. First, they had to determine whether the complainant consented. Secondly, a matter which the Court held "clearly arose on the facts [of the case] was as to whether the accused knew she did not consent or was reckless as to whether she did consent or not". In the view of the Court, "[t]he existence of the second issue ... clearly brought the case within the category provided for in [s 2(2)]". The trial judge had not drawn the jurors' attention to the section or to the factors which they should consider in determining whether it was established beyond reasonable doubt that the defendant did not believe that the complainant was consenting to sexual intercourse. Thus, the Court of Criminal Appeal held that it was unsafe to let the defendant's conviction stand. Finlay CJ stated that the court was satisfied that:

> "... in this particular case, and it must not be taken to be that it will apply in every rape case, but in this particular case, having regard to the particular issues which were raised on the evidence given by both the complainant and the accused...subsection (2) did become relevant and that the specific directions along the lines indicated should have been given in the course of the charge to the jury."

[1–48] In *People (DPP) v F*,[112] the CCA noted that not every charge of rape will involve a real issue as to whether the defendant knew that the complainant did not consent or was reckless as to whether she did not consent. However, in cases where knowledge possessed by the defendant of the fact that the woman concerned was not consenting to sexual intercourse or recklessness on his part as to whether she was or not arises as something which the prosecution must establish, s 2(2) will apply. The Court also pointed out that in relation to knowledge or recklessness, s 2(2) does not make the presence or absence of reasonable grounds for a belief that the woman was consenting the determining or only factor—it is merely something which the jury must have regard to in conjunction with any other relevant matters. In *F*, the trial judge had appropriately explained s 2(2) to the jury. However, he did not link this explanation to any particular matters raised in the course of the evidence in the case which would constitute potential reasonable

---

[111] Unreported, Court of Criminal Appeal, 10 May 1991. Note there are no paragraph numbers available in this judgment.

[112] Unreported, Court of Criminal Appeal, 27 May 1993. Note that there are no paragraph numbers in this judgment.

grounds for such a belief. While the Court held that in many instances it will be sufficient to charge a jury on s 2(2) without further linking in any relevant evidence raised during the course of the trial, in *F* such a linkage was necessary. Accordingly, the appellant's conviction was set aside.

In *People (DPP) v Creighton*,[113] the complainant and the accused gave vastly different accounts of the sexual encounter which had taken place. The complainant asserted that she "had at all times made it unambiguously clear by what she said and did that she was not consenting".[114] The defendant contended that the complainant was "a willing and expressly agreeing participant in the acts of intercourse and other acts of sexual contact which occurred".[115] He did not offer evidence that he had reasonable grounds for believing that the complainant was consenting because his position was that she "plainly and expressly" consented.[116] The Court held that, in circumstances like this, a trial judge should state in full the statutory provisions applicable to rape, and explain in simple language the constituent elements of the charge. However, "it is not necessary, and might well be confusing", to direct the jury on the issue of whether there were reasonable grounds for a belief that a complainant was consenting if that issue did not arise from the evidence in the case.[117] Thus, it was held that in this case it had not been necessary for the trial judge to direct the jury on the application of s 2(2). **[1–49]**

The decision in *Creighton* conflicts with that in *DPP v Rock.*[118] Here, the defendant and complainant's accounts of the impugned incident flatly contradicted each other on the issue of consent. The Court of Criminal Appeal nonetheless held that this did not render s 2(2) irrelevant. Counsel for the State had argued that because of the facts (i.e. the complainant's allegation that there was no consent and the defendant's contention that the intercourse was consensual), the issue was "intentional rape or no rape at all". There was no need to direct the jury on honest belief. However, the Court held that as the defendant's contention was that the complainant consented, "it would follow that he believed that she had consented, and while the complainant's evidence was that she had not this did not exclude the possibility that the defendant believed that she had". Although the jury had two very different versions of the facts before them, the Court held that "it cannot be assumed that in coming to a conclusion on the facts they **[1–50]**

---

113 [1994] 1 ILRM 551.
114 *ibid*, 554.
115 *ibid.*
116 *ibid.*
117 [1994] 1 ILRM 551, 554.
118 Unreported, Court of Criminal Appeal, 29 July 1993. Note that there are no paragraph numbers in this judgment.

were limited to accepting one version and rejecting the other as they could have accepted parts of each version and rejected other parts". Since the jury could have held that the complainant did not consent and still found that the defendant believed that she consented, they should have been appropriately guided on s 2(2). Consequently, the conviction was set aside.

[1–51] By the mid-1990s, as a result of these Court of Criminal Appeal decisions, there was confusion about precisely how a trial judge should approach directing the jury on s 2(2). The Supreme Court considered the section for the first time in *People (DPP) v McDonagh.*[119] The appellants had been convicted of rape. As with many of the earlier cases cited above, the complainant and the appellants gave very different accounts of the events which led to the rape charge. The complainant asserted that she had been gang-raped by six men. The appellants had denied this, claiming that the woman had offered to have sex with all the men in return for IR£30. At trial, the jury accepted the complainant's account of events and convicted the appellants. The appellants appealed on the grounds that the trial judge had inadequately charged the jury on s 2(2). They argued that the judge should have read s 2(2), explained it to the jury and then instructed them on its significance, linking principles of law to the evidence in the trial which might have constituted grounds for an honest belief in consent on the part of the appellants.

[1–52] The Supreme Court held that the provisions of s 2(2) are only applicable when an issue of mistaken belief arises. According to Costello P:

> "Sub-section 2 contains principles which are applicable only in those cases in which the existence of the accused's belief has to be considered by the jury, that is those cases in which, the jury having found that the complainant had not in fact agreed to intercourse, an issue is raised that the accused had mistakenly believed that she had consented. If such an issue arises (and as the reported cases show the issue does not arise in every case in which it is claimed that a complainant consented to intercourse) then the trial judge will be required to explain to the jury the law as set out in the sub-section."[120]

[1–53] In the present case, the Supreme Court held that, if the jury concluded that, as a matter of fact, the complainant had not consented to intercourse in return for the payment of money as alleged by the appellants, then there was no basis on which it could be concluded that the appellants had believed that she had consented to intercourse. Accordingly, it was not necessary for the trial judge to have directed the jury on the provisions of s 2(2).

[119] [1996] 1 IR 565.
[120] *ibid*, 573.

As a Supreme Court decision, *McDonagh* provides some clarification of the conflicting judgments offered by the Court of Criminal Appeal on the application of s 2(2). However, the guidance offered here is still vague. Much is left to the discretion of the trial judge who must decide on a case-by-case basis whether an issue of honest belief arises. Commenting on *McDonagh*, Ní Raifeartaigh suggests that the judgment appears to lean against opening the subsection to the jury except in the clearest of cases.[121] That s 2(2) should only be explained to jury in exceptional cases was again emphasised by the Supreme Court in the more recent judgment in *DPP v O'R.*[122] Charleton J noted that cases in which honest belief in consent would be relevant would be few and far between: **[1–54]**

> "It is to be emphasised that in the vast majority of cases no specific issue as to any belief aspect of the mental element in rape arises. ... The circumstances are very rare indeed where a genuine issue could arise that even though the woman did not consent, the man nonetheless believed that she was consenting."[123]

The learned judge also highlighted that where the defendant's assertion was that the complainant consented, it would not also be open for him to claim that he held an honest belief in consent: **[1–55]**

> "In the ordinary course of prosecutions, rape cases tend to follow a predictable pattern. The woman says that she was raped and indicates the circumstances whereby she did not consent. The man denies this and puts forward a version of events telling of a sexually charged encounter participated in willingly by both sides. The task of the jury is to assess if the external elements of the offence have been proved beyond all reasonable doubt and whether, on the resolution of those facts in favour of the prosecution, a fact may be found beyond reasonable doubt that the accused knew of the lack of consent or was reckless as to whether the woman was or was not consenting. In those circumstances, the appropriate direction by the trial judge does not need to go beyond the presentation to the jury of the elements of the offence ... It is unnecessary in those cases to embark on the issue of mistaken belief as it simply does not arise. Nor can anyone credibly plead alternative facts: that there was a consensual sexual encounter but if there was not then that the accused nonetheless believed that the woman consented."[124]

Where, however, the defence is relied upon by the defendant, "then the jury should examine all of the facts which may support or which may undermine the claimed belief" and "[t]hey should consider all of the circumstances **[1–56]**

---

[121] Ní Raifeartaigh, "Comment on *People (D.P.P.) v. McDonagh*" (1997) 7(1) *Irish Criminal Law Journal* 81, 82.

[122] [2016] IESC 64.

[123] *ibid*, para 40.

[124] *ibid*, para 41.

and focus on whether there are, or are not, any reasonable grounds for that belief".[125] Charleton J also articulated that, although a defendant's belief need not be objectively reasonable to exculpate, irrational unfounded assertions of honest belief need not be accepted by jurors:

> "[s 2(2)] means that where the accused believed genuinely, albeit unreasonably, that the woman was consenting, on this statutory definition he must, even though she did not consent, be acquitted. It needs also to be stated by trial judges, however, that no jury is under any obligation to believe an obviously false story. A jury is entitled to accept or reject any prosecution or defence evidence. In these cases, every jury is entrusted, using shrewdness and commonsense, to judge what the accused claims as to his mistaken belief against their view of what an ordinary or reasonable man would have realised in the circumstances. This defence requires genuine belief."[126]

[1–57] The *O'R* judgment emphasises that the honest belief defence should only be raised where there is a solid base for claiming an honest belief in consent on the facts of the case. Moreover, the judgment makes clear that the defendant cannot claim that there was consent and also seek to rely on the defence of honest belief. The judgment places significant faith in jurors' ability to see through a clearly spurious claim of honest belief, thereby suggesting that the defence is not open to abuse and that the subjective construction of the defence is not creating injustice. However, given the complexities of rape cases, jurors may not be as impervious to spurious claims of honest belief as the Supreme Court would seem to believe. Thus, the defence may have greater practical impact than the judgment suggests. Consequently, there remains a case for reform of the current formulation of the defence, particularly in light of the introduction of the statutory definition of consent. Given the strong inter-linkage between both aspects of the law, to reform one element and not at least review the other would be incongruous.

Reform of the Honest Belief Defence

[1–58] There are strong arguments for reform of the current subjective approach to defining the honest belief defence, especially given that the English provision on which it has been based has since been abandoned in that jurisdiction. The practical difficulty with the current law is that it is very easy to raise the defence, as a defendant is not obliged to meet any objective minimum standard of appropriate behaviour to avail of it. Of course, as was highlighted by the Supreme Court in *O'R* and as stated by Hanly, the jury is not obliged to believe the defendant. The absence of reasonable grounds for the belief will increase the likelihood that the jury will disregard the

---

125 *ibid*, para 51.
126 *ibid*.

defendant's assertions of honest belief.[127] While it is certainly logical to suggest that the jury is free to accept or reject a defendant's claim to have had an honest belief in consent, in practice, where the defence is raised it has the propensity to cast doubt in the minds of jurors.. Convincing a jury that there was no way in which the defendant honestly believed that the complainant had given consent may prove difficult. For example, in some cases, the complainant may have been frozen in fear and may not have screamed or cried for help.[128] In such situations, the defendant could argue that he took the complainant's silence as consent. Consequently, it is clear that the subjective formulation of the honest belief defence can contribute to the difficulties of proof in sexual offence trials. At the very least, the defence creates a space for spurious assertions of honest belief which, even if not credible, can needlessly complicate the jury's deliberations.

Even if the practical problems with the current formulation of the honest belief defence are minimal, there is a principled argument against maintaining the subjective approach. An objective construction of the honest belief defence sends a message that forming a unilateral view about a sexual partner's consent is unacceptable. Redefining the honest belief defence could have an important symbolic effect.[129] As seen above, there was a view that the decision in *R v Morgan* was a "Rapists' Charter". Allowing the subjective construction of the defence to remain in force creates a sense that the current law is biased against complainants and favours a defendant's perspective on the incident.[130] There is thus a sound principled basis for a move towards a subjective construction of the defence. Based on both the practical and principled objections to the current law, there is a clear case for **[1–59]**

[127] Hanly, *supra* note 34, p 326.

[128] Victims of rape and sexual assault may often freeze during the attack and thus offer no physical or verbal resistance. Lees notes that the response of "freezing" is not uncommon where victims are often terrified for their lives: Lees, *Carnal Knowledge: Rape on Trial* (2nd ed, Women's Press Ltd, London, 2002), p xliii. The notion of "frozen fright" whereby victims do not offer resistance to the efforts of their attacker in rape and sexual assault cases has been recognised by the European Court of Human Rights: *MC v Bulgaria* (2005) 40 EHRR 20, para 164.

[129] Ashworth, *Principles of Criminal Law* (3rd ed, Oxford University Press, Oxford, 1999), p 355. However, Ashworth is clear that it is necessary to make sure that such a symbolic measure translates into practical effects. Thus, it would be necessary to publicise the new provision and educate the public about its significance.

[130] This is certainly the view of feminist commentators such as MacKinnon who argues that the problem with the subjective construction of the honest belief defence is that "while the injury of rape lies (or should lie) in the meaning of the act to its victim, the standard for its criminality lies in the meaning of the act to the defendant": MacKinnon, *Toward a Feminist Theory of the State* (Harvard University Press, Cambridge, Massachusetts, 1989), p 180. Lees makes a similar assessment, stating that the decision in *R v Morgan* "explicitly denies a woman's 'no' if a man reads it as consent'": Lees, *supra* note 128, p xxx (*Reader please note that this refers to a Roman numeral page within this text*). See also Temkin, *supra* note 40, pp 122–127.

considering the introduction of an objective standard. Indeed, the RCNI has repeatedly called for the honest belief defence to be objectively defined.[131]

[1–60] Of course, a move towards an objective construction of the honest belief defence raises concerns about protecting defendants' rights. There may be fears that such a reformulation could result in conviction of what Glanville Williams termed "the stupid man" (i.e. the defendant who is not capable of behaving reasonably). In his view, "to convict the stupid man would be to convict him for what lawyers call inadvertent negligence—honest conduct which may be the best that this man can do but that does not come up to the standard of the so-called reasonable man".[132] Many commentators have, however, expressed doubts about the potential for unfairness which an objective construction of the honest belief defence may pose. As Gardner and Shute note, stupidity is a vice, not an excuse.[133] Temkin also suggests that since it is very easy to confirm whether one's sexual partner is consenting and the harm caused where a mistake is made is grave, a requirement of reasonableness is not draconian.[134] There is strong academic support[135] for the view that an individual who forms a unilateral and unreasonable belief in consent has a culpable mindset and the unavailability of a defence is these circumstances is not disproportionate.

[1–61] A possible template for reform of the Irish law may be found in the English Sexual Offences Act 2003.[136] Honest belief is no longer a defence in English

---

[131] Rape Crisis Network of Ireland, *Agenda for Justice: Towards Ending Injustice for Survivors of Sexual Violence* (Rape Crisis Network of Ireland, Galway, 2005), p 4; *Consent on Sexual Contact: RCNI Discussion Document*, (Rape Crisis Network of Ireland, Galway, 2008), p 4; *RCNI Agenda for Justice Discussion Document* (Rape Crisis Network of Ireland, Galway, 2009), p 12.

[132] Glanville Williams, in a letter to *The Times* (London), 8 May 1975, quoted in Estrich, *Real Rape: How the Legal System Victimizes Women Who Say No* (Harvard University Press, Harvard, 1987), p 97.

[133] Gardner and Shute, "The Wrongness of Rape" in Horder, *Oxford Essays in Jurisprudence* (Oxford University Press, Oxford, 2000), p 213.

[134] Temkin, "Rape and Criminal Justice at the Millennium" in Nicolson and Bibbings (eds), *Feminist Perspectives on Criminal Law* (Cavendish Publishing, London, 2000), p 190.

[135] Archard, "The *Mens Rea* of Rape: Reasonableness and Culpable Mistakes" in Burgess-Jackson, *A Most Detestable Crime: New Philosophical Essays on Rape* (Oxford University Press, New York, 1999), p 225; Ashworth, *Principles of Criminal Law* (6th ed, Oxford University Press, Oxford, 1999), pp 354–355; Burgess-Jackson, *supra* note 102, p 142.

[136] For a full and detailed discussion of the feasibility of introducing the English approach to honest belief in Irish law, see: Leahy, "When Honest is Not Good Enough: The Need for Reform of the Honest Belief Defence in Irish Law" (2013) 23(1) *Irish Criminal Law Journal* 2.

law. Instead, it is now a constituent element of the *mens rea* of rape.[137] Thus, to satisfy the *mens rea* requirement for rape in English law, the defendant must have intended to commit the impugned sexual activity[138] and must not have reasonably believed that the complainant consented.[139] However, although honest belief is not formulated as a defence in the 2003 Act, the approach to its construction provides a model of how to objectively construct honest belief as a defence in Irish law. The requirement that a defendant have a reasonable belief in consent introduces an objective construction of honest belief into English law, but any potential unfairness for defendants who may not be able to reach an objective standard of behaviour is offset by the meaning attached to "reasonable". The 2003 Act provides that the reasonableness of a belief must be assessed with regards to "all the circumstances, including any steps which he has taken to ascertain whether the complainant was consenting".[140] The phrase "all the circumstances" requires an assessment of the context in which the sexual activity occurred. Thus, the jury should look at the actions of both parties, what the relationship between them was prior to the alleged incident, the circumstances in which they had placed themselves, and the level of responsibility exercised by both parties.[141] Further, the explicit reference to steps which the defendant has taken to ascertain whether the complainant was consenting emphasises the importance of sexual communication. While a defendant is not required to have taken steps to establish consent, Rook and Ward note that "this is something the jury will consider when considering the reasonableness of his belief" and that "[i]t is likely that police interviews with those suspected of rape will now focus more than in the past on what steps, if any, the suspect took to ascertain whether the complainant was consenting".[142]

Perhaps the most important issue relating to the interpretation of the English formulation of the honest belief defence is the protection it affords to defendants who are not capable of reaching an objectively reasonable standard of behaviour. The Crown Prosecution Service *Guidelines on the Sexual Offences Act 2003* provide that "all the circumstances" includes a defendant's attributes, such as disability or extreme youth, but not any particular fetishes which he may possess.[143] Thus, it would seem that in deciding whether the defendant's belief in consent was reasonable, any **[1–62]**

---

137 It is also a constituent element of the *mens rea* for assault by penetration (s 2); sexual assault (s 3) and causing sexual activity without consent (s 4).

138 For rape under English law, this would require the defendant to have intentionally penetrated the vagina, anus or moth of the complainant: s 1(1)(a).

139 s 1(1)(c).

140 s 1(2).

141 Home Office, *Protecting the Public: Strengthening protection against sex offenders and reforming the law on sexual offences*, (Home Office, London, 2002), p 17.

142 Rook and Ward, *supra* note 72, p 171.

143 Crown Prosecution Service, *Guidelines on the Sexual Offences Act 2003*, (Crown

characteristic of the defendant, transient or permanent, which might affect his ability to perceive or understand whether or not the complainant was consenting must be taken into account.[144] Examples of such characteristics include, learning disabilities, mental illness, impairment of sight or hearing, level of maturity or level of sexual experience or inexperience. The jury must determine whether a reasonable person clothed with the characteristics of the defendant would have believed that the complainant was consenting. However, in *R v B*,[145] it was made clear that the mere fact that a defendant was suffering from a mental illness or disorder of some kind does not mean that his belief in consent will be exculpatory: the condition must affect his ability to understand whether the complainant consented. According to Hughes LJ:

> "… unless and until a state of mind amounts to insanity in law, then under the rule enacted in the Sexual Offences Act beliefs in consent arising from conditions such as delusional psychotic illness or personality disorders must be judged by objective standards of reasonableness and not by taking into account a mental disorder which induced a belief which could not reasonably arise without it."[146]

The learned judge went on to clarify that:

> "It does not follow that there will not be cases in which the personality or abilities of the defendant may be relevant to whether his positive belief in consent was reasonable. It may be that cases could arise in which the reasonableness of such belief depends on the reading by the defendant of subtle social signals, and in which his impaired ability to do so is relevant to the reasonableness of his belief."[147]

[1–63] Thus, it is difficult to determine with any degree of accuracy which illnesses or disorders might be taken into account in determining whether a defendant's belief that consent was given is reasonable.[148] This uncertainty is regrettable but will no doubt be resolved as further cases are brought to the courts. Hughes LJ makes clear that where a condition genuinely affects an individual's capacity to understand whether a complainant was consenting, it can be taken into account by a jury. Thus, defendants are protected, but the legislation and its subsequent interpretation in the courts make clear

Prosecution Service, London, 2003), p 7. Available at: http://www.cps.gov.uk/legal/p_to_r/rape_and_sexual_offences/consent/#a04 (last accessed: 24 August 2017).

144 Card, *Sexual Offences: The New Law* (Jordan Publishing Ltd, Bristol, 2004), p 39.

145 [2013] EWCA Crim 3.

146 *ibid*, para 40. "The defendant's medical condition, and its impact on his behaviour, is of course, extremely relevant to sentence": *ibid*.

147 *ibid*, para 41.

148 Wortley, "Case Comment: Reasonable belief in consent under the Sexual Offences Act 2003" (2013) 77(3) *Journal of Criminal Law* 184, 188.

that irrational assertions of honest belief will not be entertained.

The English formulation of honest belief provides a possible template for reform of Irish law. Informed by the English provision, a reformed defence in Irish law should be phrased as follows: [1–64]

> "A defendant will not be guilty of rape where he held a reasonable belief that the complainant was consenting. Whether a belief was reasonable is to be determined according to all the circumstances, including any steps which the defendant took to ascertain whether the complainant was consenting."

Of course, as the English experience has shown, the introduction of such a provision in itself will not preclude the potential for inappropriate or irrational claims of honest belief to be raised and, indeed, entertained by juries. To be effective, very careful interpretation and application of the new provisions on the part of the judiciary would be essential. Significantly, mock jury research conducted by Finch and Munro on the English provision suggests that, without guidance, the looseness of the phrase "all the circumstances" is likely to be interpreted by jurors in a broad manner which will greatly reduce the significance of the more objective approach to *mens rea*.[149] Likewise, it would be very important that an approach similar to *R v B* would be adopted to ensure that a defendant's conditions or characteristics are only deemed to be relevant to belief in consent where they genuinely affected the defendant's ability to form a reasonable belief. However, with careful implementation, this reformed approach to honest belief could yield important symbolic and practical benefits. It is unfortunate that the Irish legislature did not opt to reform the honest belief in consent defence to accompany the new definition of consent in the Criminal Law (Sexual Offences) Act 2017. However, the government has referred this issue for consideration by the LRC[150] and an examination of the defence in light of any recommendations from the LRC has been promised in the *National Strategy for Women and Girls 2017-2020*.[151] It is to be hoped that these commitments will lead to prompt and meaningful reform in this area. [1–65]

Rape within Marriage

Previously, under common law, a husband could not be guilty of raping his wife. The historic justification behind this rule was explained by the seventeenth century jurist Sir Matthew Hale in the following terms: [1–66]

149 Finch and Munro, "Breaking Boundaries?: Sexual Consent in the Jury Room" (2006) 26(3) *Legal Studies* 303, 303.

150 Bardon, "State to review use of honest belief of consent as rape defence", *The Irish Times*, 24 January 2017.

151 Department of Justice and Equality, *National Strategy for Women and Girls 2017-2020* (Department of Justice and Equality, Dublin, 2017), objective 5.10.

> "But the husband cannot be guilty of rape committed by himself upon his lawful wife, for by their mutual matrimonial consent and contract, the wife hath given herself up in this kind unto her husband which she cannot retract."[152]

[1–67] The presumption that a man could not rape his wife remained law until the enactment of s 5(1) of the Criminal Law (Rape) Act 1990 which abolished "... any rule of law by virtue of which a husband cannot be guilty of the rape by him of his wife ...". However, s 5(2) of the Act provides that criminal proceedings against a man in respect of the rape by him of his wife shall not be instituted except by or with the consent of the DPP. The reasoning for this condition is unclear. As Bacik et al comment, "since the consent of the DPP is required in order to prosecute any indictable crime ... this 'special rule' is somewhat meaningless and it seems to create an unnecessary distinction between marital and other forms of rape".[153] Campbell et al argue that requiring the DPP's consent for prosecution, "a factor that is absent in other offences", "may betray a sentiment on the part of the legislature that such a crime perpetrated by a woman's husband is not truly comparable to rape per se".[154] There have been a number of calls for removal of this requirement from Irish law. The Joint Oireachtas Committee on Justice, Defence and Equality recommended that s 5(2) should be repealed in its *Report on hearings in relation to Domestic and Sexual Violence*.[155] The RCNI has also called for s 5(2) to be repealed, labelling the section "anachronistic".[156]

---

[152] Hale, *The History of Pleas of the Crown: Volume 1*, 629: reproduced in Temkin, *supra* note 40, p 77.

[153] Bacik, et al, *The Legal Process and Victims of Rape: A comparative analysis of the laws and legal procedures relating to rape, and their impact upon victims of rape, in the fifteen member states of the European Union*, (Dublin Rape Crisis Centre, Dublin, 1998), p 244. At the time of the passage of the Bill, a private prosecution could reach a preliminary hearing in the District Court without the DPP's intervention. s 5(2) would prohibit this, thereby preventing "the institution of spiteful or mischievous proceedings by a spouse or an interfering third party": Minister for Social Welfare (Dr Woods), presenting the Criminal Law (Rape) (Amendment) Bill 1988 on behalf of the Minister for Justice, *Dáil Debates*, 18 May 1989, Vol 390, col 601.

[154] Campbell et al, *supra* note 11, p 588. Fennell notes that it is difficult not to perceive s 5(2) as representative of "the lingering suspicion that a woman, devious as she is with all the traditions and myths of Eve hanging about her, would once again use rape within marriage as some way of getting back at her husband"; Fennell, *supra* note 33, 32–01 to 32–02.

[155] Joint Oireachtas Committee on Justice, Defence and Equality, *Report on Hearings in Relation to Domestic and Sexual Violence*, (Joint Oireachtas Committee on Justice, Defence & Equality, Dublin, 2014), p 5.

[156] Rape Crisis Network of Ireland, *RCNI Agenda for Justice: Discussion Document* (Rape Crisis Network of Ireland, Galway, 2009), p 14. A similar call for reform was made by the RCNI in 2005: *Agenda for Justice: Towards Ending Injustice for Survivors of Sexual Violence: RCNI Legal Position Paper*, (Rape Crisis Network of Ireland, Galway, 2005), p 4.

Although the marital exemption has been abolished, the difficulties in obtaining a conviction for marital rape are illustrated by the case in which the first conviction for marital rape was obtained in the State. This conviction was secured in January 2006.[157] The defendant was sentenced to six years in prison. The incident had occurred in July 1997. The defendant was first convicted in 2002 but this was overturned by the Court of Criminal Appeal who ordered a retrial. The delays involved in this case, along with the fact that the first conviction for marital rape occurred so long after the removal of the marital rape exemption, demonstrate that, despite the change in the law, effectively punishing rape within the marital relationship remains challenging. These challenges are further evidenced in the fact that there have only been three other convictions for marital rape in Ireland. In October 2015, a man was sentenced to six years' imprisonment for marital rape. Significantly, when arrested, he told the gardaí that he did not think it was possible for a man to rape his wife.[158] More recently, in 2016, there were two convictions for marital rape in this jurisdiction. In July 2016, a man was sentenced to 10 years' imprisonment for marital rape.[159] This case received a lot of attention in the media, serving as a grim reminder of the abuse which women can be subjected to within intimate relationships. The husband in this case was also found guilty of separate offences of threatening to kill his wife and pleaded guilty to assaulting her with a hammer. A further conviction in October 2016 once again involved significant levels of violence. The man in this case punched his wife in the face several times during the rape. In December 2016, he was sentenced to seven years' imprisonment with the final two years suspended.[160] **[1–68]**

There are no official statistics available on the number of complaints of marital rape made to the gardaí or of the number of prosecutions which have been taken since the 1990 Act commenced. However, statistics show that a substantial number of rape victims were attacked by current or former partners (necessarily including husbands). In *SAVI*, 23.6 percent of perpetrators of sexual violence against women as adults were intimate partners, or ex-partners.[161] Further, statistics from Women's Aid show that there were 616 disclosures of sexual abuse by women engaging with their **[1–69]**

---

[157] McCartaigh, "First man convicted for marital rape jailed for six years", *Irish Examiner*, 31 January 2006.

[158] "Six-year sentence for man convicted of raping his wife", *The Irish Times*, 30 November 2015.

[159] Gallagher, "Man jailed for 10 years for threatening, assaulting and raping his wife", *The Irish Times*, 25 July 2016.

[160] Hayes, "Man gets five years in jail for raping and beating his wife", *Irish Independent*, 21 December 2016.

[161] McGee, et al, *The SAVI Report: Sexual Abuse and Victimization in Ireland* (The Liffey Press, Dublin, 2002) p 98.

services in 2015. This included 212 reports of rape.[162] The Dublin Rape Crisis Centre *Annual Report 2015* also revealed that 24.36 percent of victims who had used their service had been sexually abused by a boyfriend or partner.[163] These statistics suggest that rape within intimate relationships, including marriage, happens more frequently than the conviction rate suggests.

162 Women's Aid, *Impact Report 2015* (Women's Aid, Dublin, 2016), p 19.

163 Dublin Rape Crisis Centre, *Annual Report 2015* (Dublin Rape Crisis Centre, Dublin, 2016), p 15.

Chapter Two

Sexual Assault Offences against Adults

Introduction

This chapter focusses on the sexual assault offences which can be committed against adults. The most serious of these offences is rape under s 4 which was enacted to punish non-consensual penetrative sexual activity other than vaginal sexual intercourse. The remaining offences are sexual assault and aggravated sexual assault. The three offences may be referred to as "assault-based" offences as they all stem from the basic offence of sexual assault which has assault as a constituent element of the *actus reus*. They are discussed here in ascending order of gravity, beginning with sexual assault. [2–01]

Sexual Assault

Prior to 1990, indecent assault against a female and indecent assault against a male were two separate offences. Both punished all non-consensual sexual activity other than common law rape. Until the introduction of the Criminal Law (Rape) Act 1981, there were different maximum penalties depending on the sex of the victim. Section 62 of the Offences against the Person Act 1861 provided for a maximum penalty of 10 years' imprisonment[1] for indecent assault upon a male. However, s 52 of the same Act only provided for a maximum penalty of two years' imprisonment for the equivalent offence upon a female. Section 52 was later repealed by s 6 of the Criminal Law (Amendment) Act 1935, which provided for a penalty of two years' imprisonment for a first offence or for three to five years' imprisonment for a subsequent offence. Section 10 of 1981 Act increased the maximum penalty for indecent assault upon a female to 10 years' imprisonment, creating parity of punishment for both offences.[2] [2–02]

1 The text of the original Act refers to "penal servitude". Criminal Law Act 1997, s 11, abolished penal servitude and removed all references to penal servitude from Irish legislation. Where terms of penal servitude are prescribed in legislation, these punishments must now be read as terms of imprisonment: s 11(2).

2 In *SM v Ireland* [2007] 4 IR 369, the discrepancy in punishments for indecent assault upon a male and indecent assault upon a female in s 62 of the 1861 Act was declared to be inoperative. Laffoy J held that the varying punishments violated the equality guarantees in Art 40.1 of the Constitution. Article 50 of the Constitution declares

[2–03] The term "indecent assault" was also eventually found to be unsatisfactory. In its *Consultation Paper on Rape*, the Law Reform Commission (LRC) noted that the term "indecent" "seriously understate[d] the gravity and enormity of the defendant's conduct" where the conduct involved is at the far-end of the scale of conduct which was covered by the term "indecent assault" (e.g. where there is unwanted sexual touching accompanied by significant violence).[3] The offence was re-labelled as sexual assault in the Criminal Law (Rape) (Amendment) Act 1990. Section 2(1) provides that "the offence of indecent assault upon any male person and the offence of indecent assault upon any female person shall be known as sexual assault". The maximum penalty for sexual assault is 10 years' imprisonment.[4] However, if the victim is aged under 17 years at the time of the assault, the maximum penalty increases to 14 years' imprisonment.[5]

[2–04] Section 2 is basically a statutory re-labelling of the offence of indecent assault on a woman and indecent assault on a man, amalgamating these two offences into one offence of "sexual assault". The basic elements of the offence are not altered. It has simply been re-named and introduced to the statute books. This approach is not uncomplicated and, perhaps unsurprisingly, s 2 has been challenged in the courts. In *Doolan v DPP*,[6] it was argued that there was no offence of indecent assault known to common law and that consequently, s 2 did not effectively create an offence. O'Hanlon J dismissed this argument, noting that:

> "An indecent assault … was an offence at common law, and in my opinion, it was permissible for parliament to prescribe a special range of penalties for assault, or assault and battery, of this particular kind without having to spell out the creation of a new statutory felony or misdemeanour in the process."[7]

---

that any laws preceding the enactment of the Constitution which are incompatible with constitutional provisions would no longer be enforceable once the Constitution became operative. Thus, the varying punishments for indecent assault upon a male and indecent assault upon a female did not survive after the Constitution was enacted in 1937. This did not, however, affect the offence itself, which was held to be a common law offence. The only effect was that there would be no statutory penalty applicable should the plaintiff in this case be convicted of the allegations of sexual assault (alleged to have occurred in the period 1966 to 1976) which were pending against him.

3 Law Reform Commission, *Consultation Paper on Rape*, (Dublin: Law Reform Commission, 1987), para 57.

4 Criminal Law (Rape) (Amendment) Act 1990, s 2(2)(a)(ii), as amended by s 37 of the Sex Offenders Act 2001.

5 Criminal Law (Rape) (Amendment) Act 1990, s 2(2)(a)(i), as amended by s 37 of the Sex Offenders Act 2001. For the purposes of the section, a child is defined as someone under 17 years of age: s 2(b).

6 [1993] ILRM 387

7 *ibid*, 392.

This interpretation was confirmed by the Supreme Court in *People (DPP) v EF.*[8] Egan J held that: [2–05]

> "the offence of indecent assault remains but as and from the 21st January 1991 it became known as sexual assault. It still remains a common law offence for which punishment is provided by statute".[9]

Most recently, in *S O'C v Governor of Curragh Prison,*[10] Hardiman J held that "it seems clear that the effect of section 2 of the Act of 1990 was simply to change the name of the offence while leaving its nature and constituents unaltered".[11] In effect then, sexual assault is "a mixed statutory and common law offence".[12] Since the 1990 Act simply re-labels the common law offence, the existing law surrounding indecent assault is equally applicable to sexual assault.[13] The *actus reus* and *mens rea* of sexual assault must be determined according to common law. [2–06]

Actus Reus

In *R v Court,* the House of Lords held that on a charge of indecent assault, [2–07]

> "... the prosecution must prove (1) that the accused intentionally assaulted the victim, (2) that the assault, or the assault and the circumstances accompanying it, are capable of being considered by right-minded persons as indecent, (3) that the accused intended to commit such an assault as is referred to in (2) above."[14]

Therefore, to demonstrate the *actus reus* of sexual assault, there must be (1) an assault and (2) circumstances of indecency. Each of these elements will be considered in turn. [2–08]

Assault

There is some uncertainty as to whether the definition of assault which applies to sexual assault is the statutory definition in s 2(1) of the Non-Fatal [2–09]

---

8 Unreported, 24 February 1994 (Egan J).
9 *ibid.* Note that there are no paragraph numbers in this judgment.
10 [2002] 1 IR 66.
11 *ibid,* 69.
12 McIntyre and McMullan, *Criminal Law* (Thomson Round Hall, Dublin, 2005), p 153.
13 Charleton points out that the use of the words "shall be known as sexual assault" in s 2(1) make it clear that the common law of indecent assault must be applied to the new offences of sexual assault and aggravated sexual assault: Charleton, *Offences Against the Person* (Round Hall, Dublin, 1992), p 285.
14 [1988] 2 All ER 221 at 232; Charleton, McDermott and Bolger, *Criminal Law* (Butterworth, Dublin, 1999), p 647.

Offences against the Person Act 1997. O'Malley suggests that as sexual assault is based upon the common law offence of indecent assault, "the better view probably is that ... the assault element should continue to be defined as at common law".[15] However, as O'Malley also asserts, "[t]he question is not of great moment because there is little difference between the common law and present statutory definitions".[16] Given the similarity between the common law and legislative definitions, for ease of discussion here, the s 2 offence is used to articulate the ways in which assault may be understood for the purposes of sexual assault. Section 2(1) of the Non-Fatal Offences against the Person Act 1997 provides that:

> "A person shall be guilty of the offence of assault who, without lawful excuse, intentionally or recklessly:
> (a) directly or indirectly applies force to or causes an impact on the body of another, or:
> (b) causes another to believe on reasonable grounds that he or she is immediately to be subjected to any such force or impact,
> without the consent of another".

[2–10] There are thus two forms of assault. The first is where the victim is subjected to an impact upon her person and the second involves causing the victim to reasonably believe she will be immediately subjected to force or impact. The former mirrors the offence of battery at common law and the latter resembles the common law offence of assault. Consequently, two potential scenarios may arise in the context of sexual assault. The victim may be subjected to physical impact in circumstances of indecency. For example, the defendant may stroke the victim's breasts or genitals without her consent. Such touching need not necessarily involve threats or hostility. In *Faulkner v Talbot*,[17] it was held that "[a]n assault is any intentional touching of another person without the consent of that person and without lawful excuse. It need not necessarily be hostile or rude or aggressive".[18] The alterative scenario involves behaviour which causes the victim to reasonably believe that such unwanted physical impact will be inflicted upon him/her. An example of such a scenario may be taken from *R v Rolfe*.[19] The complainant was sitting alone in a train carriage when the appellant joined her. He then exposed his penis to her and moved towards her, "inviting her to have connection with him".[20] The English Court of Appeal upheld his conviction for indecent assault as the behaviour constituted an assault. Lord Goddard CJ noted that:

---

15 O'Malley, *Sexual Offences* (2nd ed, Round Hall, Dublin, 2013), p 102.
16 *ibid*, p 101.
17 [1983] 3 All ER 468.
18 *ibid*, 471.
19 (1952) 36 Crim App R. 4.
20 *ibid*, 5.

> "One always thinks of an assault as the giving of a blow to somebody, but that is not necessary. An assault may be constituted by a threat or hostile act committed towards a person, and if a man indecently exposes himself and walks towards a woman with his person exposed and makes an indecent suggestion to her that, in the opinion of this court, can amount to an assault."[21]

Thus, causing someone to believe that they will be subject to touching in circumstances of indecency can amount to a sexual assault. What has proved problematic, however, are cases where the defendant has not touched the complainant or necessarily caused her to believe she will be touched, but rather has invited or suggested sexual touching. This scenario has arisen in circumstances where adult defendants have invited children to touch them sexually. The courts have held that an invitation to touch is not sufficient to constitute an assault for the purposes of sexual assault. For example, in *Fairclough v Whipp*,[22] the defendant was urinating by the bank of a canal when a group of young girls aged between six and nine passed by. The defendant exposed his penis to one of the girls, aged nine, and asked her to "[t]ouch it". The girl complied with his request. Lord Goddard CJ held that an invitation to touch such as this was not tantamount to an assault: **[2–11]**

> "An assault can be committed without there being battery, for instance, by a threatening gesture or a threat to use violence made against a person, but I do not know of any authority that says that, where one person invites another person to touch him, that can amount to an assault … [B]efore we come to the question whether there was an indecent assault we must consider whether there was an assault, and I cannot hold that an invitation to somebody to touch the invitor can amount to an assault on the invitee."[23]

As there was no assault, there could be no indecent assault. Hanly submits that if the defendant had forced the girl to touch him, or advanced towards her, the situation would have been different, as these actions could be taken as assault.[24] A similar outcome to *Fairclough v Whipp* may be seen in *R v Burrows*.[25] The defendant exposed himself to a boy and asked the boy to masturbate him. Lord Goddard CJ held that if the defendant only invited the boy to touch him, "and did not in any way threaten the boy or commit a hostile act against the boy, that did not amount in law to an indecent **[2–12]**

---

[21] *ibid*, 6.

[22] [1951] 2 All ER 834. (1951) 35 CR APP R 138.

[23] (1951) 35 CR APP R 138, 139–140.

[24] Hanly, *An Introduction to Irish Criminal Law* (3rd ed, Gill and MacMillan, Dublin, 2015), p 291. Similarly, if on refusing to touch the defendant, the victim is reasonably under the apprehension that on refusal she would be grabbed by the accused in indecent circumstances, there would then be a sexual assault: Charleton, *supra* note 13, p 288.

[25] [1952] 1 All ER 58; (1951) 35 Crim App R 180.

assault".[26] A more controversial case is *R v Rogers*.[27] The defendant, on two occasions, put his arm around his 11-year-old daughter, led her upstairs, exposed his penis and asked her to masturbate him. His daughter complied with these requests. The defendant did not use force or compulsion. Confirming that the defendant was rightly acquitted of indecent assault, Lord Goddard CJ noted that:

> "If one could show here that the respondent had done anything towards his child which by any fair use of language could be called compulsion, or acted, as I have said in other cases, in a hostile manner towards her, that is, with a threat or gesture which could be taken as a threat, or by pulling the child, after she had shown reluctance, towards him, that would undoubtedly be assault, and if it was accompanied by an act of indecency, it would be an indecent assault."[28]

[2–13] It was held that because the defendant had not used force or compulsion or acted in a hostile manner, there was no assault.

[2–14] The foregoing case-law demonstrates a worrying gap in the protection which common law offers for children in the context of sexual assault. Fortunately, this gap in protection has now been filled by the Criminal Law (Sexual Offences) Act 2017 which provides for the punishment of passive or "invitation to touch" sexual assaults of children. Section 4(1) of the Act creates an offence of "invitation etc. to sexual touching", providing that:

> "A person who, for sexual purposes, invites, induces, counsels or incites a child[29] to touch, with a part of the body or with an object, the body of any person, including the body of the person who so invites, induces, counsels or incites and the body of the child, shall be guilty of an offence ..."

[2–15] The maximum penalty for this offence is imprisonment for a term not exceeding 14 years.[30] The introduction of this offence responds to calls for reform made by the LRC[31] and the Joint Oireachtas Committee on Child Protection[32] and provides welcome protection for children from this form of sexual abuse.

---

[26] (1951) 35 Crim App R 180, 183. Lord Goddard CJ suggested that the appropriate charge to have brought in this case would have been one of procuring or attempting to procure an act of gross indecency: *ibid*.

[27] [1953] 3 All ER 644; [1953] 1 WLR 1017; (1953) 37 Crim App R 137.

[28] [1953] 3 All ER 644, 645.

[29] For the purposes of the section, "child" means a person under the age of 15: s 4(2).

[30] Criminal Law (Sexual Offences) Act 2017, s 4(1).

[31] The LRC criticised this gap in the law: Law Reform Commission, *Report on Child Sexual Abuse*, (Dublin: Law Reform Commission, 1990), paras 4.16–4.20.

[32] Joint Oireachtas Committee on Child Protection, *Report Child Protection* (Joint Oireachtas Committee on Child Protection, Dublin, 2006), para 4.6.12.

Indecency

Whether the circumstances accompanying the assault are "indecent" is an objective fact to be decided by the jury. In *R v Court*,[33] Lord Ackner stated that: **[2–16]**

> "... the jury must be asked 'to decide whether right-minded persons would consider the conduct indecent or not'. It is for the jury to decide whether what occurred was so offensive to contemporary standards of modesty and privacy as to be indecent."[34]

Accordingly, it is clear that what constitutes indecency can vary from case to case and can, indeed, change over time as public sensibilities change and develop. As a result of this, it is very difficult to frame a precise definition of "indecency" but the decision in *Court* is instructive. In that case, Lord Ackner identified and discussed three types of situation that can arise in the context of deciding whether conduct was indecent, so as to satisfy the test for indecent assault. **[2–17]**

The first is a situation where "the circumstances of the assault are *incapable* of being regarded as indecent".[35] If an act is inherently decent, an "undisclosed intention of the accused could not make the assault an indecent one".[36] By way of support for this statement, Lord Ackner cited the case of *R v George*.[37] In that case, the defendant had, on a number of occasions, removed a young girl's shoe from her foot. He admitted that this action provided him with sexual gratification. The court held that the defendant was not guilty of indecent assault as an assault became indecent only if it was accompanied by circumstances of indecency towards the person alleged to have been assaulted. The removal or attempted removal of shoes, without more, did not satisfy this test of indecency. However, while the defendant's undisclosed intention cannot make an assault indecent, the fact that the complainant was not aware of the circumstances of indecency, or did not appreciate the indecency of the circumstances, does not mean that an indecent assault has not been committed.[38] Thus, if a complainant was asleep or unconscious when she was indecently assaulted and thus did not apprehend either the assault or the indecent circumstances, an indecent assault will still have been committed. **[2–18]**

The second type of situation is where there is an assault which is *inherently* **[2–19]**

---

33 [1988] All ER 221.
34 *ibid*, 229.
35 *ibid.*
36 *ibid.*
37 [1956] Crim LR 52.
38 [1988] All ER 221, 229.

indecent, such as, for example, where the defendant removes a woman's clothing against her will. Lord Ackner noted that "those facts, devoid of any explanation, would give rise to the irresistible inference that the defendant intended to assault his victim in a manner which right-minded persons would clearly think was indecent".[39] Conduct in this category is indecent by its very nature, irrespective of whether the defendant engages in the conduct for sexual or other reasons.[40]

[2–20] The final type of situation which can arise is where the conduct of the defendant is *capable* of being an indecent assault, depending on the facts of the case. Lord Ackner notes that, in deciding whether or not right-minded persons might think that an assault was indecent, the following factors are relevant:

> "(i) the relationship of the defendant to victim (i.e. were they relatives, friends or virtually complete strangers);
> (ii) the way in which the defendant had come to embark on this conduct and;
> (iii) why the defendant was behaving in this way?"[41]

[2–21] Armed with this information, the jury can determine the true nature of the assault. Hanly notes that a guilty verdict should only be returned where the jury is sure that the circumstances of the assault lead to an irresistible inference that the defendant had intended to commit the assault in an indecent manner.[42]

[2–22] The facts of *Court* fell within the third category. The appellant, a 26-year-old shop assistant, pulled a 12-year-old girl visitor to the shop across his knees and smacked her with his hand 12 times on her bottom outside her shorts for no apparent reason. If the defendant's behaviour had been a disciplinary measure, it would have been a common assault. However, if it was done for sexual gratification, it would be an indecent assault. The appellant pleaded guilty to assault but denied that it was indecent. When asked by the police to explain his behaviour, he had replied "I don't know—buttock fetish". However, at trial, he contended that his statement regarding his "buttock fetish" should be excluded as evidence as it was a secret uncommunicated motive and as such, could not make indecent an assault which was not overtly indecent. This contention was rejected by the House of Lords which held that any evidence of the accused's explanation for assaulting the victim, regardless of whether it reveals an indecent motive, is admissible

---

39 *ibid*, 230.
40 Simester and Sullivan., *Criminal Law: Theory and Doctrine* (2nd ed, Hart Publishing, Oxford, 2003), p 416.
41 [1988] All ER 221, 230.
42 Hanly, *supra* note 24, p 330.

both to support or negative that the assault was an indecent one and was so intended by the accused.[43] Thus, the defendant was rightly convicted of indecent assault.

Consent

Originally, the 1990 Act did not clarify the relevance of consent for the assault-based sexual offences.[44] While the legislation was being discussed in the Dáil, concern was expressed at the non-inclusion of the words "non-consensual" in the definition of sexual assault and aggravated sexual assault. However, the then Minister for Justice defended this omission on the basis that an assault is by definition non-consensual.[45] The non-inclusion of the words "non-consensual" in s 4 was similarly justified.[46] This reasoning would appear to be based on the notion that because these offences involve "assaults", it would be impossible for a defendant to successfully argue that the complainant consented due to the level of violence or force involved. This may well be true in some instances, especially for allegations of aggravated sexual assault. However, the slightest touching may constitute an assault. Violence need not be involved. Consider the example of a defendant who fondled a complainant's breast. The presence of consent may be very believable if, for example, the defendant was the complainant's date for the evening and there was no additional force other than the unwanted touching. Similarly, the type of sexual activity which would form the basis of a charge of rape under s 4 could easily give rise to a doubt about the presence of consent as it covers penetration, however slight, and this requires no additional elements of force or violence. For example, it is easy to imagine that a defendant might credibly argue that the complainant who was his on-off girlfriend at the time was consenting to oral sex with him. **[2–23]**

Despite the failure of the 1990 Act to address the relevance of consent for the assault-based offences, it was generally understood that, since the absence of consent is a prerequisite for an assault and assault is a constituent element of sexual assault, it is axiomatic that the presence of consent will exculpate a defendant charged with any form of sexual assault upon an adult with full mental capacity (including aggravated sexual assault and rape under s 4). A case which illustrates the applicability of the rules on consent to **[2–24]**

43 [1988] All ER 221, 232, per Lord Ackner.

44 This omission has been criticised by the Rape Crisis Network of Ireland (RCNI): *RCNI Submission on Substantive and Procedural Legal Reforms in relation to Sexual Offences*, (RCNI, Galway, 2012), p 9.

45 Fennell, "Annotation of the Criminal Law (Rape)(Amendment) Act 1990", *Irish Current Law Statutes Annotated*, 32–01 at 32–06. See comments of Minister for Justice (Deputy Burke), *Dáil Debates*, 4 December 1990, (vol 403), col 944.

46 *ibid*, 32–01 at 32–10.

sexual assault is *R v Tabassum*[47] which was discussed in chapter one. The complainant in this case consented to an examination of her breasts in the belief that the defendant possessed medical qualifications, when in fact he did not. The defendant was found guilty of indecent assault as his fraud vitiated the complainant's apparent consent to his touching. Fortunately, the Criminal Law (Sexual Offences) Act 2017 has now confirmed that the definition of consent introduced in s 48 of that Act applies to an act described in s 3(1) or s 4(1) of the 1990 Act (i.e. aggravated sexual assault and rape under s 4), as well as "an act which if done without consent would constitute a sexual assault". This clarification is significant, and provides welcome transparency in this area of the law.

[2–25] There are, however, two exceptions to the applicability of the rules on consent to the assault-based offences which remain after the clarification provided in the 2017 Act. First, consent is irrelevant where the complainant is under 15 years of age. Section 14 of the Criminal Law Amendment Act 1935 provides that a child under the age of 15 is not legally capable of consenting to the act which constitutes the sexual assault.[48] Second, consent is irrelevant where an assault causes "serious harm". The irrelevance of consent where sexual activity causes serious harm is clearly evident in the now infamous English case of *R v Brown*.[49] The appellants in this case were appealing their convictions for wounding and assaults occasioning actual bodily harm under ss 20 and 47 of the Offences against the Person Act 1861, respectively. The appellants were homosexual sadomasochists who had engaged in consensual sadomasochistic sexual activity whereby they committed acts of violence against each other for sexual pleasure.[50] No complaint had been made to the police, but charges were preferred on the appellants after the police became aware of their activities. The appellants were convicted of offences under the 1861 Act, but appealed on the grounds that a conviction for an assault-offence is not possible where the alleged victim has consented to the activity in question. This argument was dismissed by the House of Lords who held that there may be limits on the types of activity to which an individual can legally consent. The majority in the House of Lords was of the view that it was not in the public interest

---

47 [2000] 2 Cr App R 328.

48 Sexual offences against individuals who are under the age of consent are discussed fully in chapter three.

49 [1994] 1 AC 212; [1993] 2 All ER 75.

50 The activity involved was described by Lord Templeman:

> "The charges against the appellants were based on genital torture and violence to the buttocks, anus, penis, testicles and nipples. The victims were degraded and humiliated, sometimes beaten, sometimes wounded with instruments and sometimes branded. Bloodletting and the smearing of human blood produced excitement. There were obvious dangers of serious personal injury and blood infection.": [1994] 1 AC 212, 236.

that one individual should wound or cause actual bodily harm to another without a legitimate reason. Thus, an individual's consent to such infliction of harm will not exculpate a defendant.[51] Consequently, if in the course of sexual activity, serious harm is inflicted on a complainant, there can be no question of the complainant's consent (alleged or actual) exculpating the defendant.

An example of this rule in practice can be seen in *R v Emmett*.[52] The appellant was convicted of assault occasioning actual bodily harm in relation to two incidents of sexual activity with his girlfriend. In the first incident, the appellant, with his girlfriend's consent, covered her head with a plastic bag, tied it at her neck with a ligature and tied her up whilst he performed oral sex on her. His girlfriend became distressed as a result of the lack of oxygen. Although the appellant removed the bag immediately, the woman suffered from subconjunctival haemorrhages in both eyes and bruising around her neck. She presented at a doctor's surgery for treatment, but none was prescribed, and her injuries healed within a week or so. The second incident occurred when the appellant poured lighter fuel on his partner's breasts and set light to it, inflicting a burn upon her which became infected. Again, the woman attended the doctor for treatment, at which point the doctor made a report to the police. The appellant's appeal against conviction was dismissed as his partner's consent was held not to be capable of exculpating him from liability in light of the harm inflicted upon the victim. **[2–26]**

Mens Rea

In order to prove a defendant's guilt in a sexual assault case, it is necessary to prove that the defendant had the requisite *mens rea* for both elements of the *actus reus*, that is, both the assault and the element of indecency. The *mens rea* for assault in s 2 of the 1997 Act is intention or subjective recklessness. However, in a sexual assault case the issue becomes more complicated as it is also necessary to prove that the defendant had *mens rea* regarding the indecency aspect of the offence. In *Court*, the Lord Ackner held that, **[2–27]**

> "... on a charge of indecent assault the prosecution must not only prove that the accused intentionally assaulted the victim, but that in so doing he

---

51 This case was taken to the European Court of Human Rights, the applicants arguing that a conviction in these circumstances, where the parties were willing participants in the activity, was a contravention of their right to a private life under Art 8 of the European Convention on Human Rights. However, the Court held that it was within the margin of appreciation of Member States to intervene in the private lives of citizens in circumstances such as this and thus, there was no violation of the Convention: *Laskey, Jaggard and Brown v UK* (1997) 24 EHRR 29.

52 [1999] EWCA Crim 1710.

intended to commit an indecent assault, i.e. an assault which right-minded persons would think was indecent."[53]

[2–28] It is clear that Lord Ackner takes the *mens rea* of sexual assault to be intention. The prosecution must show that the defendant *intended* to commit an assault which is capable of being considered by right-minded persons as indecent. As a result, it would seem that recklessness will not suffice as the *mens rea* for a sexual assault. As Hanly correctly asserts, if intention is necessary for the indecency element of the offence, it is difficult to see how recklessness could realistically be sufficient for the assault element, as it is hard to imagine how a defendant could recklessly assault a person while intending to do so indecently.[54] Consequently it appears that in order to make out the offence of sexual assault, the prosecution must show that the defendant *intended* to commit an assault which is capable of being considered by right-minded persons as indecent. Since sexual assault is the base offence for all the assault-based offences , it would seem that recklessness will not suffice as the *mens rea* for any of these offences.

[2–29] The legislation does not make clear whether the honest belief defence applies to the assault-based offences. However, as the *mens rea* for the assault-based sexual offences is intention, and consent is a constituent element of the offence, a defendant who honestly believed that the complainant had consented to the impugned activity could not be found guilty as he did not possess the requisite intent. Consequently, while the legislation does not explicitly provide that the honest belief defence applies to the assault-based offences, in practice it is likely that it will avail a defendant who is on trial for one of these offences. In support of this supposition, O'Malley points to the case of *R v Kimber*,[55] where the English Court of Appeal applied reasoning similar to *R v Morgan*[56] to the offence of indecent assault, holding that if the defendant believed that the complainant was consenting, he could not be found to have intended to touch the victim without her consent, and therefore could not be guilty of indecent assault.[57]

Aggravated Sexual Assault

[2–30] Section 3(1) of the 1990 Act defines aggravated sexual assault as "... a sexual assault that involves serious violence or the threat of serious violence or is such as to cause injury, humiliation or degradation of a grave nature to the person assaulted". The maximum penalty upon conviction for

53 [1988] 2 All ER 221 at 228.
54 Hanly, *supra* note 24, p 331.
55 [1983] 1 WLR 1118; [1983] 3 All ER 316; [1983] 75 Cr App R 225.
56 [1976] AC 182; [1975] 2 WLR 913; [1975] 2 All ER 247; [1975] 61 Cr App R 136.
57 P 112.

aggravated sexual assault is life imprisonment.[58] In an aggravated sexual assault case, the prosecution must, as in a sexual assault case, show that there was an assault accompanied by circumstances of indecency. However, one of the aggravating factors listed in s 3(1) must also be shown to be present. Whether the "aggravating circumstances" (i.e. serious violence or the threat thereof, or injury, humiliation or degradation of a grave nature) which are necessary to make out the offence are present is an objective fact for the jury to decide. The standards prevalent among the community should be taken into account in assessing whether or not this additional external factor is present.[59]

An aggravated sexual assault "will typically consist of a non-penetrative sexual assault accompanied by significant physical violence, or else a sexual assault during which the victim is subjected to particularly degrading treatment, even if no significant or lasting physical injury is inflicted".[60] If in an aggravated assault case the jury decides that the offence of sexual assault has been made out, but the aggravating factors necessary for a finding of aggravated sexual assault are not present, the defendant can still be found guilty of sexual assault. **[2–31]**

For an aggravated sexual assault to be proved the defendant must have intended an assault of that nature. Therefore, as with sexual assault, recklessness will not suffice as the mental element for aggravated sexual assault. Accordingly, the defendant must have intended to commit a sexual assault which involved serious violence or the threat of serious violence, or a sexual assault which would cause injury, humiliation, or degradation of a grave nature to the person assaulted. **[2–32]**

Rape under Section 4

Rape under s 4 is defined as a sexual assault that includes: **[2–33]**

> "(a) penetration (however slight) of the anus or mouth by the penis, or
> (b) penetration (however slight) of the vagina by any object held or manipulated by another person."[61]

The offence of rape under s 4 was enacted in response to criticism of the traditional gender-specific definition of rape which is encapsulated in s 2 of the 1981 Act. In its Report *Rape and Allied Offences*, the LRC noted that the main objection to a gender-specific definition of rape is that rape, **[2–34]**

---

58 Criminal Law (Rape)(Amendment) Act 1990, s 3(2).
59 Charleton, *supra* note 13, p 293.
60 O'Malley, *supra* note 15, p 115.
61 Criminal Law (Rape) (Amendment) Act 1990, s 4.

when confined to non-consensual vaginal intercourse, "arbitrarily selects for special classification a form of sexual assault which is no more distinctive than other similarly serious forms of sexual assault which are grouped together within a single offence".[62] It was pointed out in the Report that victims of penetration other than in the vagina, or by, for example, knives or bottles, rightly saw themselves, and indeed were seen by society, as having been "raped". Similarly, to treat, for example, the forcible buggery of males as anything other than "rape" was deemed to be "wholly unreal".[63]

[2–35] As a result of these observations, the LRC concluded that the definition of rape should be extended to include non-consensual sexual penetration of the major orifices of the body[64] by the penis of another person or of a person's vagina or anus by an inanimate object held or manipulated by any other person.[65] In this form, the crime of rape should be capable of being committed against both men and women.[66] However, rather than interfere with the traditional definition of rape, the legislature opted to introduce a new offence of "rape under section 4" in the Criminal Law (Rape) (Amendment) Act 1990.[67] The then Minister for Justice asserted that the new offence would "provide the psychological reassurance sought for victims of rape without attracting any of the disadvantages of interfering with the existing definition".[68] The maximum penalty on conviction for rape under s 4 is life imprisonment.[69]

Actus Reus

[2–36] Rape under s 4 is limited to serious sexual assaults involving penetration of the body by a sexual organ, or penetration of a sexual organ by an object. Penetration of the anus by an object is not included. The Minister for Justice[70] at the time of the introduction of the new offence of rape under s 4 justified this exclusion as follows:

---

62 Law Reform Commission, *Report on Rape and Allied Offences*, (Law Reform Commission, Dublin, 1988), para 10.
63 *ibid*, para 7.
64 That is, the vagina, anus and mouth.
65 Law Reform Commission, *supra* note 62, para 14.
66 *ibid*.
67 The Criminal Law (Rape) (Amendment) Bill 1988 contained no reference to the offence of "rape under section 4". The offences which would later form s 4 were originally contained in the Bill as acts included under the new offence of "aggravated sexual assault". However, during its passage through the Oireachtas, the Bill was amended to create the offence of "rape under section 4"; Charleton, McDermott and Bolger, *supra* note 14, p 652.
68 402 *Dáil Debates* Col 1255 (13 November 1990).
69 Criminal Law (Rape) (Amendment) Act 1990, s 4(2).
70 Mr Ray Burke TD.

> "The penetration of the anus by an object will not constitute rape under section 4 because in certain circumstances such an occurrence may not constitute a serious offence. For example, one could have horseplay among schoolboys where an object, for example, a pencil, could penetrate the anus and a person would not be charged with rape in such circumstances."[71]

The Minister went on to say that if there was a serious indecent assault involving penetration of the anus by an object, the offender could be charged with aggravated sexual assault. Therefore, non-consensual penetration of the anus by an object would amount to sexual assault or aggravated sexual assault. The Joint Committee on Child Protection recommended that rape under s 4 be extended to include penetration of the anus by an object, expressing a view that: **[2–37]**

> "[t]he possibility of horseplay between boys accidentally resulting in such an act being committed is not … a reason to exclude what in other circumstances would be a very serious penetrative sexual assault from the definition of that type of offence".[72]

It would also be beneficial if the definition of this offence was amended to clarify whether digital penetration is punishable under this provision. As Hanly notes, "a finger is arguably an object that can be manipulated by another person, and on that basis digital rape could be included in section 4".[73] Nonetheless, statutory clarification on this issue would be welcome. Overall then, it is clear that there is space for some firming up of the definition of rape under s 4. Admittedly, the maximum penalty for aggravated sexual assault is the same (i.e. life imprisonment) and many penetrative sexual assaults could be punished under this provision as well. However, it would be preferable if all forms of non-consensual penetrative sexual activity were dealt with within the same offence. As noted in the Department of Justice's *Discussion Paper on The Law of Sexual Offences*: **[2–38]**

> "… it is somewhat artificial to attempt to distinguish penetration of any of the body orifices because the attack on the dignity and bodily integrity of the victim, and his or her utter and complete humiliation, is the same in all cases of penetration."[74]

Of course, the bigger definitional issue with regard to rape under s 4 is whether it should be amalgamated with "common law rape" in s 2 of the **[2–39]**

---

71 402 *Dáil Debates*, Col. 1273 (13 November 1990).

72 *ibid.*

73 Hanly, *supra* note 24, p 328.

74 Department of Justice, Equality and Law Reform, *Discussion Paper on the Law on Sexual Offences* (Department of Justice, Equality and Law Reform, Dublin, 1998), para 6.3.4.

1981 Act to allow for one overarching rape offence. Noting "the general tendency nowadays is to have a single offence of rape defined in such a way as to include various forms of bodily penetration of a sexual nature", O'Malley has suggested that "[a] similar approach could usefully be adopted in Ireland".[75] A discussion of the merits or otherwise of this approach is outside the scope of this text, raising complex issues regarding not only appropriate labelling but also debates regarding the appropriateness of retention of the nomenclature of "rape" in sexual offences legislation. With regard to the latter point, it is noteworthy that some common law jurisdictions have abandoned the word "rape" in legislation, instead opting to grade sexual offences according to severity under a general heading of "sexual assault".[76] Given that rape under s 4 and common law rape carry the same penalty and there is no evidence that the law as currently constructed is not working well,[77] a discussion about appropriate nomenclature in Irish sexual offences legislation may not be terribly urgent. However, it is likely that debates on these points may arise in future reform efforts.

Mens Rea

[2–40] Section 4 does not address the issue of *mens rea*. However, since rape under s 4 is essentially a serious sexual assault with certain characteristics,[78] the rules on *mens rea* which apply to the offences of sexual assault and aggravated sexual assault are also applicable to rape under s 4. Therefore, in order to make out the offence of rape under s 4, it would seem to be necessary for the prosecution to show that the defendant intended to commit the act in question. Hanly suggests that "if the prosecution can show that the defendant intentionally carried out any of the acts in section 4 upon the complainant without her consent and did so not caring whether he or she consented, the offence has been made out".[79] As with the other sexual assault offences, it is likely that an honest belief in consent will exculpate a defendant charged with rape under s 4, in spite of the fact that the section makes no reference to this defence.

Alternative Verdicts

[2–41] Alternative verdicts are provided for in the Criminal Law (Rape) (Amendment) Act 1990. Section 8(1) provides that:

---

75 O'Malley, *supra* note 15, p 69.

76 Canada and New South Wales are two common law jurisdictions that have adopted this approach.

77 Department of Justice, Equality and Law Reform, *supra* note 75, para 6.2.3.

78 That is, the penetration of the body by a sexual organ or penetration of a sexual organ by an object.

79 Hanly, *supra* note 24, p 290.

> "[a] person indicted for rape may, if the evidence does not warrant a conviction for rape but warrants a conviction for rape under section 4 or aggravated sexual assault or sexual assault, be found guilty of rape under section 4 or of aggravated sexual assault or of sexual assault, as may be appropriate."

Likewise, a defendant indicted for rape under s 4 may, if the evidence does **[2–42]** not warrant a conviction for that offence, be found guilty of either aggravated sexual assault or sexual assault, as appropriate, where the evidence warrants a conviction for those offences.[80] Finally, if a defendant is charged with aggravated sexual assault, and the evidence does not support a conviction for that offence, the defendant may be found guilty of sexual assault.[81]

---

80 Criminal Law (Rape) (Amendment) Act 1990, s 8(3).
81 *ibid*, s 8(4).

CHAPTER THREE

Capacity-Related Offences: Offences Against Children and Individuals with Limited Decision-Making Capacity

Introduction

Individuals may lack the capacity to consent to sexual activity on a transient basis because of their age or due to a more permanent limitation on their decision-making capacity such as an intellectual disability or mental illness. Sexual offences against such individuals are viewed as particularly abhorrent as children or those with limited decision-making capacity are especially vulnerable to abuse, and may find it more difficult to report this abuse and seek protection. It is important that the law is sufficiently robust to safeguard vulnerable individuals from sexual abuse and exploitation. As will be seen in this chapter, not all individuals who lack capacity to consent to sexual activity may be treated in the same way. Although children and adults with limited decision-making capacity are both vulnerable groups requiring special protection from sexual abuse and exploitation, children's lack of capacity to consent is transient and will end when they reach the age of capacity to consent (i.e. 17 years). Further, it is indisputable that sexual activity with children is harmful and should be deterred and punished when it occurs.[1] Contrarily, legislating to protect individuals whose capacity to consent to sexual activity is subject to permanent limitation poses far greater difficulties. Although these individuals require protection and may be particularly susceptible to sexual abuse and exploitation, the law in this area must be sufficiently nuanced to allow this group to exercise their [3–01]

1 The only exception to this is sexual activity between mature adolescents (e.g. those between the ages of 15 and 17 years) who engage in sexual experimentation with peers of a similar age. As O'Sullivan notes, "while the assumption that children lack sexual competence is unproblematic when applied to six-year-olds it is debatable whether it is equally applicable to 16-year-olds given the range of sexual activities that are prohibited until the age of 17 [by Irish law]": O'Sullivan, "Protecting Young People from Themselves: Reform of the Age of Consent Law in Ireland" (2009) *Dublin University Law Journal* 386, 386. Consequently, there are some limited exemptions from criminal liability for non-abusive peer adolescent sexual relationships.

sexual autonomy where this is appropriate. Thus, the law in this area must be delicately balanced to ensure that these individuals are afforded adequate protection without being barred indefinitely from engaging in meaningful sexual relationships.

[3–02] This chapter explores the current Irish law which applies to the protection of children and those with limited decision-making capacity. The Irish legislature has struggled to get the balance right with the law in this area and the current rules have been subject to both judicial and academic criticism. The laws protecting children and vulnerable adults from sexual abuse and exploitation have undergone significant changes with the enactment of the Criminal Law (Sexual Offences) Act 2017. While the previous laws in these areas will be outlined to provide context, the discussion in the chapter will focus on the current legal position post the commencement of the relevant provisions of the 2017 legislation.

Offences Against Children

[3–03] Sexual offences against children may be divided into two categories, that is, sexual activity with children who are below the age of consent, and offences which involve the sexual exploitation of children. Both categories of offences will be discussed in turn in this section.

Sexual Activity with Children

[3–04] The prohibition of sexual activity with children has proved problematic for the Irish legislature, with the law in this area undergoing significant changes in the last decade or so. Until 2006, the rather antiquated Criminal Law (Amendment) Act 1935 applied. Section 1(1) of this Act provided that it was an offence for a male person of any age to have sexual intercourse with a girl younger than 15 years of age. The maximum punishment for this offence was life imprisonment. Section 2(1) provided for an offence of sexual intercourse with a girl aged between 15 and 17 years.[2] The maximum penalty for this offence was five years' imprisonment for a first offence. A higher maximum penalty of 10 years' imprisonment applied for any subsequent offence under this section. The complainant's consent was irrelevant for the purposes of these offences. More significantly, the defendant had no defence even if he was mistaken as to the age of the

[2] The section was amended by s 13 of the Criminal Law Act 1997 (in conjunction with the First Schedule of that Act) so that it provided simply for an offence of sexual intercourse with a girl aged under 17 years. However, it was subsequently held in *ZS v DPP* [2011] IESC 49 that this amendment was not effective as s 2(1) did not survive the enactment of the Constitution. Fennelly J held that as s 2(1) was not in force in 1997, it could not be amended by the Criminal Law Act of that year: [2011] IESC 49, para 45.

complainant. The offence was one of strict liability: once it was proved that the defendant had engaged in sexual intercourse with a girl who was under the age of consent, he was guilty.

The statutory rape provisions in the 1935 Act were fundamentally flawed. The Act was inherently gender-biased, displaying a particularly paternalistic attitude towards female children and offering far inferior protection to boys who were under the age of consent. The paternalistic attitude towards young girls is evidenced clearly in the oft-cited words of Maguire CJ in *Attorney General (Shaughnessy) v Ryan*[3] where he stated that the offences in ss 1 and 2 of the 1935 Act "were designed to protect young girls, not alone against lustful men, but against themselves".[4] The only gender-neutral aspect of the 1935 Act was s 14, which provided that "[i]t shall not be a defence to a charge of indecent assault upon a person under the age of 15 years to prove that such person consented to the act alleged to constitute such indecent assault". Thus, both boys and girls under the age of 15 were treated as incapable of consenting to activity which would constitute a sexual assault. In the absence of a specific legislative provision prohibiting sexual intercourse with boys under the age of consent, s 14 provided the only potential liability for an adult who engaged in sexual activity with a male child. Since s 14 only applied to those under the age of 15, this effectively created a different age of consent for boys and girls. This situation was remedied somewhat with the introduction s 3 of the Criminal Law (Sexual Offences) Act 1993 which created the offence of buggery with males or females under the age of 17.[5] As with the offences in the 1935 Act, consent was irrelevant for the purposes of this offence and the defendant could not raise a defence of mistake of age. However, overall, the law prior to 2006 was deeply gendered, offering highly varying levels of protection to boys and girls and, above all, demonstrating some erroneous attitudes about the susceptibility of young boys to sexual exploitation. As Doyle notes: **[3–05]**

> "the gender-biased nature of ss. 1 and 2 of the 1935 Act rested on the false presumption that young boys were not as vulnerable to sexual exploitation as young girls during this period, and we now know that this certainly was not the case. The irony is that, despite the fact that the 1935 Act was on the statute book for 71 years, between 1935 and 2006, there was more 'widespread, persistent and callous sexual abuse during this period than we

---

3 [1960] IR 181.

4 *ibid*, 183.

5 Criminal Law (Sexual Offences) Act 1993, s 2, abolished the common law offence of buggery between consenting adults, thus creating the need for a provision which protected those under the age of consent from this form of sexual abuse. s 4 also created an offence of gross indecency with a boy under the age of 17 years of age.

> ever could have imagined'.[6] Inevitably, children of both sexes suffered this abuse, albeit the perpetrators were predominantly male."[7]

[3–06] Although the gendered nature of the pre-2006 law was problematic, this was not what ultimately led to the downfall of the statutory rape provisions in the 1935 Act, which were ultimately declared unconstitutional in *CC v Ireland*[8] because of the absence of a mistake of age defence. The potential unfairness of this aspect of the 1935 Act for young males who were not engaging in predatory behaviour is well articulated by Doyle who notes that:

> "The young male, in such circumstances, could not advance a reasonable belief defence and was guilty of an offence carrying enormous social stigma and serious penalties of imprisonment simply by reason of the fact that the girl was under the age of consent- even if on the facts he was actually "morally innocent" of the offence and took every reasonable step to satisfy himself that the girl was not underage."[9]

[3–07] The problems posed by the absence of such a defence had been identified by the Law Reform Commission (LRC) in its *Report on Child Sexual Abuse* in 1990. Commenting on the responses to the consultation process in relation to this question, the LRC noted that:

> "There appeared to be little dissent from the view that the Irish law in this area was unduly harsh and wholly out of step with the law in other jurisdictions. While it may be again that a combination of prosecutorial and judicial discretion is ensuring that no problems arise, the possibility of serious injustice should none the less...be removed."[10]

[3–08] Consequently, it was recommended that a defence should be available to an accused "that he genuinely believed at the time of the act on reasonable grounds that the girl had attained the age of consent or an age attracting a less serious penalty".[11]

[3–09] The applicant in *CC* had been charged with four counts of unlawful carnal knowledge with a girl under the age of 15, contrary to s 1(1) of the 1935 Act. When arrested, the applicant had admitted that the sexual activity occurred but stated that the girl had told him that she was 16. Judicial review

---

6 Here Doyle is citing O'Malley: "Should there be strict criminal liability for adults who have sex with children?", *The Irish Times*, 5 May 2008.

7 Doyle, "Reasonable belief and unlawful carnal knowledge: a historical perspective" (2012) 47(1) *Irish Jurist* 49, 75.

8 [2006] 4 IR 1.

9 Doyle, *supra* note 7, 73.

10 Law Reform Commission, *Report on Child Sexual Abuse*, (Dublin: Law Reform Commission, 1990), para 4.14.

11 *ibid.*

proceedings were instituted on his behalf, challenging the constitutionality of s 1 as it did not provide for a mistake of age defence. The case was dismissed by the High Court but, on appeal, the Supreme Court granted a declaration that s 1(1) was unconstitutional.[12] Delivering the Supreme Court judgment, Hardiman J noted that it was "necessary to restate the absolute nature of the offence" which "affords absolutely no defence once the *actus reus* is established, no matter how extreme the circumstances".[13] The learned judge highlighted that "[s]o absolute an offence is rare, even by comparison with other offences which address serious social problems, and offences that are the subject of serious societal condemnation".[14] Further, he emphasised that there could be no doubt but "that this is explicitly a provision capable of criminalising and of jailing, the mentally blameless".[15] Thus, the Court concluded that:

> "It appears to us that to criminalise in a serious way a person who is mentally innocent is indeed 'to inflict a grave injury on that person's dignity and sense of worth' and to treat him as 'little more than a means to an end'...[16] It appears to us that this in turn, constitutes a failure by the State in its laws to respect, defend and vindicate the rights to liberty and to good name of the person so treated, contrary to the State's obligations under Article 40 of the Constitution."[17]

The Criminal Law (Sexual Offences) Act 2006 was enacted on 2 June 2006, **[3–10]** just 10 days after the Supreme Court decision. As well as providing for a mistake of age defence, "[t]wo of the key developments in the 2006 Act were the establishment of a uniform age of consent regardless of gender ... and the increase of the range of sexual activities that are captured in the newly defined [offences]".[18] The provisions of the 2006 have since been reformed again by the Criminal Law (Sexual Offences) Act 2017, most notably with further reform of the mistake of age defence. The newly amended offences

---

12 Although s 2(1) of the 1935 Act was repealed and replaced by the Criminal Law (Sexual Offences) Act 2006, it is noteworthy that the absence of a mistake of age defence for that offence was also subsequently challenged and held by the Supreme Court to be inconsistent with the Constitution: *ZS v DPP* [2011] IESC 49. Thus, as O'Malley notes, "[p]rosecutions may not therefore be brought under either s. 1 or 2 of the 1935 Act even for offences alleged to have been committed before the repeal date in 2006": O'Malley, *Sexual Offences* (2nd ed, Round Hall, Dublin, 2013), p 123.

13 [2006] 4 IR 1, 73.

14 *ibid.*

15 *ibid*, 74.

16 Here, Hardiman J was quoting from the judgment of Wilson J in the Canadian case *Hess and Nguyen v The Queen* [1990] 2 SCR 906, where a Canadian statutory rape law which did not allow for a mistake of age defence was struck down.

17 [2006] 4 IR 1, 77–78.

18 O'Sullivan, "Protecting Young People from Themselves: Reform of the Age of Consent Law in Ireland" (2009) 31(1) *Dublin University Law Journal* 386, 392.

will now be discussed. Reference to the original provisions of the 2006 will be included where relevant to highlight the changes entailed in the 2017 reforms.

Sexual Act with a Child under 15 Years of Age[19]

[3–11] Section 2(1) of the Criminal Law (Sexual Offences) Act 2006[20] provides that:

> "A person who engages in a sexual act with a child who is under the age of 15 years shall be guilty of an offence and shall be liable on conviction on indictment to imprisonment for life or a lesser term of imprisonment."

[3–12] Further, s 2(2) (as amended) provides that:

> "A person who attempts to engage in a sexual act with a child who is under the age of 15 years shall be guilty of an offence and shall be liable on conviction on indictment to imprisonment for life or a lesser term of imprisonment."

[3–13] For the purposes of the 2006 Act, a "sexual act" is defined as: (a) an act consisting of: (i) sexual intercourse, or (ii) buggery, between persons who are not married to each other, or (b) an act described in ss 3(1) or 4(1) of the Act 1990 (i.e. aggravated sexual assault or rape under s 4).[21] Where an individual engages in activity which would constitute a sexual assault, this remains governed by the 1935 Act meaning that the age of consent to this level of sexual activity remains at 15.

[3–14] Section 2 makes clear that the consent of the complainant is irrelevant for the purposes of this offence.[22] However, the mistake of age defence is provided for as follows:

> "It shall be a defence to proceedings for an offence under this section for the defendant to prove that he or she was reasonably mistaken that, at the time of the alleged commission of the offence, the child against whom the offence is alleged to have been committed had attained the age of 15 years."[23]

---

19 The offences in the 2006 Act were originally referred to as "defilement of a child under 15 years of age" and "defilement of a child under the age of 17 years". The relabelling of these offences as part of the 2017 reforms is to be welcomed, the language of defilement representing quite an outdated description of these offences.

20 The entirety of s 2 was substituted by s 16 of the Criminal Law (Sexual Offences) Act 2017.

21 Criminal Law (Sexual Offences) Act 2006, s 1.

22 Criminal Law (Sexual Offences) Act 2006, s 2(6), provides that:

> "It shall not be a defence to proceedings for an offence under this section for the defendant to prove that the child against whom the offence is alleged to have been committed consented to the sexual act of which the offence consisted".

23 Criminal Law (Sexual Offences) Act 2006, s 2(3) (as amended).

Originally, prior to the 2017 reforms of the 2006 Act, the defence was to be construed according to the following guidance: [3–15]

> "Where in proceedings for an offence under this section, it falls to the court to consider whether the defendant honestly believed that, at the time of the alleged commission of the offence, the child against whom the offence is alleged to have been committed had attained the age of 15 years, the court shall have regard to the presence or absence of reasonable grounds for the defendant's so believing and all other relevant circumstances."[24]

Thus, the offence was defined subjectively, that is, "all the accused need prove is that he or she *honestly* believed that the other party had reached the specified age; the belief need not be reasonable".[25] However, as per the guidance in the 2006 Act, the absence of reasonable grounds for such a belief and all other relevant circumstances would have to be considered by the court in deciding where the belief was honestly held, thereby limiting the potential for groundless assertions of the defence. [3–16]

The correct application of the original incarnation of the mistake of age defence was considered in *People (DPP) v Egan.*[26] The applicant in this case was appealing his conviction under s 3 for engaging in a sexual act with a child under 17 years of age. The applicant argued that the trial judge had misdirected the jury about the mistake of age defence in s 3(5). During the trial, "the defence took no active steps in the course of the trial directed at establishing a defence by reference to s. 3(5)".[27] The Court of Criminal Appeal noted that "[t]he applicant gave no evidence on the point and no cross-examination was directed to establishing that the applicant had an honest belief that [the complainant] had attained the age of 17 years".[28] Despite this, the trial judge of his own motion had directed the jury on the mistake of age defence. The question for the Court of Criminal Appeal to decide was what burden of proof s 3(5) could be interpreted as placing on the defendant. There were three possible approaches to interpretation of the section identified in the judgment. The first was that proposed by the applicant in this case, which was that the defence only has an evidential burden to discharge. An evidential burden "is an obligation to raise an issue, or to make out a prima facie case and so get the issue past the trial judge and before the trier of fact".[29] Thus, Fennell suggests that "[t]o describe the evidential burden as a burden of proof is something of a misnomer", as "[t] [3–17]

24 Criminal Law (Sexual Offences) Act 2006, s 2(4).
25 O'Malley, *supra* note 12, p 132.
26 [2010] IECCA 28; [2010] 3 IR 561.
27 [2010] 3 IR 561–567.
28 *ibid.*
29 Fennell, *The Law of Evidence in Ireland* (3rd ed, Bloomsbury Professional, Dublin, 2009), p 111.

he evidential burden is discharged by evidence sufficient to warrant, but not necessarily to require, an affirmative finding by a reasonable jury".[30] Thus, this interpretation of the defence places the minimum burden possible on the defence.

[3–18] The second approach which was discussed in the judgment was the one actually adopted by the trial judge in this case, which was to interpret s 3(5) as placing a persuasive burden of proof on the defendant. This required the defendant to prove the mistake of age defence "by reference to some evidence in the case, whether by cross-examination or otherwise, but not necessarily by giving evidence himself".[31] The burden here "is no higher than to establish a reasonable doubt in the mind of the jury".[32] Shifting the burden of proof to the defendant is not uncontroversial as it raises concerns about interference with the presumption of innocence and infringement of defendants' rights. Traditionally, provisions placing a burden of proof on the accused in a criminal trial are generally interpreted as placing an evidential burden such as that proposed by the applicant in this case. However, the approach adopted in this case, which places a heavier onus on the defendant, is a new method of interpreting reverse onus provisions which can be traced to the case of *People (DPP) v Smyth*.[33] McGrath notes that the judgment in *Smyth* "departs from the orthodoxy" in relation to the interpretation of reverse onus provisions:

> "... by drawing a distinction between 'a burden of adducing evidence' and an 'evidential burden of proof', the decision in *Smyth* suggests some form of enhanced obligation whereby an accused bearing an evidential burden in respect of a defence or constituent element of an offence is required to establish the existence of a reasonable doubt, rather than simply identifying evidence that might leave the jury with a reasonable doubt."[34]

[3–19] Thus, this new interpretation of the evidential burden of proof creates an intermediate approach between the traditional understandings of the evidential burden of proof and the legal burden of proof, placing a higher obligation on the defendant. McGrath suggests that:

> "[t]he emergence of this higher threshold may be driven, at least in part, by a concern that the bar has been set too low in respect of the discharge of an evidential burden in respect of defences such as provocation and self-defence, so that merely requiring an accused to discharge an evidential burden in

30 *ibid.*
31 [2010] 3 IR 561–572.
32 *ibid.*
33 [2010] IECCA 34; [2010] 3 IR 688; [2010] 1 ILRM 81.
34 McGrath, *Evidence* (2nd ed, Round Hall, Dublin, 2014), p 38.

accordance with the traditional approach would open the door to the raising of unmeritorious defences".[35]

This justification is particularly pertinent in the context of the mistake of age defence. The Court of Criminal Appeal's decision to opt for this higher threshold in the context of this defence seems both sensible and justified. **[3–20]**

The third approach to interpreting the mistake of age defence identified in *Egan* was that advanced by the prosecution, that is, "that section 3(5) of the Act requires the accused to show by way of proof on the balance of probabilities that he had an honest belief that the complainant was more than the age specified".[36] This would place the heaviest onus of proof—a legal burden of proof—on the defence. The Court of Criminal Appeal rejected the interpretation of s 3(5) which was advanced by the applicant, noting that the defence had not raised the defence and that the trial judge had not been asked to rule on whether the defence might be raised. Moreover, the Court held that if the trial judge had been so asked, "it seems more than doubtful that he could have concluded, on the state of the evidence, that there was a basis for raising it".[37] In light of this, the Court felt that it was "probably unnecessary" to proceed to consider the other possible interpretations of s 3(5). However, the Court endorsed the interpretation of s 3(5) adopted by the trial judge, noting that: **[3–21]**

> "[The Court] cannot ignore the fact that the Oireachtas requires the accused person to prove the state of his 'honest belief'. The learned trial judge gave effect to that statutory requirement. He did not go so far as to adopt the submission of the prosecution to the effect that the burden must be discharged on the balance of probabilities. He held that the defence must show that there is a reasonable doubt as to whether he had the required 'honest belief'. This, as he described it, is a 'reversed onus of proof'. As such, it is a novelty in our criminal law. It proceeds, however, from an interpretation of the statutory provision which goes no further than to require the accused to prove that there is a reasonable doubt as to whether he had an honest belief that the complainant was 17 years of age or more … the learned trial judge was correct to require that the applicant discharge at least that burden."[38]

Since the trial judge's stricter interpretation of the honest belief defence was held to be the correct one, there could be no question as to whether the applicant's conviction was safe. Significantly, the Court noted that "[i] t may be that the section, correctly interpreted, places a heavier burden on the accused person, namely to prove, on the balance of probabilities that he **[3–22]**

---

35 *ibid.*

36 [2010] 3 IR 561–572.

37 *ibid*, 573.

38 *ibid*, 574.

had the requisite honest belief".[39] Thus, the Court did not outright dismiss the interpretation of the mistake of age defence which was advanced by the prosecution, but noted that "it [was] neither necessary nor appropriate for the Court to decide whether the section requires proof to that higher standard".[40]

[3–23] The 2017 Act has reformed the mistake of age defence, replacing the subjective construction of the defence in the 2006 Act with an objective formulation. Section 2(4) now provides that:

> "Where, in proceedings for an offence under this section, it falls to the court to consider whether the defendant was reasonably mistaken that, at the time of the alleged commission of the offence, the child against whom the offence is alleged to have been committed had attained the age of 15 years, the court shall consider whether, in all the circumstances of the case, a reasonable person would have concluded that the child had attained the said age."

[3–24] Moreover, s 2(5) provides that:

> "The standard of proof required to prove that the defendant was reasonably mistaken that the child had attained the age of 15 years shall be that applicable to civil proceedings."

[3–25] This new formulation of the mistake of age defence places greater obligations on defendants in these cases. The move to an objective construction of the defence is welcome and offsets the potential for spurious claims of mistake of age, and should ensure that the defence is only available where an individual has been genuinely mistaken about the age of the person with whom he has engaged in sexual activity. However, shifting a legal burden of proof on the balance of probabilities to the defendant in these cases is potentially problematic. As noted in the discussion of *Egan* above, shifting a legal burden of proof to the defendant in a criminal case raises concerns about potential interference with the presumption of innocence. Consequently, the provision may be challenged as a potential infringement of defendants' rights. If this occurs, the constitutionality of the provision will be tested according to the proportionality test which typically has been applied by the Irish courts when determining the constitutionality of reverse onus provisions.[41] An example of such proportionality analysis may be seen in *McNally v Ireland*[42] where MacMenamin J stated as follows:

> "I would identify the following principles as being applicable to the

39 *ibid.*
40 *ibid*, 575.
41 McGrath, *supra* note 34, p 30.
42 [2009] IEHC 753; [2011] 4 IR 431; [2011] 1 ILRM 40.

applicable test of proportionality: (a) the necessity to establish whether the means it employs to achieve its aim correspond to the importance of the aim; (b) whether the means adopted are necessary for the achievement of the objective; (c) whether the means actually becomes an end in itself; (d) whether the objective can be attained by other methods which may be more conveniently applied; (e) whether the method chosen is the least restrictive and the disadvantage caused is least disproportionate to the aim; and (f) whether the means may be rationally connected to the objective and not be arbitrary, unfair or based on irrational considerations."[43]

How an assessment like this would be resolved in relation to the reformed mistake of age defence is difficult to predict. Whilst protecting children from sexual abuse is a very important aim, it may be questioned whether placing a legal burden of proof on the defendant in regard to mistake of age is too much of an encroachment on defendants' fair trial rights and thus is a disproportionate response which goes further than is necessary to protect children. Given the recent history of the law in this area, this constitutional uncertainty is an unfortunate side effect of the 2017 reforms. **[3–26]**

Sexual Act with a Child under 17 Years of Age

Section 3(1) of the 2006[44] Act provides that: **[3–27]**

"A person who engages in a sexual act with a child who is under the age of 17 years shall be guilty of an offence and shall be liable on conviction on indictment-
(a) To imprisonment for a term not exceeding 7 years, or
(b) If he or she is a person in authority, to imprisonment for a term not exceeding 15 years."[45]

Section 3(2) provides that: **[3–28]**

"A person who attempts to engage in a sexual act with a child who is under the age of 17 years shall be guilty of an offence and shall be liable on conviction on indictment-
(1) to imprisonment for a term not exceeding 7 years, or
(2) if he or she is a person in authority, to imprisonment for a term not exceeding 15 years."[46]

Significantly, the 2017 Act amends s 1 of the 2006 Act to include a new **[3–29]**

---

43 [2011] 4 IR 431–474.

44 A new s 3 was substituted by s 17 of the 2017 Act.

45 The 2017 Act increased the penalties for this offence which were previously maximums of five and 10 years' imprisonment, respectively.

46 The 2017 Act also increased the penalties for this offence. Previously the relevant punishments were a maximum of five years and 10 years' imprisonment, respectively.

definition of "person in authority".[47] In relation to a child against whom an offence is alleged to have been committed, a "person in authority" means:

> "(a) a parent, grandparent, uncle or aunt whether of the whole blood, of the half blood or by affinity of the child,
> (b) a current or former guardian or foster parent[48] of the child,
> (c) a current or former step-parent of the child,
> (d) a current or former partner of a parent of the child who lives or has lived in an enduring family relationship with the parent,
> (e) any person who is for the time being, or has been, in *loco parentis* to the child, or
> (f) any other person who is or has been responsible for the education, supervision, training, care or welfare of the child."[49]

[3–30] As with the s 2 offence, the complainant's consent is irrelevant for the purposes of this offence.[50] The defence of mistake of age is also provided for in exactly the same terms as it is in s 2. For the sake of completeness, the relevant provisions of s 3 are set out here in full. The discussion of the application of these provisions in the consideration of s 2 applies equally here so will not be repeated. Sections 3(3) to 3(5) provide as follows:

> "(3) It shall be a defence to proceedings for an offence under this section for the defendant to prove that he or she was reasonably mistaken that, at the time of the alleged commission of the offence, the child against whom the offence is alleged to have been committed had attained the age of 17 years.
>
> (4) Where, in proceedings for an offence under this section, it falls to the court to consider whether the defendant was reasonably mistaken that, at the time of the alleged commission of the offence, the child against whom the offence is alleged to have been committed had attained the age of 17 years, the court shall consider whether, in all the circumstances of the case, a reasonable person would have concluded that the child had attained the said age.
>
> (5) The standard of proof required to prove that the defendant was

---

47 Criminal Law (Sexual Offences) Act 2017, s 15.

48 "Foster parent" means a person other than a relative of a child who is caring for the child on behalf of the Child and Family Agency in accordance with regulations made under the Child Care Act 1991: s 1 of the Criminal Law (Sexual Offences) Act 2006 (as amended).

49 The original definition of "person in authority" was much more restrictive, including only the following:
"(a) a parent, step-parent, guardian, grandparent, uncle or aunt of the victim,
(b) any person who is, for the time being, in loco parentis to the victim, or
(c) any person who is, for the time being, responsible for the education, supervision or welfare of the victim. "

50 Criminal Law (Sexual Offences) Act 2017, s 3(6). The only exception to this is in relation to the age proximity exemption in s 3(8). Further, O'Malley notes that consent may be relevant to sentence, particularly in circumstances where the parties are of the same age group and all the more so when the female party is close to the age of consent: O'Malley, *supra* note 12, p 128.

> reasonably mistaken that the child had attained the age of 17 years shall be that applicable to civil proceedings."

Given the older age category of complainants involved in this offence, there is greater potential for non-abusive sexual activity between peers to be inappropriately criminalised and punished by this provision. Two concessions are contained within s 3 to prevent this arising. Section 3(7) states that the consent of the Director of Public Prosecutions (DPP) is required to bring proceedings for an offence under this section against a child under the age of 17. O'Malley notes that this provision is of limited significance as all prosecutions on indictment must be brought by the DPP in any event.[51] However, this provision prevents the possibility of a private prosecution being brought under s 3. **[3–31]**

The 2017 Act also introduced an age proximity provision into s 3 which allows for an exemption from punishment for non-abusive sexual activity between peers. Section 3(8) provides that: **[3–32]**

> "Where in proceedings for an offence under this section against a child who at the time of the alleged commission of the offence had attained the age of 15 years but was under the age of 17 years, it shall be a defence that the child consented to the sexual act of which the offence consisted where the defendant-
> (a) is younger or less than 2 years older than the child,
> (b) was not, at the time of the alleged commission of the offence, a person of authority in respect of the child, and
> (c) was not, at the time of the alleged commission of the offence, in a relationship with the child that was intimidatory or exploitative of the child."

This represents a significant advance on the original concession for non-abusive peer relationships in the 2006 Act which merely provided that where a person convicted under s 3 was not more than 24 months older than the child under the age of 17 years with whom he engaged or attempted to engage in a sexual act, then he would not be subject to the provisions of the Sex Offenders Act 2001.[52] **[3–33]**

While s 3 applies to sexual activity with a child under the age of 17 years, it is not limited to children who are over the age of 15 years old but under the age of 17. Thus, there is an overlap between s 2 and s 3. The DPP has discretion whether to bring a prosecution under s 2 or s 3. For example, in *MD (a minor) v Ireland, Attorney General and DPP*,[53] although the **[3–34]**

---

51 O'Malley, *supra* note 12, p 136
52 This was provided for in the original s 3(10) of the 2006 Act.
53 [2012] 2 ILRM 305.

complainant was aged 14 at the time of the alleged offence, a prosecution was brought under s 3, not s 2. The Supreme Court noted that this was an appropriate exercise of prosecutorial discretion and that the DPP "clearly considered the facts ... and decided to prosecute the appellant for the offence with the lower penalty under s. 3".[54]

Offence by a Person in Authority

[3–35] Prior to the 2017 reforms, abuse by persons in authority was identified as an aggravated form of sexual abuse of children by the creation of higher maximum penalties where the defendant was a person in authority. As seen above, to strengthen further the law in this area, the 2017 Act increases these maximum penalties. However, additionally, the 2017 Act creates a new offence of abuse by a person in authority where the complainant is aged between 17 and 18 years old. The 2017 Act inserts a new s 3A into the 2006 Act which states that:

> "A person in authority who engages in a sexual act with a child who has attained the age of 17 years but is under the age of 18 years shall be guilty of an offence."[55]

[3–36] A person who attempts to commit such an offence will also be guilty of an offence.[56] The mistake of age defence applies to this offence in the same way as for the offences in s 2 and s 3:

> "3A(3) It shall be a defence to proceedings for an offence under this section for the defendant to prove that he or she was reasonably mistaken that, at the time of the alleged commission of the offence, the child against whom the offence is alleged to have been committed had attained the age of 18 years.
>
> 3A(4) Where, in proceedings for an offence under this section, it falls to the court to consider whether the defendant was reasonably mistaken that, at the time of the alleged commission of the offence, the child against whom the offence is alleged to have been committed had attained the age of 18 years, the court shall consider whether, in all the circumstances of the case, a reasonable person would have concluded that the child had attained that age.
>
> 3A(5) The standard of proof required to prove that the defendant was reasonably mistaken that the child had attained the age of 18 years shall be that applicable to civil proceedings."

[3–37] In addition, a further defence applies where the defendant can prove that he has reasonable grounds for believing that he was not a person in authority

---

54 *ibid*, 314.
55 Criminal Law (Sexual Offences) Act 2006, s 3A(1), as inserted by s 18 of the 2017 Act.
56 Criminal Law (Sexual Offences) Act 2006, s 3A(2).

in relation to the child against whom the offence is alleged to have been committed.[57] The consent of the child against whom the offence is alleged to have been committed is irrelevant for the purposes of liability.[58] A person guilty of this offence will be liable on conviction on indictment to imprisonment for a term not exceeding 10 years.[59]

Special Protection for Girls under the Age of 17

A particularly controversial aspect of the 2006 Act is s 5 which provides that "a female child under the age of 17 years shall not be guilty of an offence under this Act by reason only of her engaging in an act of sexual intercourse". The Oireachtas Joint Committee on Child Protection, which was formed just a few weeks after the introduction of the 2006 Act to review the law in this area and make recommendations for reform, noted that s 5 provoked the largest number of critical submissions.[60] The stated legislative intention behind s 5 was to avoid stigmatising girls who become pregnant as a result of an under-age sexual encounter. Speaking during the Dáil Debates during the passage of the 2006 Act, the then Minister for Justice, Michael McDowell, justified the provision on the following basis: **[3–38]**

> "[I]t was all very well from the point of view of political correctness to have gender neutrality, but … if it were not for…section [5], young women who become pregnant could find themselves criminalised for having a child. It is not pretty to avoid that in legislation but if I introduced a totally gender neutral Bill, I would have ensured for the first time that a girl aged 15 or 16 who becomes pregnant would be a criminal as well as everything else."[61]

Although concerns were raised about the constitutionality of s 5,[62] the provision was upheld by the Supreme Court in *MD (a minor) v Ireland, Attorney General and DPP*.[63] The appellant was accused of having sexual intercourse and committing an act of buggery with a female person under the age of 17, contrary to s 3(1) of the 2006 Act. At the time of the alleged offence, the appellant was 15 and the complainant was 14. He argued that s 5 was repugnant to the Constitution as it discriminated against the appellant on the basis of gender, contrary to Art 40.1 of the Constitution.[64] **[3–39]**

---

57 *ibid* s 3A(6).

58 *ibid*, s 3A(7).

59 *ibid*, s 3A(8).

60 Joint Oireachtas Committee on Child Protection, *Report Child Protection* (Dublin, 2006), para 8.5.2.

61 621(1) Dáil Debates 75 (2 June 2006).

62 Leahy, "Hard Cases and Bad Law: An Overview of the Criminal Law (Sexual Offences) Act 2006" (2008) 26 *Irish Law Times* 38, 45 and O'Sullivan, *supra* note 1, 408–410.

63 [2012] IESC 10; [2012] 2 ILRM 305.

64 There were also arguments based on the European Convention on Human Rights but

He argued that the provision was "gender biased and discriminatory and that it expose[d] the underage male to the real risk of criminal sanctions based on the traditional sexual stereotype where it is legislatively assumed that the male is the guilty predator and the female is the innocent comely maiden".[65] He submitted that "the fact that the female alone can become pregnant is not a ground which justified an immunity of this kind".[66] Article 40.1 of the Constitution provides as follows:

> "All citizens shall, as human persons, be held equal before the law.
> This shall not be held to mean that the State shall not in its enactments have due regard to differences of capacity, physical and moral, and of social function."

[3–40] Assessing Art 40.1 in the context of s 5, Denham CJ noted that:

> "... the article recognises that perfectly equal treatment is not always achievable, rather the article recognises that applying the same treatment to all human persons is not always desirable because it could lead to indirect inequality because of the different circumstances in which people find themselves."[67]

[3–41] Denham CJ noted that "the second sentence of [Article 40.1] recognises that human persons have or may be perceived by the Oireachtas to have 'differences of capacity, physical and moral, and of social function'".[68] In this vein, the learned judge referenced the fact that only a woman can become pregnant and the laws prohibiting discrimination on the grounds of pregnancy "have justifiably applied to women" and that "laws such as these are not an example of the State holding men or women respectively unequal before the law".[69] Referring specifically to s 5, Denham CJ noted that "[c]ourts should be deferential to the legislative view on such matters of social policy".[70] Applying this reasoning to s 5, Denham CJ stated that:

> "The Oireachtas made a choice, and such a legislative decision reflects a social policy on the issue. While the legislature could have enacted another social policy, it was an approach the legislature was entitled to take, it was an issue in society to which the legislature had to respond. The danger of

---

the challenge was based primarily on the constitutionality of s 5, with the Supreme Court noting that it was "not satisfied that the appellant has formulated any claim based on the Convention provisions capable of being entertained by this court": *ibid*, 325.

65 [2012] 2 ILRM 305, 308.

66 *ibid.*

67 *ibid*, 320.

68 *ibid.*

69 *ibid.*

70 *ibid*, 321.

pregnancy for the teenage girl was an objective which the Oireachtas was entitled to regard as relating to 'differences of capacity, physical and moral and of social function', as provided for in [Article 40.1] of the Constitution. The court would dismiss the appeal and reject the claim that section 5...is invalid having regard to the Constitution."[71]

Although the Supreme Court upheld the constitutionality of s 5 in *MD*, it remains open to question whether a provision like this should be retained in a 21st century statute or whether it merely serves to re-inforce outdated patriarchal values about female sexuality. As Doyle notes: **[3–42]**

"Social attitudes in relation to the young unmarried mother may have changed dramatically since the early years of the Irish State, but it appears that legislative and judicial thinking on the immunity of the female party from prosecution remains unequivocally rooted in the legitimate interest of the State in preventing teenage pregnancies".[72]

Admittedly, as the Office of the Ombudsman for Children (OCO) notes, s 5 is well-intentioned, seeking "to prevent the stigmatisation or prosecution of pregnant teenagers ...". However, as the OCO rightly suggests, this is a matter which should be dealt with outside of the criminal law.[73] As Leahy notes, "whilst it is laudable to seek to protect young girls who may find themselves pregnant as a result of an underage sexual encounter ... a provision such as section 5 is wholly unacceptable in the context of a piece of legislation which aspires to gender neutrality".[74] **[3–43]**

Sexual Exploitation of Children

The 2017 Act contains a number of offences to punish the sexual exploitation of children. Section 5 creates an offence of engaging in sexual activity in the presence of a child, providing that: **[3–44]**

"A person who, for the purpose of obtaining sexual gratification from the presence of a child or corrupting or depraving a child[75], intentionally engages in sexual activity whether or not with another person-

(a) when the child is present or in a place from which the person can be observed by the child, and

---

[71] *ibid*, 324.

[72] Doyle, "'The guilty sexual predator' and the 'innocent comely maiden': Gender, paternalism and the pregnancy factor" (2011) *Irish Criminal Law Journal* 36, 40.

[73] Office of the Ombudsman for Children, *Advice of the Ombudsman for Children on the General Scheme of the Criminal Law (Sexual Offences) Bill 2014* (Dublin, Office of the Ombudsman for Children, 2014), para 3.4.11.

[74] Leahy, *supra* note 62, 45.

[75] For the purposes of the section, "child" means a person under the age of 17 years: s 5(2).

(b) knowing or believing that the child is aware, or intending that the child should be aware, that the person is engaging in sexual activity,

shall be guilty of an offence and shall be liable on conviction on indictment to imprisonment for a term not exceeding 10 years."

[3–45] A similar offence is provided for in s 11 of the English Sexual Offences Act 2003.[76] The interpretation of the English provision is thus relevant for understanding this new offence in Irish law. Commenting on the English offence, Pegg and Davies note that it:

> "... could cover a broad range of behaviour. For example, if two adults engaged in sexual intercourse in the presence of a child for their own gratification, this would be an offence. However, it would also cover the situation where an adult was alone, such as an adult who masturbated in the presence of a child for his own gratification".[77]

[3–46] Also commenting on the English provision, Rook and Ward note that whether a child is "present" when the sexual activity is being engaged in "could raise difficult questions of fact and degree depending on the precise circumstances".[78] They suggest that "[i]f [the child] is not present, [the defendant] may nonetheless be convicted if [the child] is in a place from which [the defendant] can be observed".[79]

[3–47] Section 6(1) creates an offence of causing a child to watch sexual activity, providing that:

> "A person who, for the purpose of obtaining sexual gratification or corrupting or depraving a child, intentionally causes a child[80]:
>
> (a) to watch another person engaging in sexual activity, or

---

[76] s 11(1), provides that a person aged 18 or over (A) commits an offence if—
"(a) he intentionally engages in an activity,
(b) the activity is sexual,
(c) for the purpose of obtaining sexual gratification, he engages in it—
(i) when another person (B) is present or is in a place from which A can be observed, and
(ii) knowing or believing that B is aware, or intending that B should be aware, that he is engaging in it, and
(d) either—
(i) B is under 16 and A does not reasonably believe that B is 16 or over, or
(ii) B is under 13."

[77] Pegg and Davies, *Sexual Offences: Law and Context* (Routledge, Oxon, 2016), p 86.

[78] Rook and Ward, *Rook and Ward on Sexual Offences: Law & Practice* (5th ed, Sweet & Maxwell, London), p 396.

[79] *ibid.*

[80] That is, a person under the age of 17 years: s 6(2).

> (b) to look at an image[81] of that person or another person engaging in sexual activity,
>
> shall be guilty of an offence and shall be liable on conviction on indictment to imprisonment for a term exceeding 10 years."

Commenting on a similar provision in English law (i.e. s 12 of the Sexual Offences Act 2003[82]), Rook and Ward note that the creation of an offence of this nature "has its genesis in concerns about the sexual grooming of children by paedophiles, which can begin with the exposure of children to pornography as a way of breaking down their inhibitions and accustoming them to sexual behaviour".[83] For the purposes of the English law, it has been held that the sexual gratification does not have to be taken immediately. Rather, it can extend to a "longer term plan to obtain further or greater sexual gratification in the form of the eventual working out of a particular sexual fantasy or activity involving the child".[84] A similar interpretation may well be applied to the Irish provision. **[3–48]**

The 2017 Act also creates a preparatory offence in s 7 which provides for an offence of meeting a child for the purpose of child exploitation,[85] stating that: **[3–49]**

> "A person who-
>
> (a) intentionally meets, or travels with the intention of meeting a child[86] or makes arrangements with the intention of meeting a child or for a child to travel, whether or not from within the State, having communicated by any means with that child on a least one previous occasion, and
>
> (b) does so for the purpose of doing anything that would constitute sexual exploitation of the child,
>
> shall be guilty of an offence."

---

81 "Image" is defined as any photographic, film or video representation or any other form of visual representation, and any accompanying sound or any documents: s 2.

82 s 12(1), provides that a person aged 18 or over (A) commits an offence if—

> "(a) for the purpose of obtaining sexual gratification, he intentionally causes another person (B) to watch a third person engaging in an activity, or to look at an image of any person engaging in an activity,
>
> (b) the activity is sexual, and
>
> (c) either—
>
> (i) B is under 16 and A does not reasonably believe that B is 16 or over, or
>
> (ii) B is under 13."

83 Rook and Ward, *supra* note 78, p 397.

84 *R v Abdullahi* [2007] 1 Cr App R 14, 206–210.

85 This is not quite a new offence as a similar offence was provided for in s 3(2A) and s 3(2B) of the Child Trafficking and Pornography Act 1998 (as amended by the Criminal Law (Sexual Offences) (Amendment) Act 2007)). These sections were repealed by the 2017 Act and are replaced by the stand-alone offence in s 7.

86 For the purposes of this section, a child means a person under the age of 17 years.

[3–50] A person guilty of an offence under this section will be liable on conviction on indictment to a maximum of 14 years' imprisonment.[87]

[3–51] The new legislation also seeks to modernise the law in this area by recognising the potential for information and communication technology to be used to exploit and groom children. Section 8 of the 2017 Act creates an offence of using information and communication technology to facilitate sexual exploitation of a child, providing that:

> "A person who by means of information and communication technology communicates with another person (including a child) for the purpose of facilitating the sexual exploitation of a child by that person or any other person shall be guilty of an offence and liable on conviction on indictment to imprisonment for a term not exceeding 14 years."

[3–52] Further, s 8(2) provides that:

> "Any person who by means of information and communication technology sends sexually explicit material to a child shall be guilty of an offence and shall be liable-
> (a) on summary conviction, to a class A fine or to imprisonment for a term not exceeding 12 months or both, or
> (b) on conviction on indictment, to imprisonment for a term not exceeding 5 years."

[3–53] "Sexually explicit material" means any indecent or obscene images or words.[88] Section 8 provides some protection for a child who sends sexually explicit messages to another child (e.g. where teenagers engage in "sexting"). Section 8(3) provides that proceedings for an offence under s 8 cannot be brought "except by, or with the consent of, the [DPP]".

Incest

[3–54] Incest refers to sexual intercourse between individuals who are closely related by blood. Unlike other sexual offences, incest is punished not because one individual's consent is lacking but because the individuals are blood relatives. Eugenic considerations are traditionally thought to be the primary motivation for the punishment of incest. However, as Temkin notes, when the Punishment of Incest Act 1908 (which still governs incest in Ireland) was passed, eugenic considerations were not the central reason for the legislation and "the protection of children from sexual exploitation

87 Criminal Law (Sexual Offences) Act 2017, s 7(2).
88 *ibid*, s 8(4).

by parents was regarded as far more significant".[89] This offence is discussed here as it may be used in situations where a relative has abused a child within the family. Indeed, O'Malley notes that the majority of incest cases which come before Irish courts have an abusive element and involve young victims.[90] However, the number of incest cases is small. Between 2003 and 2011, court proceedings were instituted for incest in only 12 cases.[91] There were eight convictions for incest in this time period.[92] Despite the small number of convictions, the offence of incest is not uncontroversial and there have been a number of calls for reform.

Actus Reus

The offence of incest is provided for in the Punishment of Incest Act 1908. [3–55] One of the most controversial aspects of this legislation is its differential treatment of males and females which is evident in both the definition of the offence and its punishment. Section 1 makes it an offence for a male to have vaginal sexual intercourse with a female who is to his knowledge his granddaughter, daughter, sister (including half-sister) or mother. Section 2 prohibits any female person aged 17 or over from consenting to vaginal sexual intercourse with her grandfather, father, brother (including half-brother) or son. Significantly, females under 17 cannot be found guilty of incest[93] whereas there is no such exemption for males. Hanly notes that girls under the age of 17 are conclusively regarded as victims rather than offenders and this applies even where there is evidence that the under-age girl initiated the encounter.[94] Boys under the age of 17 are afforded no such protection and can be charged with incest once they reach the age of criminal responsibility (i.e. 12 years of age[95]). As Hanly notes, this leads to the somewhat anomalous situation whereby a 16-year-old girl who convinces her 15-year-old brother to have intercourse will not be guilty of incest, while her brother will be.[96] McIntyre and McMullan note that the gender-bias in the legislation owes to the fact that the bulk of incest cases concern

---

89 Temkin, *Rape and the Legal Process*, (2nd ed, Oxford University Press, Oxford, 2002), p 59.

90 O'Malley, *supra* note 12, p 161.

91 "Criminal Law (Incest)(Amendment) Bill 2012, Private Members Bill – Second Stage, Speech by Alan Shatter T.D. Minister for Justice, Equality and Defence", 7 March 2014: available at: http://www.justice.ie/en/JELR/Pages/SP14000062 (last accessed: 21 August 2017).

92 *ibid.*

93 Punishment of Incest Act 1908, s 2, as amended by s 12 of the Criminal Law Amendment Act 1935.

94 Hanly, *An Introduction to Irish Criminal Law* (3rd ed, Gill and MacMillan, Dublin, 2015), p 339.

95 Children Act 2001, s 52(1) (as amended).

96 Hanly, *supra* note 93, p 339.

fathers abusing their daughters.[97] While this may be true, it is questionable whether this level of inequality between males and females is acceptable in modern society, especially in light of recent efforts to ensure that sexual offences legislation in general is gender-neutral.

[3–56] Consent is not a defence to a charge of incest. Accordingly, an incestuous relationship between two consenting adult relatives will result in both parties being criminally liable. However, consent "may be relevant to sentence, especially where both parties are adults".[98]

Mens Rea

[3–57] The key element of the *mens rea* for incest is that the defendant must have known that his/her sexual partner was a blood relative as defined by the Act. In *R v Carmichael*,[99] the defendant at trial was not permitted to adduce evidence to support his contention that he did not believe that the female he had sexual intercourse with was his daughter.[100] On appeal it was held that the trial judge's refusal to admit this evidence was incorrect and his conviction for incest was quashed:

> "Proof that [the female party] was in fact his daughter would not be sufficient to justify a conviction unless it was also proved that the appellant knew that she was his daughter. If the appellant could have proved to the satisfaction of the jury that he believed that she was not his daughter, or even if the jury had reasonable doubt about that matter, he would have been entitled to a verdict of acquittal."[101]

[3–58] The law was similarly interpreted in the later case of *R v Baillie-Smith*[102] where it was held that a man's conviction for incest should be quashed because he had not been permitted to adduce evidence at trial that when he had sex with his 13-year-old daughter, he had done so because he had mistaken her for his wife.[103]

---

97 McIntyre and McMullan, *Criminal Law* (2nd ed, Thomson Round Hall, 2005), p 113.

98 O'Malley, *supra* note 12, p 164.

99 [1940] 1 KB 630.

100 The man's evidence was that his wife had been having an affair around the time that his daughter was conceived and that she had subsequently told him that he was not the girl's father.

101 *ibid*, 634.

102 (1977) 64 Cr App R 76.

103 It is notable that this was one of two grounds on which the conviction was quashed. The other ground was that indirect evidence of the complainant's statement had been allowed during the trial, despite the fact that she had withdrawn her allegation and had not been called as a witness. The Court of Appeal held that for both these reasons, the appellant's conviction was unsafe.

Punishment

Differential treatment of males and females is again evident in the punishment of incest. As originally enacted, the 1908 Act made incest by a male and incest by a female punishable by up to seven years' imprisonment.[104] However, the maximum punishment for incest by a male was increased to life imprisonment in the wake of the Kilkenny Incest case where a man who had sexually abused his daughter over a period of 15 years could only be sentenced to a maximum of seven years' imprisonment.[105] The lesser maximum punishment for incest by a female came under harsh criticism in 2009 in relation to a particularly egregious case of incest which was committed by a woman in Roscommon. The offender was a mother who had forced her 13-year-old son to have sex with her on four occasions. This abuse took place in the context of severe neglect and abuse of all six children within the family, and further charges against her included two charges of sexual abuse and six charges of neglect and wilful ill-treatment of her children. She pleaded guilty to all the charges and was sentenced at Roscommon Circuit Court. When sentencing this woman for the maximum seven years' imprisonment for the incest offences, Judge Miriam Reynolds was critical of the law in this area and the low maximum penalty for incest by a female.[106] As this offender was the first female to be convicted of incest in the State, the differential sentencing for male and female offenders in this context had not proven controversial prior to this case but the need for parity of punishment for both offences is now clearly evident. **[3–59]**

Reform

The most obvious reform which is necessary in the area of incest is alignment of the penalty structure so that both males and females are subject to the **[3–60]**

[104] Where incest by a male was committed with a girl who was younger than 15 years, the maximum punishment was life imprisonment: s 1 of the 1908 Act, as amended by the Criminal Law Amendment Act 1935.

[105] The penalty was first increased to 20 years' imprisonment by s 12 of the Criminal Justice Act 1993 and then to life imprisonment by s 2 of the Criminal Law (Incest Proceedings) Act 1995. The failure of State agencies to intervene to protect the victim in this case was the subject of an inquiry: *Kilkenny Incest Investigation Report* (Stationery Office, Dublin, 1993). Available at: http://lenus.ie/hse/bitstream/10147/46278/4/zkilkennyincestinvestigation.pdf (last accessed: 23 March 2017).

[106] The Health Service Executive also came under sharp criticism for their failure to intervene more promptly to protect the children in this case. An investigation of the failures in this case was undertaken by the Roscommon Childcare Inquiry who published a Report in 2010: *Roscommon Child Care Case: Report of the Inquiry Team to the Health Service Executive*, available at: http://www.hse.ie/eng/services/publications/Children/RoscommonChildCareCase.pdf (last accessed: 23 March 2017).

same maximum punishment on conviction.[107] It had been proposed that this reform would be included in the Criminal Law (Sexual Offences) Act 2017. The General Scheme of the Criminal Law (Sexual Offences) Bill 2014 had proposed to repeal and replace s 1 and s 2 of the 1908 Act and to apply a maximum penalty of life imprisonment for both incest by a male and incest by a female.[108] This amendment was not included in the final version of the Act. The failure to align the punishments for incest by a male and incest by a female is regrettable and indeed, it is arguable that the continuing disparity between the maximum punishments is unconstitutional.[109] However, it is hoped that this inconsistency in the law will be remedied in the not-too-distant future as the government has recently committed to addressing this issue in forthcoming legislation.[110]

[3–61] The only reform of the substantive rules relating to incest included in the 2017 Act is the substitution of a new s 1 (incest committed by a male), which merely clarifies the current law in the area, providing that[111]:

> "(1) Any person who has carnal knowledge of a female person, who is to his knowledge his grand-daughter, daughter, sister or mother, shall be guilty of an offence and shall be liable on conviction on indictment to imprisonment for life or a lesser term of imprisonment.
>
> (2) It shall not be a defence to proceedings for an offence under this section for the defendant to show that the carnal knowledge was had with the consent of the female person."

[3–62] This provision has not, however, been commenced.

---

107 This has been recommended by the Rape Crisis Network of Ireland (RCNI): RCNI, *RCNI Agenda for Justice Discussion Document*, (RCNI, Galway, 2009), p 13.

108 A previous attempt to align the punishments for incest by a female and incest by a male was made via the Criminal Law (Incest) (Amendment) Bill 2012. However, this was a private members' Bill and appears to have floundered due to the impending introduction of the government-sponsored Criminal Law (Sexual Offences) Bill.

109 See Hanly, *supra* note 94, p 340 and O'Malley, *supra* note 12, p 169. In *SM v Ireland* (No 2) [2007] 4 IR 369 the different maximum penalties applicable for indecent assault upon a male (10 years' imprisonment) and indecent assault upon a female (two years' imprisonment) in the Offences against the Person Act 1861 were held to be unconstitutional and thereby invalid as they breached the principle of equality before the law enshrined in Art 40.1 of the Constitution and thus, as a result of Art 50 of the Constitution, did not continue into force once the Constitution became operative.

110 Department of Justice and Equality, "Press Release: Government approves proposals to strengthen penalties for repeat sexual offenders and to amend existing incest laws", 11 July 2017. Available at: http://justice.ie/en/JELR/Pages/PR17000233 (last accessed: 21 August 2017).

111 Reform to the procedural rules relating to the trial of incest are also included in the 2017 Act. These reforms are discussed in chapter 4.

Aside from the issues surrounding the punishment of incest, further criticisms of this offence relate to its rather narrow construction, applying only to blood relatives. Thus, it is not incest where individuals who are legally related by adoption or by marriage engage in sexual intercourse. For example, where an adoptive parent has sexual intercourse with his/her adoptive child, or where adopted siblings have sexual intercourse, or where a step-parent has sexual intercourse with a step-child, or where step-siblings engage in sexual intercourse, incest is not committed. In light of traditional eugenic justifications for the offence of incest, these limitations within its definition are understandable, but since incest may also be used to punish exploitative sexual activity within familial settings, there is a case for considering extending both the types of sexual activity covered by the offence and the relationships within which this activity is prohibited.[112] However, as incest is generally understood as involving blood relatives, concerns about fair labelling may arise if it is to be extended to cover other familial relationships.[113] Moreover, with the introduction of a new offence of abuse of a position of authority in relation to children (discussed above), it seems that familial abuse involving non-blood relatives might be more accurately captured under this offence rather than an extension of the offence of incest. With regard to extending the categories of sexual activity to which the offence of incest applies, in *The Law of Sexual Offences: A Discussion Paper*, the Department of Justice noted that since one of the main reasons the offence exists is to avoid genetic defects, the focus on heterosexual sexual intercourse is justifiable. While the definition could be broadened to include other forms of sexual activity and abuse this might "undermine the reason for a separate incest offence and, in any event, other laws provide adequate protection for children in such situations".[114] **[3–63]**

A final concern which might be raised about the offence of incest relates to whether there should be exceptions to liability for incest where adult relatives engage in consensual sexual relationships, especially where this arises in situations where the individuals have first met as adults. An **[3–64]**

---

[112] The RCNI has previously recommended a complete review of the 1908 Act to reflect the changing nature of "families", for example, categories of prohibited persons covered by this legislation ought to be enlarged to protect persons within a wider definition of "family", such as step-parents: RCNI, *Agenda for Justice I: Towards Ending Injustice for Survivors of Sexual Violence*, (RCNI, Galway, 2005), p 4. The RCNI also recommended that the 1908 Act be amended to take account of current and evolving understandings or definitions of family members, such as foster-children/parents or step-children/parents: RCNI, *supra* note, 107 p 13).

[113] Home Office, *Setting the Boundaries: Reforming the Law on Sexual Offences* (Home Office, London, 2000), para 5.5.5.

[114] Department of Justice, Equality and Law Reform, *Discussion Paper on the Law on Sexual Offences* (Dublin: Department of Justice, Equality and Law Reform, Dublin, 1998), para 7.5.1.

example of such a scenario would be where "long lost" siblings have met for the first time as adults having been raised by adoptive parents. This was the scenario which arose for consideration by the European Court of Human Rights in *Stübing v Germany*.[115] The applicant in this case had had a sexual relationship with his biological sister who he met for the first time when he was reunited with his biological family as an adult, having been raised by adoptive parents. The applicant and his sister had lived together for several years and had four children together. He was convicted of incest and sentenced to one year and four months' imprisonment.[116] The applicant alleged that the German law prohibiting incest was incompatible with his right to private life in Art 8 of the European Convention on Human Rights (ECHR).[117] The Court held the applicant's right to respect for his private life was interfered with but that this interference was compatible with Art 8(2) which provides that:

> "There shall be no interference by a public authority with the exercise of [the right to respect for one's private and family life] except such as in accordance with the law and is necessary in a democratic society in the interests of national security, public safety or the economic well-being of the country, for the prevention of disorder or crime, for the protection of health or morals, or for the protection of the rights and freedoms of others."

[3–65] The Court noted that "there must exist particularly serious reasons before interference on the part of public authorities concerning a most intimate aspect of private life, such as the manifestation of a person's sexuality, can be legitimate for the purposes of [Art 8(2)]".[118] However, such interference was acceptable in this instance. The Court noted that:

> "... there is no consensus between the member States as to whether the consensual commitment of sexual acts between adult siblings should be criminally sanctioned ... .Still, a majority of altogether twenty-eight out of the forty-four States reviewed[119] provide for criminal liability. The Court

---

115 (2012) 55 EHRR 24.

116 It is notable that a sentence was not imposed on his sister. It was held that she was only partially responsible for her actions as she suffered from a serious personality disorder which, together with an unsatisfying family situation and mild learning difficulties, led to her being considerably dependent on the applicant: *ibid*, para 64.

117 s 6 of the 1908 Act expressly provides that all prosecutions for incest require the consent of the DPP.

118 *ibid*, para 59.

119 The Court notes that out of 31 Council of Europe Member States, 16 States criminalised the performance of consensual sexual acts between adult siblings (Albania, Austria, Bosnia and Herzegovina, Bulgaria, Croatia, Cyprus, the Czech Republic, Finland, Greece, Iceland, Ireland, Liechtenstein, Macedonia, Moldova, San Marino and Slovakia). Contrarily in 15 States, such activity was not punishable under criminal law (Armenia, Azerbaijan, Belgium, Estonia, Georgia, Latvia, Lithuania, Luxembourg, Malta, Monaco, Montenegro, Portugal, Serbia, Slovenia and

further notes that all the legal systems, including those which do not impose criminal liability, prohibit siblings from getting married. Thus, a broad consensus transpires that sexual relationships between siblings are neither accepted by the legal order nor by society as a whole. Conversely, there is no sufficient empirical support for the assumption of a general trend towards a decriminalisation of such acts. The Court further considers that the instant case concerns a question about the requirements of morals. It follows from the above principles that the domestic authorities enjoy a wide margin of appreciation in determining how to confront incestuous relationships between consenting adults, notwithstanding that this decision concerns an intimate aspect of an individual's private life."[120]

Thus, it remains for individual Member States to exercise their discretion under the margin of appreciation on whether to maintain the prohibition on sexual activity between adult relatives and its retention is not a breach of Convention rights. There are no clear arguments for the decriminalisation of consensual incestuous sexual activity and it is very unlikely that the Irish legislature would ever move to decriminalise it as it "might lead to a perception that the State condones such relationships".[121] Thus, the primary concern with this aspect of the law from a reform perspective is the disparate sentences which apply to incest by a male and incest by a female. **[3–66]**

Offences Against Individuals with Limited Decision-Making Capacity

Until the recent commencement of the Criminal Law (Sexual Offences) Act 2017, the law protecting individuals with limited decision-making capacity from sexual abuse was the subject of much criticism and was clearly not fit for purpose. Section 5 of the Criminal Law (Sexual Offences) Act 1993 provided that a person who (a) has or attempts to have sexual intercourse or (b) commits or attempts to commit an act of buggery with a person who is mentally impaired (other than a person to whom he is married or to whom he believes with reasonable cause he is married) will be guilty of an offence.[122] An individual found guilty of this offence would be liable on conviction on indictment to: **[3–67]**

Ukraine): para 28. Further, an expert report prepared by the Max Planck Institute for Foreign and International Criminal Law in November 2007 for the domestic German proceedings in this case found that sexual acts were criminalised in a further eight countries (Denmark, Italy, Poland, Romania, Sweden, Switzerland, Hungary and the UK) and were not subject to liability in five other countries (France, the Netherlands, the Russian Federation, Spain and Turkey): *ibid*, para 30.

120 *ibid*, para 61.

121 Department of Justice, Equality and Law Reform, *supra* note 113, para 7.4.2.

122 Criminal Law (Sexual Offences) Act 1993, s 5(1).

"(i) in the case of having sexual intercourse or committing an act of buggery, imprisonment for a term not exceeding 10 years, and

(ii) in the case of an attempt to have sexual intercourse or an attempt to commit an act of buggery, imprisonment for a term not exceeding three years in the case of a first conviction, and in the case of a second or any subsequent conviction imprisonment for a term not exceeding five years."[123]

[3–68] Section 5 also provided that it was an offence for a male person to commit or attempt to commit an act of gross indecency[124] with another male person who is mentally impaired.[125] The maximum penalty on conviction on indictment for this offence was two years' imprisonment.[126]

[3–69] For the purposes of s 5, "mentally impaired" was defined as "suffering from a disease of the mind, whether through mental handicap or mental illness, which is of such a nature or degree as to render a person incapable of living an independent life or of guarding against serious exploitation".[127] An accused was entitled to a defence if he could "show that at the time of the alleged commission of the offence he did not know and had no reason to suspect that the person in respect of whom he is charged was mentally impaired".[128] The complainant's consent was, however, irrelevant and could not exculpate. Notably, proceedings against a person charged with an offence under s 5 could not be taken except by or with the consent of the DPP.[129]

[3–70] As the primary protection from sexual abuse for individuals with limited decision-making capacity, s 5 was inherently flawed, and it was subject to review by LRC,[130] resulting in a number of recommendations for its

---

[123] *ibid*, s 5(1).

[124] Gross indecency has never been statutorily defined. O'Malley notes that the offence "was generally accepted to involve two males acting in concert in such a way as represented a "marked departure from the decent conduct expected from the average [person] in the circumstances that existed"": O'Malley, *supra* note 12, p 138. He cites mutual masturbation as an activity which might be capable of amounting to gross indecency: *ibid*.

[125] Criminal Law (Sexual Offences) Act 1993, s 5(2).

[126] *ibid*.

[127] *ibid*, s 5(5).

[128] *ibid*, s 5(3).

[129] *ibid*, s 5(4).

[130] Law Reform Commission, *Consultation Paper: Sexual Offences and Capacity to Consent*, (LRC CP 63–2011) (Law Reform Commission, Dublin, 2011) and *Report: Sexual Offences and Capacity to Consent*, (LRC 109–2013) (Law Reform Commission, Dublin, 2013). This topic was also considered by the LRC in an earlier consultation process which focussed on the law on capacity as it applied in a civil law context. See: Law Reform Commission, *Consultation Paper on Vulnerable Adults and the Law: Capacity* (LRC CP 37–2005), (Dublin, Law Reform Commission, 2005), chapter 6. Ultimately, given the complexities of the issues raised during the

reform. Since s 5 has now been repealed, it is superfluous to provide too much detail about its shortcomings. However, some comments on the perceived failings of the section are worthwhile to provide a context for discussion and critique of the reforms in the 2017 Act. The first, and perhaps most troubling, issue with s 5 was that consent did not provide a defence. This meant that an individual who was categorised as "mentally impaired" within the meaning of the section was effectively legally barred from engaging in a sexual relationship. This paternalistic stance was founded in a desire to protect these individuals from exploitation and abuse, but its absolutist nature failed to provide for the situation where an individual with an intellectual disability or mental illness was capable of exercising sexual choice. Instead, these individuals' rights to sexual autonomy were overlooked which was in direct conflict with the rights-based approach to disability which is required by the United Nations Convention on the Rights of People with Disabilities (UNCRPD),[131] the ECHR[132] and the equality provisions of the Irish Constitution.[133]

The use of the term "mentally impaired" was also problematic, being both outdated and inappropriate. Moreover, the criteria it set for capacity to consent to sexual activity (i.e. the ability to live independently) was highly questionable. As the LRC observed, capacity to consent to sexual activity is not predicated on an ability to live independently. Competence is local. It must be judged in a context-sensitive manner with reference to each decision which the relevant person needs to make or each activity which s/he wishes to engage in. It is neither accurate nor sufficiently respectful of autonomy to assert that an individual who does not have capacity to live independently necessarily does not have capacity to consent to sexual activity. **[3–71]**

Another problem with s 5 was the focus on sexual intercourse and buggery. The LRC highlighted research showing that sexual touching, rather than penetrative sexual activity, was the most common type of abuse suffered by people with intellectual disability. The failure of s 5 to provide for all forms of sexual abuse (penetrative and non-penetrative) was highlighted in *People (DPP) v XY.*[134] In this case, the accused was alleged to have forced a woman with an intellectual disability to perform oral sex on him. As this **[3–72]**

consultation on this point, the LRC opted not to provide recommendations for reform in its Report: *Report on Vulnerable Adults and the Law: Capacity* (LRC 83–2006) (Law Reform Commission, Dublin, 2006), chapter 3.

131 Art 12(1) of the UNCRPD provides that: "States Parties reaffirm that persons with disabilities have the right to recognition everywhere as persons before the law". Further, Art 12(2) states that: "States Parties shall recognize that persons with disabilities enjoy legal capacity on an equal basis with others in all aspects of life".

132 Art 8: *X v The Netherlands* (1986) 8 EHRR 235.

133 Art 40.1.

134 Central Criminal Court, 23 November 2010.

form of sexual activity was not included within s 5, the defendant was charged under s 4 of the Criminal Law (Rape) (Amendment) Act 1990 which makes no provision for individuals with limited decision-making capacity. Since under s 4 the complainant's intellectual disability per se could not be taken into account, some evidence of assault or of a hostile act(s) would be necessary to ground a conviction. As the complainant's evidence did not support such a finding, White J was forced to direct the jury to acquit the defendant, noting that "the Oireachtas when they introduced the 1993 Act did not fully appreciate the range of offences needed to give protection to the vulnerable".[135] Finally, the defence of marriage was criticised, with the LRC recommending that it be abolished.[136] Given the problems with s 5, it is unsurprising that the LRC recommended that it be repealed in its entirety and replaced with a more modern, rights-based provision.

Reform

[3–73] The Criminal Law (Sexual Offences) Act 2017 repealed s 5 of the 1993 Act[137] and replaces it with two new offences, that is, "a sexual act with a 'protected person'" and an "offence against a 'relevant person' by a person in authority". Proceedings for either offence cannot commence without the consent of the DPP.[138]

Sexual Act with a Protected Person

[3–74] Section 21(1) of the 2017 Act provides that:

> "A person who engages in a sexual act with a protected person knowing that

135 This case is not reported but is discussed by the LRC: *Consultation Paper: Sexual Offences and Capacity to Consent*, (LRC CP 63–2011), (Law Reform Commission, Dublin, 2011), para 6.29. See also: "Jury directed to find man not guilty of sex assault on mentally disabled woman", *The Irish Times*, 16 November 2010.

136 Law Reform Commission, *Report: Sexual Offences and Capacity to Consent*, (LRC 109–2013) (Law Reform Commission, Dublin, 2013), para 4.36.

137 Criminal Law (Sexual Offences) Act 2017, s 24. This provision of the 2017 Act also repeals s 6(2) of the 1993 Act which was substituted into that Act by s 2 of the Criminal Law (Sexual Offences) (Amendment) Act 2007. As amended, s 6(2) provided for an offence of soliciting or importuning a person who is mentally impaired (whether or not for the purposes of prostitution) for the purposes of the commission of an act that would constitute an offence (a) under s 5, or under s 2 of the Criminal Law (Rape)(Amendment) Act 1990 (i.e. sexual assault). A person guilty of an offence under this section would be liable:

> "(a) on summary conviction to a fine not exceeding €5,000, or imprisonment for a term not exceeding 12 months, or to both, or
> (b) on conviction on indictment to a fine, or imprisonment for a term not exceeding 5 years, or to both: s 6(3) (as amended)."

138 Criminal Law (Sexual Offences) Act 2017, s 23.

> that person is a protected person or being reckless as to whether that person is a protected person shall be guilty of an offence."

The penalty for engaging in a sexual act with a protected person varies depending on the type of sexual activity which is involved. Where the sexual act concerned consisted of sexual intercourse, buggery or an act described in s 3(1) or s 4(1) of the 1990 Act, the maximum penalty on conviction on indictment is life imprisonment.[139] Where the relevant sexual act is one which done without consent would constitute a sexual assault, the maximum penalty on conviction on indictment is 14 years.[140] **[3–75]**

Actus Reus

The *actus reus* of this offence consists of engaging in a sexual act with a protected person. For the purposes of the section, a "sexual act" is defined as: an act consisting of sexual intercourse[141] or buggery; an act described in s 3(1) or s 4(1) of the 1990 Act (i.e. aggravated sexual assault or rape under s 4), or; an act which if done without consent would constitute a sexual assault.[142] Thus, the new offence covers a greater variety of sexual activity, addressing one of the criticisms of the 1993 Act. A "protected person" is a person who lacks the capacity to consent to a sexual act. An individual will be found to lack such capacity

> "if he or she is, by reason of a mental or intellectual disability or a mental illness, incapable of—
> (a) understanding the nature, or the reasonably foreseeable consequences, of that act,
> (b) evaluating relevant information for the purposes of deciding whether or not to engage in that act, or
> (c) communicating his or her consent to that act by speech, sign language or otherwise."[143]

The use of the term "protected person" in the legislation is likely a direct response to what the LRC referred to as the "euphemism treadmill" which applies in this particular area whereby "terminology that appears at a given time to be respectful, or at least acceptable, runs the risk that it eventually comes to have a derogatory or insulting meaning".[144] By using neutral **[3–76]**

---

139 Criminal Law (Sexual Offences) Act 2017, s 21(4).
140 *ibid*, s 21(5).
141 Criminal Law (Sexual Offences) Act 2017, s 20, , provides that sexual intercourse should be construed in accordance with s 1(2) of the Criminal Law (Rape) Act 1981, that is, penetration is all that needs to be proved.
142 Criminal Law (Sexual Offences) Act 2017, s 20.
143 *ibid*, s 21(7).
144 Law Reform Commission, *supra* note 135, p 1.

nomenclature to refer to individuals who are protected under this provision, the legislature avoided referring to those with intellectual disability or mental illness in a manner which is acceptable now but may be seen as derogatory or outdated in the future.

[3–77] The test for capacity provided in the 2017 is founded on the functional approach to determinations of capacity. This approach "defines capacity as the ability, with suitable assistance if needed, to understand the nature and consequences of a decision within the context of the available range of choices; and to communicate that decision".[145] This represents an advancement on the approach under s 5 which was "status-based", that is, once an individual was found to be suffering from mental impairment as defined in the legislation, s/he was deemed incapable of engaging in sexual activity. The adoption of a functional approach to capacity conforms more closely with the rights-based ethos of the UNCRPD and aligns with civil law in the Assisted Decision-Making (Capacity) Act 2015 which also adopts the functional approach for determinations of capacity.[146] The LRC had recommended the adoption of a functional approach to assessments of capacity and the wording chosen in the 2017 Act closely resembles the wording proposed by the LRC.[147]

[3–78] The functional test adopted in the 2017 Act is a sensible one which allows for context-sensitive assessments of capacity. With regard to "understanding" it is likely that this will be interpreted as requiring a rudimental knowledge of the relevant sexual act. For example, where sexual intercourse is involved, the individual should be able to understand the sexual nature of the act and "reasonably foreseeable consequences" is likely to involve understanding of the possibility of pregnancy or the contracting a sexually transmitted illness. The requirement of "understanding" should also be met where an individual is capable of understanding once appropriate aids to understanding are used (e.g. use of simple language or pictorial aids).[148] Further, as noted by the LRC, effective sexual education is vital to ensure the maximum possibility that individuals with limited decision-making capacity may satisfy the understanding requirement.[149] The evaluation aspect of the test will require individuals to have "an ability to form a decision about whether or not to engage in the act", which necessarily "entails weighing relevant information that has been acquired and understood in order to arrive at a choice in the context of available choices at the time the decision is to be

---

[145] *ibid*, para 1.09.
[146] s 3.
[147] Law Reform Commission, *supra* note 135, chapter three.
[148] *ibid*, para 3.08.
[149] *ibid*, para 3.28.

made".[150] Finally, the communication requirement acknowledges that to exercise sexual autonomy, an individual must be able to communicate his/her wishes effectively. It is significant that forms of communication other than speech are specifically referenced, thus facilitating individuals who may communicate via methods such as sign language. It is to be assumed that the means of communication would have to be understood by an individual's sexual partner to satisfy the communication requirement.

Overall, the individualised approach to capacity assessments provided by this test seeks to ensure maximum respect for sexual autonomy whilst still providing a mechanism to ensure that individuals whose capacity must be assessed are capable of consenting and are not being abused or exploited. However, while this test provides useful abstract guidelines, accompanying practical policy guidance on how to carry out these assessments will be necessary to allow for proactive application of the new law and to help those who care for and/or advise individuals who may qualify as protected persons to make effective and appropriate assessments of capacity. Without such intervention, the new rules will not offer meaningful advancements in respecting the sexual autonomy of individuals whose capacity to consent to sexual activity needs to be assessed. **[3–79]**

Mens Rea

Section 21(3) provides that: **[3–80]**

> "... it shall be presumed, unless the contrary is shown, that the defendant knew or was reckless as to whether the person against whom the offence is alleged to have been committed was a protected person."

Thus, once the *actus reus* of the offence is proved (i.e. a sexual act with a protected person), then the *mens rea* is presumed unless the defendant can show that s/he did not know or was not reckless as to whether the complainant was a protected person. The legislation does not state what standard of proof the defendant must discharge in order to rebut this presumption. Thus, this will fall to be determined by the courts. However, based on the judgment in *Egan* in relation to the mistake of age defence, discussed above, it is possible to offer some observations on how s 21(3) might be interpreted by the courts. First, it would appear to be safe to suggest that the section does not place a legal burden of proof on the balance of probabilities on the defendant. Given that the mistake of age defence has been specifically reformed to shift a legal burden of proof to the defendant, it can surely be assumed that if s 21(3) were to impose such a burden on the defendant, the legislation would specifically state this. Since both **[3–81]**

[150] *ibid*, para 3.50.

defences are created in the same piece of legislation, it would seem that if the legislature wished both to apply in the same way, they would both be phrased similarly. Thus, it is necessary to determine whether, in seeking to rebut the presumption of *mens rea* in s 21(3), a defendant will merely have to raise an issue as to *mens rea* and then the legal burden of proof will revert to the prosecution, or whether the higher threshold which was approved in *Egan* will apply, requiring the defendant to establish a reasonable doubt in the mind of the jury in relation to his/her lack of *mens rea*. It is noteworthy that s 21(3) is phrased differently to the formulation of the mistake defence which prevailed at the time of the *Egan* judgment. In the original version of s 3(5) of the 2006 Act, it was stated that the defendant had to *prove* that s/he was reasonably mistaken regarding the complainant's age. However, in s 21(3), the defendant is rebutting a presumption and, further, the section states that *mens rea* is presumed unless the contrary is *shown*. McGrath suggests that this difference in terminology may be significant.[151] In *Hardy v Ireland*,[152] the use of term "show" in the provision under consideration was interpreted as placing an evidential burden on the accused which merely requires that an issue be raised as to *mens rea*. On the other hand, in *People (DPP) v Smyth*,[153] the term "prove" in the relevant provision was interpreted as applying the higher threshold of raising a reasonable doubt. This reasoning was followed in *Egan*. Consequently, it may be significant that s 21(3) uses the term "show", which may be interpreted as placing an evidential burden on an accused to raise an issue as to *mens rea* which will then cause the legal burden of proof to revert to the prosecution. Given the difficulties and controversies relating to *mens rea* of sexual offences which have already arisen in this jurisdiction, it is a pity that the legislature was not clearer about the intended interpretation of *mens rea* for this offence. Unfortunately, the true construction of the provision will not now be known until it has been interpreted by the courts.

Offence Against a Relevant Person by a Person in Authority

[3–82] Section 22(1) provides that a person in authority who engages in a sexual act with a relevant person shall be guilty of an offence.

[3–83] As with the offence of engaging in a sexual act with a protected person, the penalty for this offence varies depending upon the sexual act which is involved. Where the sexual act consists of sexual intercourse, buggery or an act described in s 3(1) or s 4(1) of the 1990 Act, the maximum penalty on conviction on indictment is 10 years. Where the sexual act involved is

151 McGrath, *supra* note 34, p 37.

152 [1994] 2 IR 550.

153 [2010] IECCA 34; [2010] 3 IR 688; [2010] 1 ILRM 81.

one which if done without consent would constitute a sexual assault, the maximum penalty on conviction on indictment is five years.

Actus Reus

For the purposes of this offence, "sexual act" has the same meaning as set out above in relation to a sexual act with a protected person. Section 22(8) provides that a "person in authority": **[3–84]**

> "in relation to a relevant person against whom an offence is alleged to have been committed, means any person who as part of a contract of service or a contract for services is, for the time being, responsible for the education, supervision, training, treatment, care or welfare of the relevant person".

A "relevant person" is one who has "(a) a mental or intellectual disability, or (b) a mental illness, which is of such a nature or degree as to severely restrict the ability of the person to guard himself or herself against serious exploitation".[154] It is no defence in proceedings for this offence for the defendant to prove that the person against whom the offence is alleged to have been committed consented to the sexual act of which the offence consisted.[155] **[3–85]**

The category of persons protected by s 22 is not intended to be the same as those protected under s 21. Although the individuals protected under this section may not have capacity to consent, the section is also concerned with those who might be capable of consenting but who, because of the relationship of trust or authority which subsists, are vulnerable to sexual abuse or exploitation. This is the reason the term "relevant person" is used here instead of "protected person", as was explained by former Minister for Justice, Frances Fitzgerald during the Dáil Debates on the passage of the Act: **[3–86]**

> "The words 'protected person' have been used in recognition of the lack of capacity of that person to consent, not the fact of a person's disability alone. We have also used the term 'protected person' to distinguish the persons protected under the section from those to whom section 22 applies. Section 22 provides for an offence by a person in authority who engages in a sexual act with a person with a mental or intellectual disability or mental illness and in respect of whom they, as part of a contract of services, have a responsibility for education, supervision, training, treatment, care or welfare. This offence targets breaches of trust by persons who may take advantage of their positions to engage in a sexual act with someone in their charge. The category of persons is where there is some confusion. The category of persons protected by section 22 is different from that under section 21 as consent is

---

154 Criminal Law (Rape) (Amendment) Act 1990, s 22(8).

155 *ibid*, s 22(4).

> not a defence under section 22. For this reason, the persons protected under section 22 are referred to as 'relevant persons'. Under section 21, where capacity to consent is an issue, we call them 'protected persons'. To be very clear sections 21 and 22 relate to two different groups of people. Therefore, to use the same words in both sections would cause confusion. That is why different terms are used."[156]

[3–87] Thus, consent is not in question in this section, as the relationship between the parties is such that the relevant person is held not to be in a position to consent to it.

Mens Rea

[3–88] The construction of s 22(1) which provides that "a person in authority who engages in a sexual act with a relevant person shall be guilty of an offence" suggests an offence of strict liability. However, a mistake defence is provided in s 22(3) which states that:

> "It shall be a defence to proceedings for an offence under this section for the defendant to prove that he or she was reasonably mistaken that, at the time of the alleged commission of the offence, the person against whom the offence is alleged to have been committed was not a relevant person."

[3–89] This defence must be proven by the defendant, s 22(5) providing that the standard of proof which will apply is that applicable in civil proceedings (i.e. the balance of probabilities).

Specific Offences Involving Inducements Etc

[3–90] The LRC had recommended that new offences created to replace s 5 should "take account of specific elements that involve exploitation or abuse, such as inducements, threats or tricks".[157] Offences along these lines are included in both ss 21 and 22. Section 21(2) provides that:

> "A person who invites, induces, counsels or incites a protected person to engage in a sexual act knowing that that person is a protected person or being reckless as to whether that person is a protected person shall be guilty of an offence".

---

156 Criminal Law (Sexual Offences) Bill 2015 [Seanad]: Report Stage (Continued), Dáil Éireann Debate *Vol. 937 No. 1*, 1 February 2017, available at: http://oireachtasdebates.oireachtas.ie/debates%20authoring/debateswebpack.nsf/takes/dail2017020100059 (last accessed: 23 August 2017).

157 Law Reform Commission, *supra* note 135, para 4.17.

A person guilty of this offence will be liable, on conviction on indictment, to a maximum term of imprisonment of 10 years. Section 22(2) provides that: **[3–91]**

> "A person in authority who invites, induces, counsels or incites a relevant person to engage in a sexual act shall be guilty of an offence."

The maximum penalty on conviction on indictment for this offence is five years. **[3–92]**

These offences are an important addition to the law and recognise that individuals whose capacity for decision-making is limited may be more vulnerable to suggestion than the general population. However, the legislature could have offered more robust protection by providing that these offences include not just inducements but also threats and deception. It must also be questioned whether this protection should have been created in a separate offence which applied to individuals with mental illness or intellectual disability who may be capable of consenting but, because of their condition, are more susceptible to the influence of threats, deceptions or inducements which would not be influential to others. Section 21 only applies to inducements etc. with a "protected person" (i.e. an individual without capacity to consent) and "relevant persons" who may have capacity to consent where the sexual activity occurs with an individual who is in a position of authority. It might have been preferable to adopt the approach taken in s 35 of the English Sexual Offences Act 2003 which creates an offence of "causing a person with a mental disorder to engage in or agree to engage in sexual activity by inducement, threat or deception".[158] Offences such as this "are designed to protect persons who are able to make a choice, but who are nevertheless vulnerable to relatively low levels of inducement, threats or deception".[159] For the purposes of the English offence, "an inducement may be, for example, the promise of sweets or a holiday; a threat may be to hurt a member of the complainant's family; and a deception may be telling the complainant that they will be in trouble if they refuse to take part or persuading him that it is expected that friends should engage in sexual activity".[160] The more robust approach in the 2003 Act would provide **[3–93]**

---

[158] s 35(1), provides that: "A person (A) commits an offence if—

"(a) by means of an inducement offered or given, a threat made or a deception practised by him for this purpose, he intentionally causes another person (B) to engage in, or agree to engage in, an activity,
(b) the activity is sexual,
(c) B has a mental disorder, and
(d) A knows or could reasonably be expected to know that B has a mental disorder."

[159] Byrne, "Sexual Offences and Capacity to Consent; Key Issues" (2015) 5(1) *Irish Journal of Legal Studies*, 22, 34.

[160] Rook and Ward, *supra* note 78, p 599. They relied on the Explanatory Notes to the

greater protection and the creation of one offence would be simpler than having two similar offences in sections 21 and 22.

A Comment on the 2017 Reforms

[3–94] There is no doubt that the 2017 reforms are a welcome improvement on s 5 of the 1993 Act. However, significant follow-up is required to ensure that the new provisions are progressively implemented and achieve the right balance between protection and respect for sexual autonomy. The LRC highlighted the policy and education changes which would be required to make sure that the introduction of a functional approach to assessments of capacity would be workable in practice and would not create the potential for exploitation or abuse. Indeed, at a base level, those who care for and/or advise individuals who may qualify as protected persons under the Act will need guidance on how to apply the new legal provisions so as to effectively assess the capacity of these individuals to consent to sexual activity for the purpose of ensuring that their right to sexual autonomy is appropriately recognised. In line with this, as the LRC identified, the delivery of high quality sex and relationships education is a vital accompaniment for the new legislative provisions. The LRC recommended that this should include "the development of a comprehensive nationwide policy and action plan regarding the delivery of sex and relationships education and … clarity as to the responsibility for the provision of educative support".[161] The LRC also recommended "that national standards should address the need for education and training for carers, staff and parents, in addition to the establishment of a communications and information campaign to raise awareness throughout the wider community of the sexual rights of persons with intellectual disability".[162] The creation of a cohesive national strategy for sex education in this context is critical to ensure that the law is applied consistently and results in appropriate recognition of the sexual rights of individuals with intellectual disability or mental illness.

[3–95] A further development in policy in the wake of the 2017 Act is the need for a fresh approach to safeguarding potentially vulnerable individuals from abuse or exploitation. The need for such safeguards is specifically recognised in Art 12(4) of the UNCRPD which states that States Parties shall ensure that all measures that relate to the exercise of legal capacity provide for appropriate and effective safeguards to prevent abuse.[163]

Act for this interpretation: *Explanatory Notes to Sexual Offences Act 2003*, Available at: http://www.opsi.gov.uk/Acts/acts2003/en/ukpgaen_20030042_en_1.htm (last Accessed: 10 August 2017), para 64.

161 Law Reform Commission, *supra* note 135, para 1.62.

162 *ibid.*

163 Such safeguards are also mandated by the general requirement imposed on States by

Thus, national standards concerning safeguards from sexual exploitation should be created to accompany the new legislative provisions. The LRC recommended that such national safeguards should be developed in consultation with stakeholders such as the Health Information Quality Authority, the Health Service Executive, An Garda Síochána, professionals such as carers and medical professionals, as well as groups who advocate for the individuals who might be affected by the 2017 Act (e.g. the National Disability Authority) and those to whom the legislation will apply.[164] The LRC recommended that the national standards should include protocols on co-operation between different agencies to provide protection. Significantly, the LRC also emphasised the importance of maintaining the balance between protection and respect for autonomy in these protocols, recommending that "[i]n addition to protective measures, emphasis should be placed on supporting the positive exercise of a person's legal right to sexual expression".[165]

The LRC had also recommended that: **[3–96]**

> "any replacement of section 5 … should provide that, to avoid any doubt on the matter, no offence occurs where (a) two relevant persons engage in or attempt to engage in a sexual act and (b) there is no exploitation or abuse (whether physical, sexual or emotional) of either relevant person, and that in such a case they need not have the same decision-making capacity as each other".[166]

The inclusion of a provision along these lines in the 2017 Act would avoid the potential for two protected persons who engage in sexual activity to incur criminal liability. Where there is no abuse or exploitation in such a relationship, it should not attract the attention of the criminal law. While the consent of the DPP is specifically required for a prosecution under s 21 and thus prosecutorial discretion is likely to avoid any inappropriate prosecutions, a provision along the lines recommended by the LRC might have been a worthwhile addition to the law for the sake of clarity. **[3–97]**

---

art 16 of the UNCRPD which requires States to guarantee "freedom from exploitation, violence and abuse".

164 Law Reform Commission, *supra* note 135, para 1.52.

165 *ibid.*

166 *ibid*, para 1.20.

Part Two

THE RULES OF EVIDENCE IN SEXUAL OFFENCE CASES

Chapter Four

Special Procedures in Sexual Offence Trials

Introduction

Involvement in the trial process, particularly giving evidence, is a distressing experience for sexual offence complainants. Special measures are necessary to ensure that complainants are protected as far as possible from the potentially negative effects of testifying. These measures also help complainants to give their best evidence. This is crucially important in light of the "oath against oath" nature of sexual offence trials, where the complainant's testimony will form the cornerstone of the prosecution's case against the defendant. Initial attempts to protect the privacy of complainants can be found in the Criminal Law (Rape) Act 1981 with the introduction of anonymity provisions and the exclusion of the public from certain trials. Later, more sophisticated measures to protect complainants while they are giving evidence (e.g. the use of television links) were introduced in the Criminal Evidence Act 1992, and the availability of such measures will be extended by when Pt 6 of the Criminal Law (Sexual Offences) Act 2017 is commenced and by the Criminal Justice (Victims of Crime) Act 2017. The existing operative measures and proposed reforms are discussed in this chapter.[1] **[4–01]**

Protection of Privacy

For sexual offence complainants, "privacy is like oxygen: it is a pervasive, consistent need at every step of recovery and within the context of the legal system, if a victim is without privacy, all other remedies are moot".[2] Protecting complainants' privacy was the theme of the first special procedures introduced in the Criminal Law (Rape)Act 1981, which included **[4–02]**

---

1 It should be noted that, as with other victims of crime, sexual offence complainants are also entitled to a range of support services such as court accompaniment and the provision of separate waiting areas in court. Victims' entitlements to these services have been strengthened in Ireland recently with the implementation of the Victims' Directive, which is given effect in Ireland by the Criminal Justice (Victims of Crime) Act 2017.

2 Seidman and Vickers, "The Second Wave: An Agenda for the Next Thirty Years of Rape Law Reform" (2004–2005) 38 *Suffolk University Law Review* 467, 473.

regulating the use of sexual experience evidence (discussed in chapter five), as well as providing for the exclusion of the public from certain sexual offence trials and protecting the anonymity of complainants and defendants. As Hedigan J noted in *LK v Independent Star Newspapers and Others*[3]:

> "Sections 6, 7 and 8 of the Criminal Law (Rape) Act 1981 (as amended) represent an attempt by the Oireachtas to balance the constitutional requirement that justice should be administered in public with the very understandable desire to encourage and facilitate victims of sexual offences to come forward and to assist in the prosecution of persons who are alleged to have committed sexual offences and to protect complainants, as much as possible, from unnecessary publicity and distress occasioned thereby."[4]

Exclusion of the Public

[4–03] Article 34.1 of the Irish Constitution guarantees the principle of "open justice", that is, that justice should be administered in public, "save in such special and limited circumstances as may be prescribed by law".[5] This principle can be departed from where this is necessary to protect privacy and/or to allow justice to be properly administered. Thus, Irish sexual offences legislation permits exclusion of the public from sexual offence trials. Section 6(1) of the 1981 Act[6] provides that in the trial of certain sexual offences, namely offences involving rape, rape under s 4, aggravated sexual assault[7] and offences under the Criminal Law (Sexual Offences) Act 2006[8]:

> "... the judge ... shall exclude from the court during the hearing all persons except officers of the court, persons directly concerned in the proceedings, *bona fide* representatives of the Press and such other persons (if any) as the judge ... may in his or her discretion permit to remain."

[4–04] Complainants and young defendants (i.e. under the age of 18) are permitted to have a parent, relative or friend in the courtroom.[9] Verdict and sentence (if any) must be announced in open court.[10]

---

3 [2011] 2 ILRM 272.
4 *ibid*, 288.
5 Art 6(1) of the European Convention on Human Rights also protects the principle of open justice, providing that "[i]n the determination ... of any criminal charge against him, everyone is entitled to a fair and *public* hearing within a reasonable time by an independent and impartial tribunal established by law". [Emphasis added].
6 As amended by s 11 of the Criminal Law (Rape)(Amendment) Act 1990.
7 Criminal Law (Rape)(Act) 1981 Act, s 6 also applies to related inchoate offences and offences of aiding, abetting, counselling or procuring these offences.
8 Criminal Law (Rape) Act 1981, s 6, as amended by s 6(3) of the Criminal Law (Sexual Offences) Act 2006.
9 Criminal Law (Rape) Act 1981, s 6(3), (as amended).
10 Criminal Law (Rape) Act 1981, s 6(4) (as amended).

Section 2 of the Criminal Law (Incest Proceedings) Act 1995 offers specific provision for exclusion of the public from proceedings under the Punishment of Incest Act 1908. The provision mirrors s 6 of the 1981 Act, apart from omitting the proviso allowing for a parent, relative or friend of the complainant or of a defendant who is under the age of 18 to remain in the court.[11] It is unclear whether this was intentional or merely an oversight. However, as O'Malley notes, "the judge has a general discretion to allow any person to remain having regard to the circumstances of the case",[12] so this omission should not cause injustice. Once commenced, Pt 5 of the Criminal Law (Sexual Offences) Act 2017 will repeal the 1995 Act in its entirety. Section 2 will be replaced by s 29 of the 2017 Act which replicates the wording of the original provision. **[4–05]**

A significant omission from the current law is the failure to provide for exclusion of the public from sexual assault trials. There has also been no provision enacted to provide for exclusion of the public from trials for offences relating to sexual acts with "protected persons" in Pt 3 of the 2017 Act (i.e. individuals with limited decision-making capacity). Section 20(3) of the Criminal Justice Act 1951[13] provides that a trial judge may exclude the public from the court if the offence is one of an "indecent or obscene nature". A judge could use this discretion to exclude the public from sexual offence trials which are not covered by s 6. There are no statistics on the extent to which s 20(3) is invoked, but the Rape Crisis Network of Ireland (RCNI) has reported that a number of sexual assault or indecent assault trials have taken place in public, which suggests that s 20(3) is not being relied upon to clear the court for these cases.[14] Thus, to offer full and equal protection to all sexual offence complainants, a consolidating provision **[4–06]**

---

[11] Criminal Law (Incest Proceedings) Act 1995, s 2(1) provides that:

> "In any proceedings for an offence under the Act of 1908, the judge or the court, as the case may be, shall exclude from the court during the hearing all persons except officers of the court, persons directly concerned in the proceedings, *bona fide* representatives of the press and such other persons (if any) as the judge or the court, as the case may be, may, in his, her or its discretion, permit to remain."

[12] O'Malley, *Sexual Offences* (2nd ed, Round Hall, Dublin, 2013), p 392.

[13] Criminal Justice Act 1951, s 20(3) provides that "in any criminal proceedings for an offence, which is, in the opinion of the Court, of an indecent or obscene nature, the Court may, subject to subsection (4), exclude from the Court during the hearing all persons except officers of the Court, persons directly concerned in the proceedings, bona fide representatives of the Press and such other persons as the Court may, in its discretion, permit to remain". s 20(4) provides that (a) where the accused is a person under 21 years, or (b) where the offence is of an indecent or obscene nature and the person with or against whom it is alleged to have been committed is under that age or is a female, a parent or other relative or friend of that person shall be entitled to remain in the Court during the whole of the hearing.

[14] Counihan, "Rape Crisis Network Ireland Perspectives on Sexual Violence and the Criminal Justice System" (2013) 23(4) *Irish Criminal Law Journal* 115, 118.

should be enacted which extends the capacity to clear the court to all sexual offences. As Counihan notes, "in light of the fact that the legislature has intervened to ensure anonymity for survivors of sexual violence, including sexual assaults, it is particularly difficult to justify not extending [s 6 of the 1981 Act] to all sexual offences".[15] Some of the problems in this area may be alleviated by the introduction of s 19 of the Criminal Justice (Victims of Crime) Act 2017 which provides for a power to exclude the public in all criminal trials. Section 20(1) states that in any proceedings relating to an offence, where a court is satisfied:

> "(a) that the nature or circumstances of the case are such that there is a need to protect a victim of the offence from secondary and repeat victimisation, intimidation or retaliation, and
> (b) it would not be contrary to the interests of justice in the case,
> the court may, on the application of the prosecution, exclude from the court during such proceedings—
> (i) the public or any portion of the public, or
> (ii) any particular person or persons,
> except officers of the court and bona fide representatives of the Press."

[4–07] This power is without prejudice to the right of: (i) a parent, relative or friend of the victim; (ii) a support worker[16] of the victim's choice; (iii) where the accused is under the age of 18 years, a parent, relative or friend of the accused; or (iv) an "appropriate person"[17] to remain in court, and: the power of a court to exclude the public or any person from the court under any other enactment or rule of law.[18] This provision provides a general catch-all power for trial judges to exclude the public from the court in criminal trials which can be used to fill any gaps in protection under the current sexual offences legislation.

---

15 *ibid*, 119.

16 "Support worker" means a volunteer of, or an individual employed under a contract of service or under a contract for services by, an organisation which provides support to victims of crime: s 20(3).

17 Criminal Justice (Victims of Crime) Act 2017, s 18(1) provides that where a victim is a child and a parent, guardian or any other person duly authorised to act on the victim's behalf—
(i) has been charged with, or is under investigation for, an offence in connection with the victim,
(ii) is, for any other reason, precluded from accompanying the victim,
(iii) is unavailable or cannot be contacted,
(iv) indicates that he or she does not wish to accompany the victim, or
(v) cannot be identified,
the Garda Síochána or the Ombudsman Commission, as the case may be, shall arrange for the victim to be accompanied by an appropriate person when attending any interviews and court proceedings at which the victim is required to be present.

18 Criminal Justice (Victims of Crime) Act 2017, s 20(2).

Anonymity: The Complainant

Section 7(1) of the 1981 Act[19] provides that after a person is charged with a "sexual assault offence"[20] or an offence under the Criminal Law (Sexual Offences) Act 2006[21]: **[4–08]**

> "... no matter likely to lead members of the public to identify a person as the complainant in relation to that charge shall be published in a written publication available to the public or be broadcast except as authorised by a direction given in pursuance of this section."

A "broadcast" "means a broadcast by wireless telegraphy of sound or visual images, intended for general reception, and cognate expressions shall be construed accordingly".[22]A "written publication" "includes a film, a sound track and any other record in permanent form but does not include an indictment or other document prepared for use in particular legal proceedings".[23] These definitions are a little outdated. In particular, "they do not include express reference to information technologies or social media".[24] In *LK v Independent Star Limited and Others*,[25] it was held that the phrase "likely to lead" in s 7(1) "means a real risk that the complainant would be identified in the minds of the public if the information is published". Whether there is such a "real risk" "depends upon the circumstances of the case".[26] The interpretation of such risk must be viewed subjectively from the perspective of the defendant media outlet. In *LK*, the information published and broadcast, viewed subjectively from the defendants' perspective, did not seem "likely" to identify the complainant. Thus, the publications and broadcasts were found not to have breached s 7.[27] **[4–09]**

Provision is made for deviation from the anonymity rule in some limited circumstances. Before the trial begins, the accused or another person against whom the complainant may be expected to give evidence at trial can apply for a direction allowing publication of the complainant's identity. O'Malley **[4–10]**

---

19 As amended by s 17(2) of the Criminal Law (Rape) (Amendment) Act 1990.

20 A "sexual assault offence" includes rape, rape under s 4, aggravated sexual assault, sexual assault, as well as related offences such as inchoate offences and aiding, abetting, counselling or procuring any of these offences: s 1(1) of the Criminal Law (Rape) Act 1981 (as amended by s 12 of the Criminal Law (Rape)(Amendment) Act 1990).

21 Criminal Law (Sexual Offences) Act 2006, s 6(3).

22 Criminal Law (Rape)(Act) 1981, s 7(7).

23 *ibid.*

24 Heffernan, *Evidence in Criminal Trials* (Bloomsbury Professional, Dublin, 2014), p 134.

25 [2010] IEHC 500; [2011] 2 ILRM 272.

26 [2011] 2 ILRM 272, 291.

27 *ibid*, 293.

notes that "such applications are very rarely made or granted".[28] To succeed with such an application, the applicant must satisfy the judge that:

> "(a) the direction is required for the purpose of inducing persons to come forward who are likely to be needed as witnesses at the trial, and
> (b) the conduct of the applicant's defence at the trial is likely to be adversely affected if the direction is not given."[29]

[4–11] The accused or other person against whom the complainant is expected to give evidence may also apply for a similar direction during the trial.[30] In this instance, the applicant will have to convince the judge of the existence of conditions (a) and (b) above in addition to providing evidence that "there was good reason for his not having made an application ... before the commencement of the trial".[31] A trial judge can also lift a complainant's anonymity protection of his/her own volition if s/he is satisfied that the effect of the anonymity "is to impose a substantial and unreasonable restriction on the reporting of proceedings at the trial and that it is in the public interest to remove or relax the restriction".[32] Importantly, such a direction must not be given "by reason only of an acquittal of an accused person at trial".[33] Finally, a convicted person may apply to the court to which he is appealing to allow publication of the complainant's identity. For this to be permitted, he must satisfy the court that (a) the direction is required for the purpose of obtaining evidence in support of the appeal, and (b) that the applicant is likely to suffer injustice if the direction is not given.[34]

[4–12] In incest proceedings, s 3 of the Criminal Law (Incest Proceedings) Act 1995 applies the same anonymity protection to both complainants and defendants. This protection continues to apply to both parties even if the defendant is convicted. This special approach is justified on the basis that, given the parties' relationship, identification of one would necessarily entail identification of the other. It is also argued "that publication of the names of the parties involved does not serve any public interest and would be a cause, at the very least, of embarrassment and distress to the entire family concerned".[35] When Pt 5 of the 2017 Act is commenced and the 1995 Act is repealed, protection of complainants' anonymity in incest proceedings will

---

28 O'Malley, *supra* note 12, p 393.
29 Criminal Law (Rape) Act 1981, s 7(2).
30 *ibid*, s 7(3).
31 *ibid*, s 7(3)(c).
32 *ibid*, s 7(4).
33 *ibid*.
34 *ibid*, s 7(5).
35 Department of Justice, Equality and Law Reform, *Discussion Paper on the Law on Sexual Offences* (Dublin: Department of Justice, Equality and Law Reform, Dublin, 1998), para 4.8.1.

be provided by s 30 of the 2017 Act. Although the new provision does not change the substance of the anonymity protection afforded to complainants and defendants in incest proceedings, it offers more modern definitions of "broadcast", "published" and "publication".[36] "Broadcast":

> "means the transmission, relaying or distribution by wireless telegraphy or by any other means or by wireless telegraphy in conjunction with any other means of communications, sounds, signs, visual images or signals, intended for direct reception by the general public, whether such communications, sounds, signs, visual images or signals are actually received or not".[37]

[4–13] "Published" "means published to any person, and includes published on the internet".[38] "Publication" "includes a film, sound track or any other record in permanent form (including a record that is not in a legible form but which is capable of being reproduced in a legible form) but does not include an indictment or other document prepared for use in particular legal proceedings".[39] These definitions are more comprehensive than the original definitions in the 1981 Act which, as noted above, are dated and fail to recognise more modern mediums of communication like the internet and social media. The new definitions in s 30 should be extended to the anonymity protections available for all offences.

[4–14] In spite of the guaranteed anonymity for complainants, there have been instances where victims have waived their anonymity after the defendant has been convicted. This has often arisen where victims are distressed about the sentence that the defendant has received.[40] However, as Gallagher notes, "[a]lthough the phrase 'the victim waived her right to anonymity' is often seen in news reports, it is not entirely accurate".[41] The legislation does not provide a mechanism by which complainants can formally waive their anonymity and publicly identify themselves. This was originally justified "on the basis that if anonymity could be waived at the instigation of a complainant this could sow confusion in the minds of complainants generally as to whether they could protect their identities in a rape prosecution".[42] There were concerns that this might deter victims from

36 The current definitions of these terms in s 3(4) of the 1995 Act are the same as those provided for in the 1981 Act.

37 Criminal Law (Sexual Offences) Act 2017, s 30(5).

38 *ibid.*

39 *ibid.*

40 The first rape victim to waive her anonymity in Ireland was Lavinia Kerwick who appeared on *The Gerry Ryan Radio Show* in 1993 to voice her distress when her rapist received a suspended sentence.

41 Gallagher, "Untangling the vexed question of anonymity in sex cases", *The Irish Times*, 3 March 2014.

42 Department of Justice, Equality and Law Reform, *supra* note 35, para 4.6.3.

reporting.[43] Also, not allowing complainants to waive their anonymity arguably protects them from "pressure or inducement to allow their identity to be revealed".[44] Gallagher notes that in practice, where a victim decides to waive her anonymity, "a barrister for the DPP will tell the court at conviction that the victim wishes 'to waive their right' and the judge consents".[45] Whether such requests are ever refused is unclear. Although there is no evidence that the lack of formalities in this area causes injustice, it would be worthwhile for the legislation to specifically provide that a victim is entitled to waive her anonymity should she wish to do so. It may, however, be prudent to maintain a practice that the exercise of this right to identify oneself must be communicated to the trial judge and that there be some mechanism which would prevent identification in exceptional cases in the interests of justice (e.g. where such identification may impact upon future proceedings against the defendant).

Anonymity: The Accused

[4–15] Section 8(1) of the 1981 Act provides that once a person is charged with a "rape offence"[46] or an offence under the Criminal Law (Sexual Offences) Act 2006,[47] "no matter likely to lead members of the public to identify him as the person against whom the charge is made shall be published in a written publication available to the public or be broadcast"[48] except for the limited exceptions created within the section. The accused can be identified after he has been convicted of the offence. The provision of anonymity for defendants is not uncontroversial. Indeed, in its 1987 *Consultation Paper on Rape*, the Law Reform Commission (LRC) provisionally recommended that anonymity for defendants be abolished.[49] However, a number of concerns were raised about this and recorded in the LRC's subsequent *Report on Rape and Allied Offences*. First, it was argued that since complainants were entitled to anonymity in rape cases, a similar protection should be afforded to defendants until they are convicted.[50] Second, it was suggested that since rape attracts significant publicity, defendants in these cases are

43 *ibid.*
44 *ibid.*
45 Gallagher, *supra* note 41.
46 This includes rape, rape under s 4 and burglary with intent to commit rape, as well as related offences of attempting, inciting, aiding, abetting or procuring these offences: s 1 of the Criminal Law (Rape) Act 1981 (as amended by s 12 of the Criminal Law (Rape) (Amendment) Act 1990).
47 Criminal Law (Sexual Offences) Act 2006, s 6, extended the anonymity provisions to the offences provided for in that Act.
48 The definitions of "broadcast" etc are the same as that for s 7: s 8(6).
49 Law Reform Commission, *Consultation Paper on Rape* (Law Reform Commission, Dublin, 1987), para 116.
50 Law Reform Commission, *Report on Rape and Allied Offences* (Law Reform Commission, Dublin, 1988), para 44.

likely to suffer greater reputational damage if named than defendants in other cases.[51] Finally, submissions raised the point that "in a significant number of cases, sexual intercourse is admitted but the defence to the charge is that the intercourse took place with [consent] and ... where the accused is acquitted, publication of the fact that he had consensual sexual relations with the complainant may represent an unwarranted intrusion into his privacy".[52] For the LRC, these justifications warranted the retention of anonymity for the accused in these cases.[53]

As with the anonymity of the complainant, the accused's right to anonymity can be lifted in certain circumstances. The accused can apply to a High Court judge before the trial commences or to the trial judge during the trial for his anonymity to be lifted.[54] Prior to the commencement of the trial, a co-accused can apply to a High Court judge for the anonymity of another co-accused to be lifted. The application can be granted if the judge is satisfied: **[4–16]**

> "(a) that the direction is required for the purpose of inducing persons to come forward who are likely to be needed as witnesses at the trial, and
> (b) that the conduct of the applicant's defence at trial is likely to be adversely affected if the direction is not given."[55]

A co-accused may also make a similar application during the trial.[56] The grounds on which such an application may be granted are the same as those in the preceding section but there is an additional requirement that must be satisfied, namely, "that there was good reason for his not having made an application ... before the commencement of the trial".[57] The Director of Public Prosecutions (DPP) may also apply to a High Court judge for the anonymity of the accused to be removed at any time after the accused is charged with a rape offence.[58] The application will be granted if the judge is satisfied that it is in the public interest to do so. As with s 7, if at **[4–17]**

---

51 *ibid.*

52 *ibid.*

53 *ibid*, para 45.

54 Such an application may be granted "[p]rovided that, if it appears to the judge that, if the direction were given, the publication of any matter in pursuance of the direction might enable members of the public to identify a person as the complainant in relation to the charge, the judge shall not give the direction unless he is satisfied that a direction could properly be given in relation to that person in pursuance of section 7": s 8(2) of the Criminal Law (Rape) Act 1981 (as amended by s 14 of the Criminal Law (Rape)(Amendment) Act 1990.

55 Criminal Law (Rape) Act 1981, s 8(3) (as amended by s 21 of the Criminal Law (Rape) (Amendment) Act 1990.

56 Criminal Law (Rape) Act 1981, s 8(4).

57 *ibid*, s 8(4)(c).

58 Criminal Law (Rape) Act 1981, s 8(8), (as inserted by s 14 of the Criminal Law (Rape)(Amendment) Act 1990).

trial the judge is satisfied that the anonymity of the accused is imposing a substantial and unreasonable restriction on the reporting of proceedings at the trial, and that the removal or relaxation of the restriction is in the public interest, then s/he can lift the anonymity of the accused.[59] Special rules for the anonymity of the accused apply in trials for incest. The Criminal Law (Incest Proceedings) Act 1995 provides for absolute anonymity for the accused which does not end upon conviction.[60] With the repeal of the 1995 Act when Pt 5 of the 2017 Act is commenced, anonymity for defendants in incest cases will be guaranteed by s 30 of the latter Act. The details of this provision are outlined in the preceding section.

[4–18] It is important to note that although a defendant's anonymity under the 1981 Act ceases on conviction, his identity will still not be revealed if this may result in the identification of the complainant. However, in *Independent Star Ltd v O'Connor*,[61] it was emphasised that "the very limited jurisdiction conferred by section 7 exists exclusively with regard to the complainant, and not the accused".[62] Thus, a trial judge can only act to prohibit the identification of the accused post-conviction if this is necessary to protect the complainant's identity. There is no residual discretion under s 8 to prohibit the lifting of the accused's anonymity for any other reason. Indeed, Kearns J indicated that a decision to protect the identity of the accused after conviction in order to protect the complainant should not be taken lightly, stressing that whilst there may be concerns "that careless or irresponsible reporting of the identity of the accused might, in certain circumstances, lead to identification of the complainant … this is a matter regulated by the Act which provides … that any such publication shall constitute an offence".[63] Thus, it appears that judges should not exercise their jurisdiction under s 7 to prohibit revealing the accused's identity merely because there is a risk that the complainant might be identified. This jurisdiction should only be exercised where this is directly necessary to protect the complainant's identity. In *LK*, Hedigan J suggested that s 8(8), which allows the DPP to apply to the High Court for directions that the accused not be identified, could allow the DPP to apply to the High Court "for directions that the accused not be identified after his conviction or that his address not be published etc on the basis that this could, indirectly, identify the complainant".[64] Thus, s 8(8) may provide another avenue for protecting the accused's anonymity post-conviction, but again only where this is necessary to protect the complainant's identity.

---

59 Criminal Law (Rape) Act 1981, s 8(5).
60 Criminal Law (Incest Proceedings) Act 1995, s 3.
61 [2002] 4 IR 166.
62 *ibid*, 175.
63 *ibid*.
64 [2011] 2 ILRM 272, 289.

The rules on anonymity for defendants are open to criticism and could be improved. Most significantly, the protection of the anonymity of the accused applies to a narrower category of offences than the complainant anonymity provisions. There are no provisions for the anonymity of the accused in trials for sexual assault and the protection in s 8 has not been amended to extend to offences relating to "protected persons". This incongruence seems to add unnecessary complication to the law, and may well lead to injustice. The inconsistency in this area has been criticised by Gallagher who notes that the omission of some offences from the anonymity protection for defendants "leaves us with the strange situation where a man accused of violently sexually assaulting a woman can be named while a man accused of raping her retains his anonymity".[65] As Gallagher argues, "surely both crimes are just as damaging to the good name of a person who is innocent until proven guilty".[66] Further, O'Malley questions whether the anonymity protections for defendants should be extended, suggesting that "a case could be made for maintaining defendant anonymity until after normal appeal procedures have been exhausted". As he notes, "[a] wrongful conviction may have a devastating impact, not only in terms of the formal penalty (almost invariably imprisonment) but also in terms of reputational damage".[67] A clarification of the law in this area and consideration of some of the criticisms highlighted here would be welcome in any future law reform effort. **[4–19]**

Punishment for Breach of Anonymity Provisions

If information is published in contravention of the anonymity protections for complainants and defendants in s 7 or s 8, the following persons will be guilty of an offence: **[4–20]**

> "(a) in the case of a publication in a newspaper or periodical, any proprietor, any editor and any publisher of the newspaper or periodical,
> (b) in the case of any other publication, the person who publishes it, and
> (c) in the case of a broadcast, any body corporate which transmits or provides the programme in which the broadcast is made and any person having functions in relation to the programme corresponding to those of an editor of a newspaper."[68]

Section 11 provides that a person who is guilty an offence under s 7 or s 8 will be liable on conviction on indictment to a maximum fine of €25,394.78 **[4–21]**

---

65 Gallagher, *supra* note 41.
66 *ibid.*
67 O'Malley, *supra* note 12, p 396
68 Criminal Law (Rape) Act 1981, s 7(6). s 8(6) provides that s 7(6) "shall have effect for the purposes of this section as if for references to that section there were substituted references to this section".

or, at the discretion of the court, up to three years' imprisonment, or to both.[69] A District Court shall have jurisdiction to try an offence to which s 11 relates summarily if—

(i) the judge is of opinion that the facts proved or alleged against a defendant charged with such an offence constitute a minor offence fit to be tried summarily,
(ii) the DPP consents, and
(iii) the defendant (on being informed by the justice of his right to be tried by a jury) does not object to being tried summarily.[70]

[4–22] In this instance, upon conviction, the defendant shall be liable to a fine not exceeding €2,500 or, at the discretion of the court, to imprisonment for a term not exceeding 12 months or to both such fine and such imprisonment.

[4–23] Where an individual is charged with an offence under s 7 or s 8, it will be a defence to prove that at the time of the alleged offence he was not aware, and neither suspected nor had reason to suspect that the publication or broadcast in question contravened s 7 and s 8.[71] In *LK v Independent Star Limited and Others*,[72] it was made clear that s 7 "does not give rise to a cause of action in damages for complainants in sexual assault cases where the media, in breach of that section publish information likely to lead to their identification".[73] However, it was held that "the fact that publication of such information is prohibited is a matter that can properly be taken into account in determining if the plaintiff can maintain an action for damages for breach of her constitutional right to privacy".[74]

[4–24] If any matter is published or broadcast in contravention of the anonymity protections in relation to incest trials in the 1995 Act, s 3(2) provides that the following persons shall be guilty of an offence:

"(a) in the case of matter published in a newspaper or periodical publication, the proprietor, the editor and the publisher thereof,
(b) in the case of matter published in any other written publication, the publisher thereof, and
(c) in the case of matter broadcast, any person who transmits or provides the programme in which the broadcast is made and any person who

[69] Criminal Law (Rape) Act 1981, s 11(1) (as amended by s 9 of the Fines Act 2010).
[70] Criminal Law (Rape) Act 1981, s 12(1), as amended by s 16 of the Criminal Law (Rape)(Amendment) Act 1990 and s 6 of the Fines Act 2010.
[71] Criminal Law (Rape) Act 1981, s 11(3).
[72] [2011] 2 ILRM 272.
[73] *ibid*, para 58.
[74] *ibid*, para 59.

> performs functions in relation to the programme corresponding to those of the editor of a newspaper."[75]

A person guilty of an offence under s 3 shall be liable— **[4–25]**

> "(a) on conviction on indictment, to a fine not exceeding €22,225 or to imprisonment for a term not exceeding three years or to both, or
> (b) on summary conviction, to a Class B fine or to imprisonment for a term not exceeding 12 months or to both."[76]

It shall be a defence for a person who is charged with an offence under s 3 to prove that at the time of the alleged offence s/he was not aware, and neither suspected nor had reason to suspect, that the matter alleged to have been published or broadcast was in breach of the anonymity provisions of the 1995 Act.[77] When the 1995 Act is repealed upon commencement of Pt 5 of the 2017 Act, s 30(2) will replace s 3(2) of the 1995 Act. The relevant punishments will be updated as follows by s 31(1) which provides that a person guilty of an offence under s 30 shall be liable- **[4–26]**

> "(a) on summary conviction, to a class B fine or to imprisonment for a term not exceeding 12 months or both, or
> (b) on conviction on indictment, to a fine or to imprisonment for a term not exceeding three years or both."

Giving Evidence: Special Protection Measures

Special measures to make the process of giving evidence easier for sexual offence complainants were first introduced in Pt III of the Criminal Evidence Act 1992, which was enacted primarily in response to concerns about the trauma which child victims experience when testifying in these cases. As Walsh notes, many cases "have been lost purely as a result of child witnesses not being able to cope with the demands of the criminal trial" and "[m]any more have not been pursued by the DPP on the basis that the key child witnesses would not be able to cope with the challenge of confronting their abuser and giving evidence against him in the unfamiliar and intimidating environment of the criminal court".[78] Part III of the 1992 Act provides protections to certain witnesses who must give evidence in "sexual offence" trials.[79] For the purposes of the 1992 Act, "sexual offence" **[4–27]**

---

75 Criminal Law (Incest Proceedings) Act 1995, s 3(2).

76 *ibid*, s 4(1) (as amended by s 9 and s 5 of the Fines Act 2010, respectively).

77 Criminal Law (Incest Proceedings) Act 1995, s 4(3).

78 Walsh, *Walsh on Criminal Procedure* (2nd ed, Round Hall, Dublin, 2016), p 1,311.

79 Criminal Evidence Act 1992, s 12 (as amended). It should be noted that Pt III also applies to witnesses giving evidence in trials for offences involving violence or the threat of violence to a person; offences under ss 3, 4, 5 or 6 of the Child Trafficking

includes rape, rape under s 4, aggravated sexual assault, sexual assault, an offence under the Criminal Law (Sexual Offences) Act 2006, incest and an offence under s 5 of the Criminal Law (Sexual Offences) Act 1993.[80] When Pt 6 of the Criminal Law (Sexual Offences) Act 2017 is commenced, a revised definition of "sexual offence" will apply, incorporating rape, sexual assault, aggravated sexual assault, rape under s 4 or an offence under: s 3 or s 6 of the Criminal Law Amendment Act 1885; s 5 and s 6 of the Criminal Law (Sexual Offences) Act 1993; s 1 or s 2 of the Punishment of Incest Act 1908; s 4A or s 5A of the Child Trafficking and Pornography Act 1998; s 249 of the Children Act 2001; the Criminal Law (Sexual Offences) Act 2006, or; s 3, s 4, s 5, s 6, s 7 or s 8 of the 2017 Act.[81]

[4–28] The special measures in the 1992 Act include: giving evidence by television link (s 13); the use of intermediaries (s 14), and; the use of video-recorded evidence (s 16). These special measures are targeted primarily at child witnesses but s 19 of the 1992 Act provides that references to children in s 13, s 14 and s 16 "shall include references to a person with mental handicap who has reached the age concerned". "Mental handicap" is not defined in the legislation. Heffernan suggests that "[t]he fact of mental handicap must be established by the express or tacit agreement of the parties or the trial judge's determination".[82] Once commenced, Pt 6 of the 2017 Act will extend the availability of special measures and introduce new protections including the possibility of giving evidence from behind a screen and prohibiting cross-examination of the complainant by an unrepresented defendant. Moreover, the Criminal Justice (Victims of Crime) Act 2017 extends the availability of special measures, making them available to a broader range of victims. Each of the current available special measures and the relevant reforms are discussed in the following sections.

Evidence through Television Link

[4–29] Common law traditionally required *viva voce* testimony to be given live in the courtroom.[83] However, the experience of facing their assailant in court in order to give evidence can be extremely traumatic for sexual offence

---

and Pornography Act 1998; offences under ss 2, 4 or 7 of the Criminal Law (Human Trafficking) Act 2008; or offences consisting of attempting or conspiring to commit, or of aiding, abetting, counselling, procuring or inciting the commission of any of the foregoing offences: *ibid.*

80 Criminal Evidence Act 1992, s 2(1) of the 1992 Act (as amended). Part III also applies to offences of attempting or conspiring to commit, or of aiding, abetting, counselling, procuring or inciting the commission of any of these offences: s 12.

81 Criminal Law (Sexual Offences) Act 2017, s 34 of the 2017 (which will substitute a new definition of "sexual offence" into s 2 of the Criminal Evidence Act 1992).

82 Heffernan, *supra* note 24, p 153.

83 Healy, *Irish Laws of Evidence* (Thomson Round Hall, Dublin, 2004), p 30.

complainants. Fortunately, s 13 of the 1992 Act attempts to minimise the trauma of complainants by allowing witnesses in sexual offence trials to give evidence via live television link.[84] Section 13(1)[85] provides that in any proceedings for an offence to which Part III applies[86] a person other than the accused may give evidence, whether from within or outside the State, through a live television link:

> "(a) if the person is under 18 years of age, unless the court sees good reason to the contrary,
> (b) in any other case, with the leave of the court."

Thus, if the person is under 18 years of age, there is a presumption that this facility will be made available "unless the court sees good reason to the contrary".[87] As per s 19, the same test will apply where the person who is to testify is an adult with a "mental handicap". Heffernan notes that s 13(1)(a) "authorises the giving of evidence by means of video-link without the need for a formal application to the court".[88] Apart from proving the age of the witness (or the fact of mental handicap), "[t]he only other substantive obstacle is a possible challenge by the other side seeking to persuade the trial judge that there is 'good reason' for him to refuse to sanction the use of video-link".[89] **[4–30]**

If the person who is to give evidence is an adult, the court will have discretion to decide whether the use of television link is permitted. No guidance is given on the circumstances in which a court would be willing to grant leave for this to occur. McGrath suggests that, in practice, an application for leave is most likely to be made and succeed where either the prosecution or the **[4–31]**

---

84 This departure from the traditional format of criminal trials naturally raised questions regarding the accused's right to a fair trial. However, the constitutionality of Pt III of the 1992 Act was upheld by the High Court in *White v Ireland* [1995] 2 IR 268 and ultimately by the Supreme Court in *Donnelly v Ireland* [1998] I IR 321; [1998] 1 ILRM 401.

85 As amended by s 18(3) of the Criminal Justice Act 1999 and s 257(3) of the Children Act 2001.

86 Also included here are proceedings under 4E (application by accused for dismissal of charge) and 4F (taking of evidence by District Court) of the Criminal Procedure Act 1967: s 13(1) as amended.

87 Criminal Evidence Act 1992, s 13(1)(a). McGrath suggests that this reflects a legislative judgment that such persons are most likely to suffer trauma if required to testify. He goes on to note that the broad application of s 13(1)(a) means that it could be potentially applicable to persons who would not run any real risk of trauma if required to testify. This, he assumes is the rationale for the caveat that the court can require a person who qualifies for special treatment under s 13(1)(a) to give evidence in open court "where it sees good reason" to do so: McGrath, *Evidence* (2nd ed, Round Hall: Dublin, 2014), p 114.

88 Heffernan, *supra* note 24, p 141

89 *ibid.*

defence can put forward an evidential basis for asserting that a particular witness is likely to suffer trauma if required to give evidence in open court.[90] However, he goes on to point out that the ambit of the subsection does not appear to be limited to that circumstance.[91] The issue of proper exercise of judicial discretion under s 13(1)(b) arose for consideration in *DPP v McManus*.[92] The applicant in this case was appealing his conviction for manslaughter. One of the grounds of appeal was the trial judge's decision to allow his daughter, who was 18 at the time of the trial, to give evidence via TV link. Macken J noted that s 13 is clear that all persons under the age of 18 may give evidence via television link "unless the court considers it appropriate, for good reason, that they should not do so".[93] He went on to note that "[i]n all other cases, including cases where the witness is over eighteen, evidence may be permitted to be given in this manner with the leave of the court" and "[n]o conditions are imposed in respect of that leave, and no restriction is set down in respect of the exercise by the trial judge of his discretion". In light of the circumstances in this case, Macken J held that the trial judge had correctly exercised his discretion to permit the witness to give evidence via television link. These circumstances included the fact that while a medical expert had "indicated that the witness was both strong and direct of personality, it was also said that she had great difficulty talking about feelings, or 'things that had happened in the past'":

> "Moreover, she had just barely reached her eighteenth birthday at the time of trial, she was giving evidence in a murder trial against her own father, concerning events that had occurred when she was only 15 years of age, was on the evidence of the social worker, a vulnerable person, and in respect of these elements, evidence was given and tested by cross-examination."

[4–32] As Heffernan notes, "[w]hereas the exceptional circumstances of this case provided compelling support for the use of video-link, it is regrettable that the Court missed the opportunity to add doctrinal flesh to the bare bones of section 13(1)(b)".[94]

[4–33] Greater guidance on the appropriate exercise of discretion under s 13(1)(b) was offered in the earlier case of *DO'D v DPP*.[95] O Néill J noted that:

> "The discretion which the court has under section 13(1)(b) to order evidence to be given in this way or to direct otherwise raises the difficult question as to how the court is to achieve the correct balance between the accused's right to

---

90 McGrath, *supra* note 87, p 114.
91 *ibid.*
92 [2011] IECCA 32.
93 *ibid* (no paragraph numbers in judgment).
94 Heffernan, *supra* note 24, p 71.
95 [2010] 2 IR 605.

> a fair trial and the prosecution's right in an appropriate case to have evidence given by video link. It is clear that what is required is a test that achieves the correct balance between these two competing interests."[96]

The learned judge provided the following guidance on how this balance might be achieved: **[4–34]**

> "Where the court reaches the conclusion that the giving of evidence in this way carries with it a serious risk of unfairness to the accused which could not be corrected by an appropriate statement from the prosecution or direction from the trial judge, it should only permit the giving of evidence by video link where it was satisfied by evidence that a serious injustice would be done, in the sense of a significant impairment to the prosecution's case, if evidence had to be given in the normal way, *viva voce*, thus necessitating evidence by video link in order to vindicate the right of the public to prosecute offences of this kind. The fact that the giving of evidence *viva voce* would be very unpleasant for the witness or coming to court to give evidence very inconvenient, would not be relevant factors. ...The real question is whether the circumstances of the witness are such that the requirement to give evidence *viva voce* is an insuperable obstacle to giving evidence in a manner that does justice to the prosecution case. The evidence must establish to the satisfaction of the court hearing the application under [section 13] that the probability is that the witness in question will be deterred from giving evidence at all or will, in all probability, be unable to do justice to their evidence if required to give it *viva voce* in the ordinary way."[97]

O Néill J acknowledged that the above test "is necessarily a high threshold" but contended that "in order to strike a fair balance between the right of the accused person to a fair trial and the right of the public to prosecute offences of this kind, it must be so".[98] In the instant case, it was held that the trial judge had erred in her decision to allow the relevant witnesses to give their evidence via television link as this test was not applied and there was "no real exploration or consideration of the ability of either complainant to give evidence *viva voce*".[99] **[4–35]**

A further issue which has arisen in relation to the use of s 13 relates to trials for sexual offences against those with limited decision-making capacity. The question which has arisen in this context was whether permitting complainants in these cases to give testimony via s 13 amounted to a pre-determination of the issue of whether they were suffering from "mental impairment" as per s 5 of the Criminal Law (Sexual Offences) Act 1993. **[4–36]**

---

96 *ibid*, 613.
97 *ibid*.
98 *ibid*.
99 *ibid*, 614.

This issue arose in *DPP v DO'D*.[100] The appellant in this case argued that where the sole issue for the jury in the case was to decide whether the complainant was mentally impaired for the purposes of s 5 of the 1993 Act, making an order for the use of television link pursuant to s 13(1)(b) amounted to a real and substantial predetermination of that issue. The Court of Criminal Appeal noted that the same potential for prejudice arose whether s 13(1)(a) or (b) was used noting that "[t]he risk (be it real or perceived) of predetermination of the mental condition of the complainant was present in either event" and probably less so where s 13(1)(b) was used:

> "... and most importantly, the clear direction given to the jury at the conclusion of the learned trial judge's charge to the jury was sufficiently strong and clear as to render any sense of pre-determination [which] may have been in the minds of the jury of little practical consequence".

[4–37] With the new terminology of "protected person" in the law protecting individuals with limited decision-making capacity from sexual abuse and the attendant functional test for capacity to consent, it is unlikely that the problems which arose in *DO'D* will arise in future cases. This is because the establishment of, for example, a mental illness or intellectual disability, is not tantamount to a lack of capacity to consent, thereby establishing that an offence has been committed. Rather, capacity to consent is a separate issue which must be determined according to the functional, context-sensitive, test for capacity established in the legislation. Thus, the fact that an individual has been held to have a vulnerability or "mental handicap", as per the 1992 Act, such that special measures have been allowed, is less likely to prejudice a jury. At the very least, it should be easier for a trial judge to direct them that the use of special measures is not a predetermination of a complainant's capacity to consent.

[4–38] It is worth pointing out that s 13(1) applies to witnesses proposed to be called by the accused and the prosecution.[101] Section 13(2) also requires that evidence given under s 13(1) must be video-recorded. While evidence is being given through a live television link pursuant to s 13(1)[102] neither the judge, nor the barrister or solicitor concerned in the examination of the witness, shall wear a wig or gown.[103] Further, where a witness testifies by video-link, s/he is not required to identify the defendant in court.[104]

---

[100] [2015] IECA 273.

[101] McGrath, *supra* note 87, p 113.

[102] Except where evidence is through an intermediary pursuant to s 14(1).

[103] Criminal Evidence Act 1992, s 13(3).

[104] Criminal Evidence Act 1992, s 18 provides that where evidence is given by a person (i.e. "the witness") through a live television link pursuant to s 13(1), then—

"(i) in case evidence is given that the accused was known to the witness before the date on which the offence is alleged to have been committed,

Evidence Through an Intermediary

Section 14(1) provides that where: **[4–39]**

> "(a) a person is accused of an offence to which [Part III] applies, and
> (b) a person under 18 years of age is giving, or is to give, evidence through a live television link,
>
> the court may, on the application of the prosecution or the accused, if satisfied that, having regard to the age or mental condition of the witness, the interests of justice require that any questions to be put to the witness be put through an intermediary, direct that any such questions be so put."

Again, s 19 operates to include adults with a "mental handicap" within this provision. Questions put to a witness through an intermediary under this section shall be either in the words used by the questioner or so as to convey to the witness in a way which is appropriate to his age and mental condition the meaning of the questions being asked.[105] An intermediary will be appointed by the court and must be a person who, in its opinion, is competent to act as such.[106] **[4–40]**

Edwards et al note that an intermediary can help to "ensure clarity of meaning between the witness and the court".[107] They also note that intermediaries may provide a range of communication supports for people with disabilities: **[4–41]**

> "... people with physical impairments, such as hearing impairments, may require communicative support in the form of sign language interpreters, or technical aids to hearing such as induction loops within courtrooms. People with intellectual impairments may require a 'cognitive interpreter'[108]...an intermediary who seeks to ensure that witnesses understand the questions that are put to them during the trial, and that their answers are also understood[109]... In the case of people with hearing impairments, where the spoken language may not be the first language, many jurisdictions make provisions to allow

---

the witness shall not be required to identify the accused at the trial of the offence, unless the court in the interests of justice directs otherwise, and

(ii) in any other case, evidence by a person other than the witness that the witness identified the accused at an identification parade as being the offender shall be admissible as evidence that the accused was so identified."

105 Criminal Evidence Act 1992, s 14(2).

106 *ibid*, s 14(3).

107 Edwards et al, *Access to Justice for People with Disabilities as Victims of Crime in Ireland* (University College Cork, Cork, 2012), p 81.

108 Cooke and Davies, "Achieving best evidence from witnesses with learning disabilities: new guidance" (2001) 29(3) *British Journal of Learning Disabilities* 84–85.

109 Plotnikoff and Woolfson, "Making best use of the Intermediary Special Measure" (2008) 2 *Criminal Law Review*, 91.

> for sign language interpreters in court… . Aids to communication such as symbols, communication boards and electronic equipment may also provide assistance… These can also help to counter the negative impacts of the prevailing principle of orality, by facilitating non-verbal evidence to be given in a court of law."[110]

[4–42] Many of the measures above will also be useful when intermediaries seek to help children, especially very young children, to give evidence.

[4–43] Unfortunately, s 14 has had a very limited impact on the practical operation of trials. Heffernan notes that this provision "has been a dead letter for the two decades in which the Act has been in force".[111] The first recorded use of an intermediary was in 2016 where a 12-year-old boy gave evidence via a video-link and through an intermediary when giving evidence in a child cruelty and sexual abuse case.[112] Thus, it is clear that greater investment in this area is required so that s 14 is fully operative. Once a properly functioning system of intermediaries is established, consideration might also be given to extending their role. For example, Counihan suggests that s 14 "should be amended to allow the complainant's responses to be relayed via an appropriately skilled intermediary".[113] In light of the increased protections available for victims under the Victims' Directive, it is very important that the availability and use of intermediaries is increased in order to offer full protection for victims.

Videorecording as Evidence at Trial

[4–44] Section 16(1) (as amended) provides that:

> "(a) a videorecording of any evidence given, in relation to an offence to which this Part applies, by a person under 18 years of age through a live television link in proceedings under Part IA of the Criminal Procedure Act, 1967, and
> (b) a videorecording of any statement made during an interview with a member of the Garda Síochána or any other person who is competent for the purpose—
> (i) by a person under 14 years of age (being a person in respect of whom such an offence is alleged to have been committed), or
> (ii) by a person under 18 years of age (being a person other than the accused) in relation to an offence under—
> (I) section 3(1), (2) or (3) of the Child Trafficking and Pornography Act 1998, or

110 Edwards et al, *supra* note 107, pp 81–82.

111 Heffernan, *supra* note 24, p 145.

112 Gallagher, "Waterford mother convicted of child cruelty following seven-week trial", *The Irish Times*, 23 May 2016.

113 Counihan, *supra* note 14, 119.

(II) section 2, 4 or 7 of the Criminal Law (Human Trafficking) Act 2008,

shall be admissible at the trial of the offence as evidence of any fact stated therein of which direct oral evidence by him would be admissible."

Any such videorecording or any part thereof shall not be admitted if the court is of the opinion that it is not in the interests of justice to do so.[114] In considering whether it is in the interests of justice to admit such videorecording, the court shall have regard to all the circumstances, including any risk that its admission will result in unfairness to the accused or, if there is more than one, to any of them.[115] It is a prerequisite for the application of s16 that the child complainant is available for cross-examination at trial.[116] This cross-examination may take place via live television link and using an intermediary.[117] Significantly, in *KD v DPP*,[118] it was confirmed that the determination of the age of the witness for the purposes of s16 "is to be had by reference to the date of the video recording of the interview".[119] The fact that a child witness or complainant is over the age specified in s 16 by the time the case gets to trial is irrelevant: the videorecording will still be admissible. Humphreys J noted that to construe s 16(1) otherwise "would create a host of anomalies": **[4–45]**

> "For example, the admissibility or otherwise of the video recording, and the necessity for child witness to have to give evidence in chief in the normal manner, would hinge on the happenstance of when the trial date happened to be fixed, or whether a particular trial ran to its conclusion or had to be recommenced or even the precise date during a particular trial on which it was sought to introduce the video evidence. To construe the section in this manner would place an enormous and irrational premium on the generation of delay on behalf of an applicant."[120]

Heffernan notes that "[t]he controversial departure which [s 16] marked from the pre-existing law is reflected in the fact that some 15 years elapsed before the section was commenced": **[4–46]**

114 Criminal Evidence Act 1992, s (2)(a).

115 *ibid*, s (2)(b).

116 *ibid*, s 16(1)(b)(ii).

117 *ibid*, s 14(1)(b) of the 1992 Act provides that where a person under 18 years of age is giving, or is to give, evidence through a live television link, the court may, on the application of the prosecution or the accused, direct that any questions be put through an intermediary. This will be done where the court is satisfied that, having regard to the age or mental condition of the witness, the interests of justice require that any such questions be so put.

118 [2016] IEHC 21.

119 *ibid*, para 16.

120 *ibid*, para 18.

> "The assumed reason for this extraordinary delay was the need to put in place resources such as specialist training for child interviewers and appropriate facilities for the video-recording of children. As a result, the video-recording of pre-trial statements remains at a fledgling stage of practice and the difficulties to which it gives rise are only beginning to emerge."[121]

[4–47] Similarly, Delahunt notes that "[t]he first cases using [s 16] took place in late 2010 and it appears that there has been no State assessment of how the provision is working in practice".[122] While she notes that "[a] significant advantage of the recording of evidence is that it allows the court to place the witness in the temporal context of the offence",[123] she highlights practical difficulties with the implementation of s 16. These include the fact that "[p]layback issues, especially with regard to the audibility of recording, occur frequently" and the potential for delays to occur "[w]hen counsel receive a file involving a vulnerable witness which does not contain a transcript, or contains a recording that will not play audibly in court, or a recording that does not contain evidence necessary to the prosecution of the offence, or a recording that requires editing".[124] It is thus clear that the infrastructure supporting the provision needs to be improved in order to ensure that it is fully effective.

[4–48] Section 37 of the 2017 Act will amend s 16 by substituting a new s 16(1)(b) which provides that the following may be admissible as evidence of any fact stated therein of which direct oral evidence would be admissible in certain circumstances:

> "video recording of any statement made during an interview with a member of the Garda Siochana or any other person who is competent for that purpose-
> (i) by a person under 14 years of age (being a person in respect of whom such an offence is alleged to have been committed), or
> (ii) by a person under 18 years of age (being a person other than the accused) in relation to-
> (I) a sexual offence, or
> (II) an offence under section 3(1), (2) or (3) of the Child Trafficking and Pornography Act 1998, or
> (III) an offence under section 2, 4 or 7 of the Criminal Law (Human Trafficking) Act 2008."

[4–49] Because the revised s 16(1)(b)(ii) will be extended to apply to sexual offences, videorecordings of evidence of child complainants in sexual

---

121 Heffernan, *supra* note 24, p 145.

122 Delahunt, "Recorded Evidence for Vulnerable Witnesses in Criminal Proceedings" (2015) 20(3) *Bar Review*, 46.

123 *ibid*, p 47.

124 *ibid*, p 48.

offence cases, and indeed any other witness in these cases, will be admissible at trial. This is a welcome extension of the current law which only permits the admission of videorecorded evidence of complainants in sexual offence trials to be admitted where the complainant is under the age of 14.

Transfer of Proceedings

Section 17 provides that in any proceedings for an offence to which Pt III applies in any Circuit or District court district in relation to which any of the provisions of s 13 to s 16 or s 29 is not in operation the court concerned may, if in its opinion it is desirable that evidence be given in the proceedings through a live television link or by means of a videorecording, by order transfer the proceedings to a Circuit or District Court district in relation to which those provisions are in operation. Where such an order is made, the jurisdiction of the court to which the proceedings have been transferred may be exercised: (a) in the case of the Circuit Court, by the judge of the circuit concerned, and; (b) in the case of the District Court, by the judge of that court for the time being assigned to the District Court district concerned. **[4–50]**

Reforms in the 2017 Act

Once Pt 6 of the 2017 Act is commenced, s 36 will provide two additions to the protections afforded to vulnerable witnesses in Pt III of the 1992 Act. First, it will insert a new s 14A into the Act which will permit evidence to be given from behind a screen. Section 14A(1) provides that where a person is accused of an offence to which Pt III applies and a person under the age of 18 years is to give evidence other than through a live television link: **[4–51]**

> "the court may, if satisfied that the interests of justice so require, direct that evidence be given from behind a screen or other similar device so as to prevent the witness from seeing the accused."

The explanatory notes on the Sexual Offences Bill noted that the consideration of "interests of justice" here would necessitate considering both the need to ensure that a child can give a full account of the acts complained of without feeling intimidated and the fact that the accused has an interest in being able to see and hear the witness giving evidence.[125] A witness giving evidence in this way must be capable of seeing and hearing and being seen and heard by: (a) the judge and jury (if any); (b) legal representatives acting in the proceedings, and; (c) an interpreter, intermediary appointed under s 14 or any other person appointed to assist **[4–52]**

---

[125] *Criminal Law (Sexual Offences) Bill 2015: Explanatory and Financial Memorandum.* Available at: https://www.oireachtas.ie/documents/bills28/bills/2015/7915/b7915s-memo.pdf (last accessed: 25 August 2017).

the witness.[126] The witness must also be capable of being seen and heard by the accused.[127] The benefits of the giving evidence from behind a screen have been explained as follows:

> "The facility of a screen will protect a child from any potential intimidation, or feeling of intimidation, by the sight of the accused while giving evidence in court. In such circumstances, it may be more appropriate for the child to give evidence through a live television link but, for various reasons, the child might wish to be heard in person before the judge, and jury when present, and this section ensures such provision is available."[128]

[4–53] Section 36 will also insert a new s 14B into the 1992 Act which provides that:

> "Where a person under the age of 18 years is giving evidence in respect of an offence to which [Part III] applies, neither the judge nor the barrister or solicitor concerned in the examination of the witness shall wear a wig or gown."

[4–54] Presently, s 13(3) provides for the removal of wigs and gowns were an individual is testifying via video-link.[129] This amendment will extend this to all situations where a child or an individual with a "mental handicap" is testifying in relation to an offence under Pt III, including a situation where no other special measures are being used.

Extension of the Availability of Special Measures

[4–55] The Victims' Directive (Directive 2012/29/EU) became operative on 16 November 2015, placing increased obligations on the State to provide special measures which deliver comprehensive protection to both adult and child victims when testifying at trial. Chapter 4 of the Directive provides for "protection of victims and recognition of victims with specific protection needs". Article 18 provides that:

> "Member States shall ensure that measures are available to protect victims and their family members from secondary and repeat victimisation, from intimidation and from retaliation, including against the risk of emotional or psychological harm, and to protect the dignity of victims during questioning and when testifying."

[4–56] The Directive provides that all child victims "shall be presumed to have

[126] Criminal Law (Sexual Offences) Bill 2015, s 14A(2).

[127] *ibid.*

[128] *Criminal Law (Sexual Offences) Bill 2015: Explanatory and Financial Memorandum*, *supra* note 125.

[129] Once s 14B is enacted, s 13(3) will be obsolete and is thus deleted by s 35 of the 2017 Act.

specific protection needs due to their vulnerability to secondary and repeat victimisation, to intimidation and to retaliation".[130] Further, it mandates that all adult victims of crime are individually assessed to identify any specific protection needs they might have.[131] Such assessment must take into account: (a) the personal characteristics of the victim; (b) the type or nature of the crime; and (c) the circumstances of the crime.[132] The Directive also requires that sexual offence victims should receive particular attention in needs assessments.[133] Where a victim is identified as having special protection needs, the Directive mandates that measures should be available to him/her in order to:

(a) avoid visual contact between victims and offenders including during the giving of evidence, by appropriate means including the use of communication technology;
(b) ensure that the victim may be heard in the courtroom without being present, in particular through the use of appropriate communication technology;
(c) avoid unnecessary questioning concerning the victim's private life not related to the criminal offence; and
(d) allow a hearing to take place without the presence of the public.[134]

These new obligations influenced the extension of the availability of special measures in the Criminal Law (Sexual Offences) Act 2017 but more significant reforms of the 1992 Act will be implemented by the Criminal Justice (Victims of Crime) Act 2017 which will implement the Directive in Irish law. Section 15(1) of the Bill provides for assessments of victims for the purpose of: **[4–57]**

(a) identifying the protection needs, if any, of the victim,
(b) ascertaining whether and to what extent the victim might benefit from protection measures, and
(c) ascertaining whether and to what extent the victim might, due to his or her particular vulnerability to secondary and repeat victimisation, intimidation and retaliation, benefit from
    (i) special measures during the course of an investigation of the alleged offence, and
    (ii) special measures during the course of any criminal proceedings relating to the alleged offence.

These assessments are to be carried out by An Garda Síochána or an officer **[4–58]**

---

130 Art 22(4).
131 Art 22(1).
132 Art 22(2). Victims must also be closely involved in such assessments and their wishes should be taken into account: Art 22(6).
133 Art 22(3).
134 Art 23(3).

of the Garda Síochána Ombudsman Commission who, when carrying out an assessment, will have regard to the following matters:

(a) the type and nature of the alleged offence;
(b) the circumstances of the commission of the alleged offence;
(c) whether the victim has suffered considerable harm due to the severity of the alleged offence;
(d) the personal circumstances of the victim, including his or her age, gender, gender identity or expression, ethnicity, race, religion, sexual orientation, health, disability, communication difficulties, relationship to, or dependence on, the alleged offender and any previous experience of crime;
(e) whether the alleged offence appears to have been committed with a bias or discriminatory motive, which may be related to the personal characteristics of the victim, including such characteristics as are referred to in paragraph (d);
(f) the particular vulnerability of victims of terrorism, organised crime, human trafficking, gender-based violence, violence in a close relationship, sexual violence or exploitation and victims with disabilities.[135]

[4–59] The views of the victim will also be taken into account.[136] If a victim is found to have special protection needs which warrant special measures during the investigation or the criminal proceedings, a range of measures are available, including:

> "measures under Part III of the Criminal Evidence Act 1992 enabling the victim to give evidence through a live television link or an intermediary or enabling a screen or other similar device to be used in the giving of evidence."[137]

[4–60] Thus, the availability of the special measures listed in Pt III will be extended beyond the special categories of witness provided for in the legislation and will be available to any victim who is deemed to have special protection needs which warrant the use of such measures.

Personal Cross-Examination by the Defendant

[4–61] Currently there is no provision in Irish law which prevents a defendant from personally cross-examining a complainant in a sexual offence trial. This omission will be rectified when the relevant sections of the 2017 Act are commenced. Although it seems unlikely that a defendant faced with a charge as serious as sexual assault or rape would opt to conduct his own

---

135 Criminal Justice (Victims of Crime) Act 2017, s 15(2). It should be noted that a child victim will be presumed to have special protection needs: s 15(7).

136 Criminal Justice (Victims of Crime) Act 2017, s 15(4).

137 *ibid*, s 19(2)(c).

defence, it remains a possibility. In Hanly et al's study of 35 transcripts of Irish rape trials,[138] there was one case in which the complainant was cross-examined by the two defendants in the case.[139] Although, as Bryan O'Sullivan highlights,[140] this case resulted in little controversy in Ireland, similar instances of defendants personally cross-examining rape complainants in England incited considerable public interest. Two of the most notorious of these were those of Ralston Edwards and Milton Brown.[141] In 1996, Edwards cross-examined his victim for six days wearing the same clothes in court as he had during the rape.[142] In 1998, Brown[143] cross-examined his two victims at trial, the trial judge commenting that the defendant's cross-examination of the complainant was "a highly regrettable and extremely sad aspect of the case".[144] After Milton Brown's trial, Jack Straw, the Home Secretary at the time, promised a "swift change in the law".[145] A Home Office Report, *Speaking Up for Justice*, also made express reference to Ralston Edwards' trial and discussed the introduction of a provision which prohibited the defendant from personally cross-examining the complainant.[146] The report noted that the trauma suffered by a sexual offence complainant who is cross-examined by a defendant arises from two factors, that is, the manner and nature of the questioning and the fact that the defendant is asking the questions.[147] It was recommended that there should be a mandatory prohibition on unrepresented defendants personally cross-examining the complainant in rape and serious sexual assault cases.[148] This recommendation found expression in ss 34–40 of the Youth Justice and Criminal Evidence Act 1999.

Allowing a defendant to personally cross-examine a complainant has **[4–62]**

---

138 Hanly, et al, *Rape & Justice in Ireland: A National Study of Survivor, Prosecutor and Court Responses to Rape* (The Liffey Press, Dublin, 2009), p 339.

139 The authors note that this case is complicated by the fact that both defendants and the complainant were foreign nationals (all from the same country), and the cross-examination was conducted in their own language which was then translated for the court: *ibid*, p 341.

140 Bryan O'Sullivan, "Protection against Cross-Examination by the Accused in Sexual Offence Trials" (2015) 25(3) *Irish Criminal Law Journal*, 54, 60.

141 For a discussion of the trials which prompted the introduction of s 34, see: Temkin, *Rape and the Legal Process* (2nd ed, Oxford University Press, Oxford, 2002), pp 320–321.

142 "Rape Victim's Foul Court Ordeal", *The London Independent*, 23 August 1996.

143 *R v Milton Brown* [1998] 2 Cr App R 364.

144 *ibid*, 368, per Judge Pontius.

145 Straw was speaking to the *Guardian* newspaper: see Lees, *Carnal Knowledge: Rape on Trial* (2nd ed, Women's Press Ltd, London, 2002), xxxix–xl.

146 Home Office, *Speaking Up for Justice: Report of the Interdepartmental Working Group on the Treatment of Vulnerable or Intimidated Witnesses in the Criminal Justice System* (Home Office, London, 1998), para 9.28–9.39.

147 *ibid*, para 9.30.

148 *ibid*, para 9.39.

the potential to be hugely traumatic for the complainant. Consequently, her ability to provide her best testimony could be seriously undermined. Indeed, a complainant faced with the prospect of being cross-examined by the defendant might refuse to testify and withdraw from the process altogether. Of course, a defendant in a sexual offence trial, as in any other trial, is entitled to take the option to represent himself and in this context it is necessary to acknowledge the defendant's right to confront and cross-examine witnesses which has been recognised under both the Irish Constitution[149] and the European Convention on Human Rights (ECHR).[150] However, the defendant's right to cross-examine witnesses is not absolute. In *Donnelly v Ireland*,[151] Hamilton CJ held that the constitutional right to confront and cross-examine witnesses does not require that the evidence is given in the physical presence of the defendant.[152] Further, in *Croissant v Germany*,[153] the European Court of Human Rights held that a requirement of German law that a defendant must be legally represented was compatible with Art 6. More recently, in *Y v Slovenia*,[154] the Court specifically noted that:

> "since a direct confrontation between the defendants charged with offences of sexual violence and their alleged victims involves a risk of further traumatisation on the latter's part … personal cross-examination by the defendant should be subject to a most careful assessment by the national courts, all the more so the more intimate the questions are."[155]

[4–63] Thus, although the defendant has rights in relation to cross-examination of the complainant in a sexual offence trial, this does not mean that a defendant who opts to defend himself should be permitted to personally cross-examine the complainant. Hanly et al point out that it is possible to permit the defendant to represent himself if he chooses but to require him to conduct a cross-examination of the complainant and other vulnerable witnesses through a professional lawyer.[156] As the RCNI highlight, in the age of legal aid for expert representation before criminal courts, it cannot be said that an accused person is at a disadvantage if he is represented

---

149 In *State (Healy) v Donoghue*, Gannon J held that Art 38.1 of the Constitution may be interpreted as giving the defendant a right "to hear and test by examination the evidence offered by or on behalf of his accuser": [1976] IR 325, 335. See also: *People (DPP) v Kelly* [2006] 3 IR 115, 136.

150 Art 6(3)(c) states that the defendant has a right "to defend himself in person or through legal assistance of his own choosing … to examine or have examined witnesses against him and to obtain the attendance and examination of witnesses on his behalf under the same conditions as witnesses against him".

151 [1998] 1 IR 321.

152 *ibid*, 357. See also: *Burke v O'Halloran* [2009] IEHC 343.

153 (1993) 16 EHRR 135.

154 [2015] EHCR 519.

155 *ibid*, para 106.

156 Hanly et al, *supra* note 138, p 83.

by counsel or a solicitor.[157] Consequently, both the RCNI[158] and Hanly et al[159] recommended that self-representing defendants be prohibited from personally cross-examining the complainant in a sexual offence trial.

These recommendations were actioned in s 36 of the 2017 Act which, once commenced, will insert a new s 14C into the Criminal Evidence Act 1992. Section 14C(1) provides that where an accused is charged with an offence to which Pt III applies and a person under 18 years is to give evidence: **[4–64]**

> "the court shall direct that the accused may not personally cross-examine the witness unless the court is of the opinion that the interests of justice require the accused to conduct the cross-examination personally".

Thus, children under 18 years of age are granted automatic protection from personal cross-examination by the accused. This protection applies whether they are the complainant or not so any child testifying in a sexual offence case is protected. **[4–65]**

Section 14C(2) provides that where a person is accused of a sexual offence, and an adult complainant is to give evidence: **[4–66]**

> "the court may direct that the accused may not personally cross-examine [the complainant] unless the court is of the opinion that the interests of justice require the accused to conduct the cross-examination personally."

Consequently, adult complainants are afforded a different level of protection to child witnesses, with the trial judge having a discretion whether to prohibit an accused from personally cross-examining an adult complainant in a sexual offence trial. **[4–67]**

Of course, if a defendant is self-representing and is not permitted to personally cross-examine a witness, provision must be made to protect his right to cross-examine. Thus, s 14C(3) provides that where a defendant is prohibited from cross-examining a witness, the court must invite the defendant to arrange for a legal representative to act for him to cross-examine the witness and require the defendant to notify the court within a specified period as to whether a legal representative is to act for the defendant for that purpose. If at the end of the specified period, the defendant has notified the court that no legal representative is to act for him, the court must consider "whether it is necessary, in the interests of justice, for the **[4–68]**

---

[157] Rape Crisis Network of Ireland, *RCNI Agenda for Justice: Discussion Document*, (Rape Crisis Network of Ireland, Galway, 2009), para 6.3.

[158] *ibid.*

[159] Hanly et al, *supra* note 138, p 354.

witness to be cross-examined by a legal representative appointed to represent the interests of the accused person".[160] If this is deemed necessary, the court must choose and appoint a legal representative to cross-examine the witness on behalf of the defendant.[161] To protect the defendant from any bias which may arise in the minds of the jury as a result of being prohibited from cross-examining a witness:

> "the court shall give the jury such warning (if any) as it considers necessary to ensure that the accused person is not prejudiced-
> (a) by any inferences that might be drawn from the fact that the accused has been prevented from cross-examining the witness in person, or
> (b) where the witness has been cross-examined by a legal representative [appointed by the court], by the fact that the cross-examination was carried out by such a legal representative and not by a person acting as the legal representative of the accused."[162]

[4–69] These safeguards should ensure that defendants are not unfairly prejudiced by the prohibition on personal cross-examination of complainants and offset any due process concerns which the prohibition might raise. Thus, once commenced, the reforms in the 2017 Act should serve to protect complainants from unnecessary trauma without any prejudice for defendants' rights.

---

160 Criminal Law (Sexual Offences) Act 2017, s 14C(4).
161 *ibid*, s 14C(5).
162 *ibid*, s 14C(6).

CHAPTER FIVE

The Admissibility of Character Evidence in Sexual Offence Trials

Introduction

Due to the nature of sexual offending, which occurs in private settings with often little to corroborate the complainant's allegation, sexual offence trials are invariably "oath against oath" contests. Consequently, the character of both the complainant and the defendant is of pronounced importance in these trials as it aids the court in assessing the credibility of the complainant's and defendant's accounts of the impugned incident. In the past, complainants in sexual offence trials were subject to much suspicion and their character, particularly their sexual reputation, was often the subject of intense scrutiny. Fortunately, this type of character assassination of complainants is no longer allowed, with special rules on the admissibility of sexual experience evidence being introduced in all common law jurisdictions in the latter decades of the 20th century. However, such evidence is still admissible upon application to a trial judge and, where not carefully controlled, it has the potential to seriously prejudice the complainant's credibility in the eyes of the jury. Further, a more recent phenomenon that has emerged is the use of complainants' personal records (e.g. counselling or social work records) as a means of testing the veracity of the complainant's testimony. The law in both of these areas will be assessed in this chapter and recommendations for reform will be discussed. **[5–01]**

There are no special rules on the introduction of evidence of the defendant's character in sexual offence trials. However, the general rules that apply in this area are worthy of discussion here given the heightened importance of character evidence in these trials. This chapter will thus include a discussion of the use of similar fact or previous misconduct evidence, as well as the rules surrounding cross-examination of the defendant on previous criminal record. **[5–02]**

Sexual Experience Evidence

Previously, at common law, evidence of the complainant's sexual past was freely admissible. Defence counsel had unlimited powers to question the **[5–03]** complainant about her prior sexual experience with the defendant and/or with third parties. Such evidence was deemed to be admissible and relevant for two purposes. Firstly, as a woman's credibility was closely allied to her perceived moral status which was largely based on her chastity, a woman's sexual past could be used to undermine this status, portraying her as "a woman of loose morals" whose credibility is consequently questionable. As Berger highlights, this tactic is based on the following syllogism: (1) an unchaste woman is apt to lie; (2) the complainant is an unchaste woman; (3) thus, she is probably lying now.[1] Secondly, sexual experience evidence was used to ground the "she did it once, she'd do it again" type of argument which would be used to support the defence contention that the complainant consented. This use of sexual experience evidence was often based on the assumption that an "unchaste" woman would be more likely to assent to sexual activity than a woman without premarital or extramarital experience.[2] Thus, evidence of sexual experience could be used to support an argument that the complainant was likely to have consented to the sexual activity which formed the basis of the charge.

[5–04] The unfettered right of the defence to adduce evidence of the complainant's prior sexual experience was the subject of much criticism. First, the supposed link between a complainant's sexual past and credibility was attacked as being based upon sexist notions of appropriate female socio-sexual behaviour. It was argued that credibility and chastity were not related concepts.[3] Second, while it was accepted that sexual history evidence may be relevant in certain instances to support the defendant's assertion of consent or honest belief in consent, it was argued that it should not be available to support bald assertions that merely because the complainant was sexually experienced, she was likely to consent to sex with anyone.[4] Finally, critics pointed out that the virtual certainty of having one's sexual history introduced at trial deterred many complainants from reporting their attacks and proceeding to trial.[5] In response to criticisms like these, "rape shield" legislation which protects complainants from unnecessary questioning about their sexual experience was widely enacted in common

---

1 Berger, "Man's Trial, Woman's Tribulation: Rape Cases in the Courtroom" (1977) 77(1) *Columbia Law Review* 1, 55.

2 *ibid*; see also Brownmiller, *Against our Will: Men, Women and Rape* (Fawcett Books, New York, 1975), p 371.

3 *ibid*, p 386.

4 Brownmiller argued that "prior sexual consensual intercourse between a rape complainant and other partners of her choosing should not be scrutinized as an indicator of purity or impurity of mind or body … and it has no place in jury room deliberation as to whether or not, in the specific instance in question, an act of forcible sex took place": *ibid*.

5 Temkin, *Rape and the Legal Process* (2nd ed, Oxford University Press, Oxford, 2002), p 197.

law jurisdictions. Irish regulation in this area was introduced via s 3 of the Criminal Law (Rape) Act 1981.[6]

Section 3 of the Criminal Law (Rape) Act 1981: Application

Section 3(1) (as amended) provides: **[5–05]**

> "If at a trial any person is for the time being charged with a sexual assault offence to which he pleads not guilty, then, except with the leave of the judge, no evidence shall be adduced and no question shall be asked in cross-examination at the trial, by or on behalf of any accused person at the trial about any sexual experience (other than that to which the charge relates) of a complainant with any person."

A "sexual assault offence" includes rape, rape under s 4, aggravated sexual assault, sexual assault and associated offences such as attempts to commit these offences,[7] as well as offences under the Criminal Law (Sexual Offences) Act 2006 (i.e. sexual offences against children)[8] and the offence of soliciting or importuning a child (whether or not for the purposes of prostitution) for the purposes of commission of an act which would constitute an offence under the 2006 Act or sexual assault.[9] The provision does not, however, extend to sexual assault, an omission which has been criticised by the Rape Crisis Network of Ireland (RCNI).[10] **[5–06]**

Under s 3(1), evidence of the complainant's sexual experience can only be adduced by the defence with the leave of the trial judge. The defence must **[5–07]**

---

6 As amended by s 13 of the Criminal Law (Rape) (Amendment) Act 1990.

7 A "sexual assault" offence means "a rape offence" and any of the following, namely, aggravated sexual assault, attempted aggravated sexual assault, sexual assault, attempted sexual assault, aiding, abetting, counselling and procuring aggravated sexual assault, attempted aggravated sexual assault or attempted sexual assault, incitement to aggravated sexual assault or sexual assault and conspiracy to commit any of the foregoing offences. A "rape offence" means any of the following, namely, rape, attempted rape, burglary with intent to commit rape, aiding, abetting, counselling and procuring rape, attempted rape or burglary with intent to commit rape, and incitement to commit rape, and ... rape under s 4, attempted rape under s 4, aiding, abetting, counselling and procuring rape under s 4 or attempted rape under s 4 and incitement to rape under s 4: s 1 of the Criminal Law (Rape) Act 1981, as amended by s 13 of the Criminal Law (Rape)(Amendment) Act 1990.

8 Criminal Law (Sexual Offences) Act 2006, s 6(1).

9 Criminal Law (Sexual Offences) (Amendment) Act 2007, s 3(3). This offence is provided for in s 6 of the Criminal Law (Sexual Offences) Act 1993 (inserted by s 250 of the Children Act 2001 and amended by s 2 of the Criminal Law (Sexual Offences) (Amendment) Act 2007.

10 Rape Crisis Network of Ireland, *Previous Sexual History Evidence and Separate Legal Representation: RCNI Position Paper*, (Rape Crisis Network of Ireland, Galway, 2012), p 9.

make an application for the admission of sexual experience evidence in the absence of the jury.[11] Notice of an intention to make such an application "shall be given to the prosecution by or on behalf of the accused person before, or as soon as practicable after, the commencement of the trial".[12] In turn, the prosecution must "notify the complainant of his or her entitlement to be heard in relation to the said application and to be legally represented, for that purpose, during the course of the application".[13] The complainant's legal representation for this purpose will be funded by legal aid.[14]

[5–08] In practice, O'Malley notes that:

> "An application to cross-examine a complainant under [s 3] should be made as early as possible in the course of the trial, preferably at the outset whenever there is material in the Book of Evidence to suggest that such an application might properly be made, but in any event no later than the end of the complainant's direct evidence."[15]

[5–09] However, "whilst postponing an application beyond this point, and particularly until after other witnesses have testified, has been declared unacceptable", he notes that the courts have indicated a willingness to consider a late application where it is in the interests of justice to do so.[16] Thus, the timing of an application "will not always be a decisive factor when adjudicating upon an application under [s 3]".[17] Further, in *The People (DPP) v McDonagh and Cawley*,[18] it was held that more than one application for the introduction of sexual experience evidence may be made. Finlay CJ noted that:

> "It is obviously desirable where it is practicable for a ruling to be made at an early stage in the trial on any such application. It may not, however, always be possible to rule it on one occasion only, and there is nothing inconsistent with the provisions of the section in a further or different application at a later stage in the trial or with the renewal of an application or the postponement of a decision on it."[19]

---

11 Criminal Law (Rape) Act 1981, s 3(2)(a).
12 Criminal Law (Rape) Act 1981, s 4A(2) (as amended by s 34 of the Sex Offenders Act 2001).
13 Criminal Law (Rape) Act 1981, s 4A(3) (as amended by s 34 of the Sex Offenders Act 2001).
14 Civil Legal Aid Act 1995, s 28(5A) (as amended).
15 O'Malley, *Sexual Offences* (2nd ed, Round Hall, Dublin, 2013), p 439.
16 *ibid*. See: *People (DPP) v Walsh*, *ex tempore*, Court of Criminal Appeal, 18 July 2008.
17 *ibid.*
18 Unreported, Court of Criminal Appeal, 24 July 1990.
19 *ibid*, 11.

Importantly, where a trial judge has granted leave for sexual experience evidence to be adduced, s/he may still exercise control over the ways in which the information is introduced at trial. The defence will not be given carte blanche to introduce and use the evidence in any way it sees fit. Section 3(3) provides that: **[5–10]**

> "If, notwithstanding that the judge has given leave in accordance with this section for any evidence to be adduced or question to be asked in cross-examination, it appears to the judge that any questions asked or proposed to be asked (whether in the course of so adducing evidence or of cross-examination) in reliance on the leave which he has given is not or may not be such as may properly be asked in accordance with that leave, he may direct that the question shall not be asked or, if asked, that it shall not be answered except in accordance with his leave given on a fresh application under this section."

The test for admission of sexual experience evidence is set out in s 3(2) (b) which provides that a judge will grant leave to admit such evidence: **[5–11]**

> "... if, and only if, he is satisfied that it would be unfair to the accused person to refuse to allow the evidence to be adduced or the question to be asked, that is to say, if he is satisfied that, on the assumption that if the evidence or question was not allowed the jury might reasonably be satisfied beyond reasonable doubt that the accused person is guilty, the effect of allowing the evidence or question might reasonably be that they would not be so satisfied."

The decision in *People (DPP) v GK*[20] suggests that the courts have taken the enactment of s 3 seriously and that trial judges should be very slow to permit sexual experience evidence to be adduced. The appellant in this case had been convicted of various sexual offences[21] against a young girl who had been aged between 10 and 15 during the years when the offences occurred. He appealed his conviction on the basis that the trial judge had erred in not allowing the complainant (who was 24 years old at the time of the trial) to be cross-examined about her previous sexual history. Evidence about the complainant's sexual history had come to light in a victim impact report which was prepared by the probation service for a sentencing hearing after the appellant's previous conviction for the same offences. These convictions had subsequently been quashed due to an error in the procedures in the trial. The victim impact report was prepared by a clinical psychologist who had counselled the complainant after she had reported her sexual abuse to the Gardaí.[22] The report "indicated that the complainant had in the course of her therapy disclosed that she 'became sexually active with boys when **[5–12]**

---

20 [2007] 2 IR 92.

21 This included charges of indecent assault, sexual assault, unlawful carnal knowledge and rape under s 4.

22 [2007] 2 IR 92, 95.

she was twelve years old'".[23] Defence counsel sought the introduction of this evidence on the basis that it "provided an explanation as to why the complainant might have made a false complaint against the accused".[24] It was also suggested that failure to introduce this evidence was likely to mislead the jury about the medical evidence in the case. The police medical examiner's evidence would reveal that the complainant had been sexually active (her hymen was broken). Without evidence of sexual activity, the jury would be led to conclude that this supported the complainant's allegations against the defendant in a situation where there was another possible explanation which may raise a doubt about the defendant's guilt.[25] The trial judge refused permission to admit the evidence on the basis that the victim impact report "was a privileged document of a confidential nature which had been brought into being solely for the purpose of sentencing after conviction" and because an application for admission of sexual experience evidence was "more appropriate to a case where consent was an issue".[26] In the Court of Criminal Appeal judgment, Kearns J noted that the "trial judge ruled on the application … for reasons which had no relevance to the statutory test".[27] However, the Court went on to consider whether the decision was justifiable on the basis of the statutory test. Commenting on s 3, the Kearns J held that:

> "Having regard to the severely restrictive terminology of the statutory provision…, in general, a decision to refuse to allow cross-examination as to past sexual history may more readily be justified in most cases than the converse. Indeed the Act is quite explicit in so providing. Furthermore, the younger the age of a complainant, the less desirable it is to ever allow cross-examination which may well be extremely traumatic for a complainant of tender years. Where a form of questioning is allowed, it should be confined only to what is strictly necessary and should never be utilised as a form of character assassination of a complainant."[28]

[5–13] Kearns J was clear that s 3 should be interpreted restrictively and that, in general, sexual history evidence should be more likely to be excluded than admitted. However, despite this strong endorsement of a restrictive approach to the use of this evidence, on the facts of this particular case, it was held that evidence of the complainant's previous sexual history should have been admitted. The failure to do so meant that:

---

23 *ibid*

24 *ibid*, 97.

25 *ibid.*

26 *ibid.* Consent was not an issue in this case as the complainant was under the age of consent when the offences occurred.

27 *ibid*, 103.

28 *ibid*, 103–104.

> "...the jury were left with only 'one suspect' in circumstances where the evidence of the ruptured hymen could only be seen as providing significant corroboration of the complainant's evidence which, because of her age, effectively conveyed to the jury the impression that the applicant was the only party with whom she was ever involved."[29]

Consequently, the appellant's convictions were quashed and, given that there had already been three trials in this case, no retrial was ordered. The judgment in this case is very important and sends a clear message that s 3 needs to be applied restrictively, with judges exercising their discretion to introduce sexual experience evidence only where this is absolutely necessary. More recent cases since *GK* also seem to support a cautious approach to the introduction of sexual history evidence. In *DPP v C*,[30] Denham J noted that the test in *GK* "is one of fairness" but emphasised that "[i]f such evidence were admitted it could have an important effect on the course of the trial, on the way counsel ran the case, on the cross examination, and on the jury".[31] Further, in *DPP v Piotrowski*,[32] Clarke J made clear that trial judges should tightly control questioning in relation to sexual experience, noting that "[t]here is ... a clear obligation on a trial judge to ensure that any permitted cross-examination on previous sexual history keeps within the bounds of what is relevant to the case".[33] This tends to suggest that s 3 has served its purpose and operates effectively to control the admission of this category of evidence. However, there are a number of problems with both the provision itself and its implementation which suggest that the practical application of s 3 does not reflect the principled strict approach to admission of sexual experience evidence which was espoused in the *GK, C* and *Piotrowski* cases. [5–14]

Section 3: Omissions and Shortcomings in Application

Section 3, and its subsequent interpretation in *GK*, are clear on the principle that sexual experience evidence should not be admitted lightly and that judges should exercise their discretion cautiously. However, there are a number of omissions within the provision which undermine its effectiveness and create space for its inappropriate application. The first problem with s 3 is that it only applies to the defence. There is no limit on the prosecution's ability to introduce evidence of the complainant's sexual experience. On its face this may not appear to be a significant omission because the prosecution is seen as being "on the complainant's side". However, the prosecution represents the interests of the State, not those of the complainant and "prosecutorial [5–15]

29 *ibid*, 104.
30 [2009] IECCA 63.
31 *ibid*, para 18.
32 [2014] IECCA 17.
33 *ibid*, para 8.

zeal might undervalue the complainant's feelings".[34] The prosecution may inadvertently bring in evidence of the complainant's sexual experience. For example, if the prosecution asserts or implies that the complainant was a virgin at the time of the attack, the defence must then be permitted to adduce evidence to the contrary. The RCNI has also highlighted that the prosecution may wish to bring in evidence of a complainant's sexual experience "where it is relevant to the case and there is a risk that the jury would be misled if it were omitted, or in order to forestall and/or minimise the impact which evidence allowed under a successful s 3 application might otherwise have upon the jury".[35] The findings in *Rape & Justice in Ireland* suggest that the introduction of sexual experience evidence by the prosecution may be a regular occurrence, with the prosecution adducing such evidence in 10 of the 35 transcripts studied.[36] Thus, the prosecution are introducing such evidence and, for the purposes of clarity and consistency, they should be included within the s 3 regime.[37]

[5–16] A second problem with the current rules in this area is the lack of a definition of "sexual experience". While it is clear that it includes evidence of sexual activity between the complainant and the defendant and third parties, it is less obvious whether indirect evidence of sexual activity is included. For example, would evidence that the complainant previously had an abortion or currently takes oral contraceptives be classified as evidence of "sexual experience"? If such information is not included, the defence is free to introduce this type of evidence without seeking leave. Such evidence may be just as prejudicial as direct evidence of the complainant's sexual past. Clarity regarding what is meant by "sexual experience" is essential if complainants are to receive appropriate protection from the unregulated introduction of sensitive information about their sexual lives at trial.

[5–17] The third problem with s 3 is the lack of detail which is provided about the process of applying to introduce sexual experience evidence. There are no special formalities regarding the initial application process. For example, there is no requirement that this application be in writing or be made within a specific time period prior to the trial. Consequently, as O'Malley's

---

34 Elliot, "Rape Complainants' Experience with Third Parties" [1984] *Criminal Law Review* 4, 9.

35 Rape Crisis Network of Ireland, *supra* note 10, p 3.

36 Hanly, et al, *Rape & Justice in Ireland: A National Study of Survivor, Prosecutor and Court Responses to Rape* (The Liffey Press, Dublin, 2009), p 355.

37 At the very least, the RCNI suggest that a formal protocol should be created or the DPP's guidelines for prosecutors should be amended to provide that the prosecution must consult the complainant before adducing sexual experience evidence: Rape Crisis Network of Ireland, *supra* note 10, p 3. Hanly et al make a similar recommendation: *ibid*, p 355. Inclusion of the prosecution within the s 3 scheme may, however, be a more transparent and streamlined approach to regulation.

comment above suggests, late applications are accepted. The RCNI notes that "one unpleasant aspect of this uncertainty is that the complainant may be surprised by a last minute section 3 application at the beginning, or even during, the trial".[38] The procedures for the hearing of the application are also vague. The only clear requirements are that the application for leave must take place in the absence of the jury[39] and that the complainant is entitled to be present and to have separate legal representation for the purposes of the application.[40] Finally, there are no criteria to guide the trial judge's discretion. The legislation states that the trial judge must only grant leave where he is satisfied that it would be "unfair" to the defendant to refuse to allow the evidence to be adduced or the question to be asked. As was seen above, the potential for "unfairness" will be assessed with reference to whether the evidence would make a difference to the jury's verdict, that is, if the evidence is adduced the effect is that it might lead the jury to acquit the defendant where they would otherwise have convicted him. This guidance is quite vague, requiring trial judges to make a determination according to their own subjective assessment of the case and, of course, the judgment in *GK* which cautions judges to take a restrictive approach to the application of s 3. Both the statutory and judicial guidance is open to interpretation by individual judges and there is space for inconsistent approaches. The RCNI has suggested that their experience supporting clients through the trial process suggests that the s 3 test "is often interpreted quite broadly".[41] Empirical evidence which further supports this contention is discussed below.

In light of these omissions, it is unsurprising that there have been calls for tightening up the procedure surrounding s 3 applications. The National Women's Council of Ireland (NWCI) have suggested that applications should be made by the defence in writing and that where the judge allows such evidence, its relevance should be explained in writing and the prosecution should receive reasonable notice in writing of its admissibility.[42] The RCNI has called for written applications and the imposition of time limitations for applications.[43] The Law Reform Commission (LRC) has **[5–18]**

[38] They note that "while this kind of application is sometimes unavoidable, it should never be the norm": Rape Crisis Network of Ireland, *supra* note 10, p 7.

[39] Criminal Law (Rape) Amendment Act 1981, s 3(2)(a), as amended by s 13 of the Criminal Law (Rape) (Amendment) Act 1990.

[40] Criminal Law (Rape) Act 1981, s 4A, as amended by s 34 of the Sex Offenders Act 2001. The DPP or her representatives will arrange for this separate representation: See Hanly et al, *supra* note 36, p 341.

[41] Rape Crisis Network of Ireland, *supra* note 10, p 7.

[42] National Women's Council of Ireland, *Report of the Working Party on the Legal and Judicial Process for Victims of Sexual and other Crimes of Violence against Women and Children*, (Dublin: National Women's Council of Ireland, 1996), para 53.

[43] Rape Crisis Network of Ireland, *supra* note 10, p 8.

also suggested that the application should be made at the beginning of the trial and that it should not be possible for such an application to be made at any later stage of the trial without the special leave of the trial judge.[44] Further guidance for judges when exercising their discretion to admit sexual experience evidence has also been called for. The NWCI has recommended that the circumstances under which evidence is admissible in relation to the complainant's sexual experience with third parties and the defendant should be codified.[45] The Task Force on Violence against Women has suggested that the rules governing the admissibility of sexual history evidence should mirror those governing the admissibility of evidence of the previous bad character of the accused. Thus, to be admissible, such evidence should be relevant, must go beyond merely tending to show that the complainant has a bad disposition or character, and must still be excluded if its prejudicial effects outweigh its probative value.[46]

[5–19] To determine whether some of the omissions highlighted here are contributing to practical problems, it is necessary to consider available empirical evidence on the operation of s 3. Unfortunately, such evidence is limited. In a study of 35 trial transcripts which was conducted for *Rape & Justice in Ireland*, applications for the introduction of sexual experience evidence were made in only seven cases and such evidence was not referred to at all in 19 cases[47], suggesting that s 3 has curbed the use of this evidence to some extent. However, there are other findings in this study which suggest that s 3 is not as effective as it could be. Six of the seven applications for the introduction of sexual experience evidence were granted[48] which may suggest that applications are granted without much difficulty. What is also troubling is the fact that although only seven s 3 applications were made, this evidence was admitted in 13 cases.[49] While it may be possible that pre-trial applications were made and granted, it is also possible that sexual experience evidence is being admitted despite the restrictions in the law. This is a worrying proposition which merits further exploration. Research by Bacik et al has also revealed that s 3 may not be achieving its objectives. Bacik et al analysed DPP files for 40 rape[50] trials which came before the Central Criminal Court in the period 2003 to 2009.[51] They found

44 Law Reform Commission, *Report on Rape and Allied Offences* (Law Reform Commission, Dublin, 1988), para 28.

45 National Women's Council of Ireland, *supra* note 42, para 53.

46 *Report of the Task Force on Violence against Women* (Stationery Office, Dublin, 1997), para 9.15–9.16.

47 Hanly et al, *supra* note 36, p 355.

48 *ibid*, 342.

49 *ibid*, 355.

50 For the purposes of the study, "rape" is defined as including rape under s 4.

51 The results of this research have yet to be published. The findings presented here are taken from a conference presentation given by Ivana Bacik at the "Rape Law

that 70 percent of s 3 applications were granted. Hence, it appears that once applications are made, they are likely to be successful. Such a high rate of successful applications would not appear to be in keeping with the spirit of s 3. The suggestion in *Rape & Justice in Ireland* that sexual experience evidence may be being admitted without going through the s 3 procedure is also worrying. Although the available empirical evidence is limited, both studies seem to suggest a more permissive attitude towards the introduction of this evidence than s 3 and the judgment in *GK* would envisage. This fact, combined with the omissions from the scheme which have been identified here, suggest that there is room for improvement of the "rape shield" in Irish law and, thus, it is worth considering possibilities for reform.

Reforming Irish Rape Shield Legislation: Achieving Effective Accommodation between Complainants and Defendants

Any attempt to reform "rape shield" legislation necessarily involves a delicate balancing of complainants' interests in the protection of privacy and avoiding unwarranted prejudice on one hand, and respect for the fair trial rights of defendants on the other. For complainants, a rape shield which does not operate to effectively eliminate unwarranted introduction of sexual experience evidence can lead to serious injustice. Most obviously, the introduction of such evidence is highly traumatic and intrusive for complainants and the prospect of such evidence being adduced may even deter them from testifying. This, in turn, impacts on societal interests in identifying and punishing those who commit sexual offences. Where complainants opt not to testify due to a fear of giving evidence, "the risk is increased that some accused of sexual crimes who should be convicted and sentenced as sex offenders, are not".[52] Sexual experience evidence also needs to be tightly controlled because of its potential to have a disproportionately prejudicial effect on juror determinations. For example, Delisle suggests a jury may give the evidence an exaggerated probative value when examining the issue of consent.[53] [5–20]

Sexual experience evidence may also skew the focus of the trial from a determination of whether an offence has occurred to an assessment of the complainant's general moral worth. The impact of "rape myths" upon juror deliberations in sexual offence trials is well-documented. One particularly pernicious myth is that of the "ideal victim", that is, a victim [5–21]

– Victims on Trial?" Conference in Dublin Castle on the 16 January 2010. The presentation may be accessed at: http://www.drcc.ie/2010/01/rape-law-victims-on-trial/ (last Accessed: 28 August 2017).

52 Rape Crisis Network of Ireland, *supra* 10, p 2.

53 Delisle, "The New Rape Shield Law and the Charter" (1993) 42 *University of New Brunswick Law Journal* 335, 335.

with a "respectable lifestyle" who is not promiscuous and does not engage in "risky" behaviour such as excessive alcohol consumption or drug use.[54] Deviations from this "ideal victim" stereotype may unfairly undermine a complainant's credibility in the eyes of the jury. There is evidence in Ireland that information about a complainant's sexual past may undermine her status as an "ideal victim". In a survey of Irish attitudes about rape conducted for the *Irish Examiner* newspaper in 2008, it was found that 23 percent of respondents believed that a woman was partially or totally responsible for being raped if she previously had had many sexual partners.[55] There also appears to be a tendency to trivialise the rape of a sexually experienced complainant. In *SAVI*, 18.3 percent of women and 23.8 percent of men believed that sexually experienced people are less traumatised by rape.[56] The danger of attitudes like this in a jury is clear. As Galvin notes, the significant danger of introducing any evidence relating to an individual's character in a criminal trial is the potential for jury misuse. It may divert the jury's attention from the issue at hand and induce them to punish or reward a party solely for having an unpleasant or attractive character, respectively.[57] Thus, introducing evidence of sexual experience evidence can unnecessarily shift the focus from a determination of whether an offence has occurred to a determination of whether the complainant is an "ideal victim" who is worthy of the law's protection.

[5–22] However, while it is vital that rape shield legislation is sufficiently robust to protect complainants' interests and to avoid the potential for injustice which has just been outlined, it is vital that any reform of s 3 is does not go so far as to infringe defendants' fair trial rights. To comply with constitutional and ECHR safeguards, any proposed changes to our rape shield laws must be sufficiently flexible to allow admission of sexual experience evidence where this is legitimately necessary to allow the defendant to make a full defence. For example, a previous sexual experience with the defendant in very similar circumstances may suggest that the complainant consented to the impugned sexual activity also or, alternatively, that the defendant had grounds for an honest belief in consent. Evidence of a previous sexual relationship may also suggest a motive to fabricate an allegation. There are instances where sexual experience evidence constitutes relevant information which jurors should have access to if they are to make a fair assessment about the defendant's guilt. At the very least, sexual experience evidence alerts the jury to the

54 Adler, *Rape on Trial*, (Routledge, London,1987), pp 119–120.

55 In this study, 1002 adults were questioned about their attitudes and beliefs about rape: Ryan, "Belief: Our Blame Culture", *Irish Examiner*, 26 March 2008.

56 McGee et al, *The SAVI Report: Sexual Abuse and Victimization in Ireland* (The Liffey Press, Dublin, 2002), p 158.

57 Galvin, "Shielding Rape Victims in the State and Federal Courts: A Proposal for the Second Decade" (1985–1986) 70 *Minnesota Law Review* 763, 779.

"context" of the alleged non-consensual sexual encounter. Duff notes that it is difficult to argue that a prior relationship with the defendant is irrelevant, particularly if it is recent and, in most cases, its existence will be essential background information necessary for the jury to make sense of the events in question.[58] As Stuart comments, in the case of prior sexual history with the defendant, when the defendant says that the complainant consented and she says she did not, or where he says that he acted reasonably and she says that he did not, it is surely part of the relevant context and essentially fair to admit evidence of the type of relationship they had.[59] Sexual experience evidence has a legitimate place in some sexual offence trials which must be accommodated in order to respect due process values.

Proposals for Reform of Section 3: Lessons from the Canadian Criminal Code

The s 3 regime is discretionary. Although some limited statutory and judicial guidance is provided, trial judges for the most part have discretion to decide whether to admit sexual experience evidence. As the discussion here shows, the breadth of this discretion, along with the uncertainties contained within s 3, allows for a permissive approach to admission of this evidence which does not provide optimum protection from its inappropriate admission. The first natural reaction to this realisation is to consider whether the creation of a stricter more "rule-bound" regime would offer a better alternative. A "rule-bound" regime only permits sexual experience evidence to be introduced where it falls within certain predefined categories. Evidence which falls outside of these categories must be excluded. This is the approach which was adopted by the English legislature in the Youth Justice and Criminal Evidence Act 1999. Prior to the introduction of this legislation, the English rape shield law was the same as the current Irish discretionary regime[60] and was the subject of much criticism.[61] The 1999 Act created "gateways" [5–23]

---

[58] Duff, "The Scottish 'Rape Shield': As Good As It Gets?" (2011) *Edinburgh Law Review* 218, 224.

[59] Stuart, "The Pendulum Has Been Pushed Too Far" (1993) 42 *University of New Brunswick Law Journal* 349, 350–351.

[60] Sexual Offences Act 1976, s 2.

[61] Kibble, "The Sexual History Provisions: Charting a Course Between Inflexible Legislative Rules and Wholly Untrammelled Judicial Discretion" [2000] *Criminal Law Review* 274, 275. Readers are directed to the following examples of commentary criticising the 1976 Act: Adler, "The Relevance of Sexual History in Rape: Problems of Subjective Interpretation" [1985] *Criminal Law Review* 769; Temkin, "Regulating Sexual History Evidence – The Limits of Discretionary Legislation" (1984) *The International and Comparative Law Quarterly* 3; Temkin, "Sexual History Evidence: The Ravishment of Section 2" [1993] *Criminal Law Review* 3; Baird, "Changes to Section 2 of the Sexual Offences Act 1976" (1999) 39 *Medicine Science Law* 198; McColgan, "Common Law and the Relevance of Sexual History Evidence" (1996) 16(2) *Oxford Journal of Legal Studies* 275.

through which sexual experience evidence could be introduced, significantly curtailing judicial discretion in this area. Although such rule-bound schemes hold the notional promise of predictability and certainty, the challenges they pose outweigh any perceived benefits. First, such schemes have the potential to undermine defendants' rights if the categories of evidence which are admissible are drawn so narrowly as to exclude relevant evidence. This problem arose quite quickly in England with the provisions of the 1999 Act being challenged the day after they came into force.[62] Although the House of Lords interpreted the provisions to avoid conflict with defendants' fair-trial rights by restoring an element of discretion to trial judges, the case demonstrates the due process challenges posed by rule-bound approaches.[63] A further problem with rule-bound schemes is the complexity which arises from seeking to provide for every situation in which sexual experience evidence may be relevant, whilst still being sufficiently prescriptive to curb the potential for discretionary judgments. The "gateway" system in the English legislation evidences the convoluted nature of this approach with the scheme being both difficult to explain and to apply in practice. Such complexity can result in the rules being misunderstood or inadvertently disregarded by the judiciary and legal professionals.[64]

[5–24] A suitable compromise between the rule-bound approach adopted in English law and the current Irish discretionary approach is the introduction of a "structured discretion" regime like s 276 of the Canadian Criminal Code which begins with an absolute prohibition on what are regarded as the illegitimate uses of sexual experience evidence,[65] providing that:

> "... evidence that the complainant has engaged in sexual activity, whether with the accused or with any other person, is not admissible to support an inference that, by reason of the sexual nature of that activity, the complainant:

---

62 *R v A (No 2)* [2002] 1 AC 45.

63 A rule-bound scheme in Canadian law which provided a blanket prohibition on the introduction of sexual history evidence which was subject to just three exceptions was challenged in *R v Seaboyer* [1991] 2 SCR 577. The Canadian Supreme Court held that the provision infringed principles of fundamental justice and the right to a fair trial guaranteed by s 7 and s 11(d) of the Canadian Charter of Rights and Freedoms, respectively, because it precluded the court from considering relevant evidence: Easton, "The Use of Sexual History Evidence in Rape Trials" in Childs and Ellison, (eds), *Feminist Perspectives on Evidence*, (Cavendish Publishing Ltd, 2000, London), p 180. The replacement legislation is discussed below.

64 Research with barristers and judges showed that there was a certain lack of understanding surrounding s 41: Temkin and Krahé, *Sexual Assault and the Justice Gap: A Question of Attitude?* (Hart Publishing, Oxford, 2008), p 146.

65 Kibble, "Judicial Discretion and the Admissibility of Prior Sexual History Evidence under Section 41 of the Youth Justice and Criminal Evidence Act 1999: Sometimes Sticking to Your Guns Means Shooting Yourself in the Foot" [2005] *Criminal Law Review* 263, 267.

(a) is more likely to have consented to the sexual activity that forms the subject-matter of the charge; or
(b) is less worthy of belief."

This opening statement is designed to counter the "twin myths"[66] which the defence may rely upon when seeking to introduce sexual experience evidence, that is, that previous sexual experience evidence can be used to support a bald "she consented once, she consented then" type of defence or to suggest that as a result of her "unchaste" character, a complainant is prone to mendacity. Of course, where there is a logical and demonstrated nexus between sexual experience evidence and the incident giving rise to the charge, it would still be admissible. For example, where the defendant had consensual sexual activity with the complainant in precisely the same circumstances on a previous occasion, this may be admissible in limited circumstances as a form of "pattern evidence" indicating her propensity to consent to sexual activity in these circumstances.[67] However, a strong link between the evidence and the impugned incident would be necessary to justify admission of the evidence. Likewise, the prohibition on the use of sexual experience evidence to undermine a complainant's credibility does not mean that a specific instance of sexual activity could never be used to challenge a complainant's version of events. For example, a previous sexual experience with the defendant or another individual might be admissible to demonstrate a motivation to fabricate. **[5–25]**

The "twin myths" prohibition is followed by the criteria which must be satisfied if sexual experience evidence is to be properly admitted. Section 276(2) provides that a trial judge may not admit evidence that the complainant has engaged in sexual activity other than the sexual activity that forms the subject matter of the charge, whether with the defendant or with any other person, unless the trial judge determines that the evidence: **[5–26]**

---

66 In *R v Seaboyer*, the case which preceded the introduction of s 276, McLachlin J referred to the traditional inappropriate uses of sexual experience evidence as the "twin myths":

> "Evidence that the complainant had relations with the accused and others was routinely presented (and accepted by judges and juries) as tending to make it more likely that the complainant had consented to the alleged assault and as undermining her credibility generally. These inferences were based not on facts, but on myths that unchaste women were more likely to consent to intercourse and in any event, were less worthy of belief. These twin myths are now discredited.": *R v Seaboyer; R v Gayme* [1991] 2 SCR 577. Note there are no paragraph numbers in this judgment. This quote may be found on p 38.

67 Of course, this type of argument would have to be carefully assessed by the trial judge to ensure that the evidence is genuinely relevant and that the similarities between the impugned sexual encounter and the evidence which it is proposed to introduce go beyond mere coincidence.

(a) is of specific instances of sexual activity;
(b) is relevant to an issue at trial; and
(c) has significant probative value that is not substantially outweighed by the danger of prejudice to the proper administration of justice.[68]

[5–27] The effect of s 276(2) is to create a three-stage cumulative test[69] for the admission of sexual experience evidence. First, the evidence must relate to a specific instance of sexual activity. Evidence of general sexual reputation is inadmissible.[70] This ensures that the defence cannot engage in a fishing expedition in order to try to find something in the complainant's sexual past which might serve to discredit her. It will be necessary to point to a particular experience of the complainant. Presumably this would entail being able to isolate a general time and/or place for this sexual activity and the identity of the complainant's partner. The second stage in the test is to demonstrate that the instance of sexual activity is relevant to an issue at trial. The sexual activity will be relevant if it "has the capacity to make the determination of any fact in issue more probable than not".[71] Thus, in a case where consent is in issue, an instance of sexual activity would be admissible if it would be relevant to determining whether or not consent was present. For example, it may demonstrate that the complainant and the defendant have always engaged in sexual activity on precisely the same terms and it has always been consensual, thereby making it significantly more probable that consent was present at the time of the impugned encounter. The final stage in the test requires the trial judge to make sure that the evidence which it is proposed to introduce has "significant probative value" which is not "substantially outweighed by the danger of prejudice to the proper administration of justice". To be "significant", the evidence must "not be so trifling as to be incapable, in the context of all the evidence, of raising a reasonable doubt".[72] Chapman suggests that the requirement of significant probative value requires only evidence which is, together with other evidence, capable of enabling a reasonable jury properly instructed to have a reasonable doubt about guilt.[73] However, this evidence may still be excluded if its significant probative value is outweighed by its potential to prejudice the proper administration of justice. Paciocco and Stuesser

---

68 Criminal Code (Canada), s 276(2).

69 This phrase is coined by Duff commenting on the Scottish equivalent of this test: Duff, "The Scottish 'Rape Shield': As good as it gets?" (2011) 15(2) *Edinburgh Law Review* 218, 228.

70 Paciocco and Stuesser, *The Law of Evidence: Revised Fifth Edition*, (Irwin Law Inc, Toronto, 2008), p 95. As will be seen below, s 277 also provides an express prohibition on the use of evidence of sexual reputation.

71 Chapman, "Section 276 of the Criminal Code and the Admissibility of 'Sexual Activity' Evidence" (1999– 2000) 25 *Queen's Law Journal* 121, 149.

72 Pacciocco and Stuesser, *supra* note 70, p 97, quoting *R v Darrach* [2000] 2 SCR 443, para 41.

73 Chapman, *supra* note 71, 128.

note that on its face, this provision contemplates that evidence capable of raising a reasonable doubt could be denied to a defendant. Although this is a "troubling proposition", they suggest that, "in practice, it is difficult to conceive of cases where a judge could find that prejudice to the administration of justice would substantially outweigh the importance of giving the accused access to evidence having such importance".[74]

The three-stage test for admissibility is followed by a list of factors which the trial judge must consider when deciding whether to admit the evidence of the complainant's sexual experience. These are as follows: **[5–28]**

> "(a) the interests of justice, including the right of the accused to make a full answer and defence;
> (b) society's interest in encouraging the reporting of sexual assault offences;
> (c) whether there is a reasonable prospect that the evidence will assist in arriving at a just determination in the case;
> (d) the need to remove from the fact-finding process any discriminatory belief or bias;
> (e) the risk that the evidence may unduly arouse sentiments of prejudice, sympathy or hostility in the jury;
> (f) the potential prejudice to the complainant's personal dignity and right of privacy;
> (g) the right of the complainant and of every individual to personal security and to the full protection and benefit of the law;
> (h) any other factor that the judge, provincial court or justice considers relevant."[75]

This checklist provision attempts to further steer judicial discretion by directing judges to consider the interests of the defendant, the complainant and society more generally. Gotell suggests that this check-list was "clearly intended to compel judges to engage in a complex balancing exercise that extends beyond the narrow contest between the privacy of the individual complainant and the legal rights claims of individual defendants".[76] Consequently, this check-list contemplates "a contextual analysis of sexual history", "an analysis in which the individual rights of complainants and defendants are set against a backdrop of sexual violence as a serious social problem and framed by a recognition of the need to curtail the circulation of discriminatory myths within sexual assault trials".[77] **[5–29]**

The test for admissibility in s 276 is also supported by s 277 which prohibits **[5–30]**

---

74 See Pacciocco and Stuesser, *supra* note 70, p 97.
75 Criminal Code (Canada), s 276(3).
76 Gotell, "When Privacy Is Not Enough: Sexual Assault Complainants, Sexual History Evidence and the Disclosure of Personal Records" (2005–2006) 43(3) *Alberta Law Review* 743, 755.
77 *ibid.*

the use of sexual reputation evidence. The provision provides that "evidence of sexual reputation, whether general or specific, is not admissible for the purpose of challenging or supporting the credibility of the complainant". This provision forbids the introduction of character evidence relating to sexual matters in order to besmirch the complainant. Setting this prohibition outside of s 276 makes it clear that such evidence must never be admitted in a trial and there can be no circumstances in which a trial judge could exercise his/her discretion to allow for it to be introduced. Given the highly prejudicial and utterly unnecessary nature of such evidence, this is an important and worthwhile provision.

[5–31] It is clear that the Canadian regime provides far greater guidance than s 3, while still respecting judicial discretion. Judges are actively discouraged from taking a permissive approach to admissibility which may lead to the unwarranted and prejudicial use of sexual experience evidence. However, defendants' rights are still adequately protected, as such evidence can still be admitted where it is legitimately relevant. Indeed, in *R v Darrach*,[78] the Supreme Court of Canada held that s 276 did not contravene the rights of defendants which are enshrined in s 7 and s 11(d) of the Canadian Charter of Rights and Freedoms, that is, the right to make full answer and defence and the right to a fair trial. The structured discretion approach would, thus, seem to offer a suitable blueprint for reform of s 3. To bolster this approach and further improve upon the current law, a number of definitional and procedural clarifications should be included in any future reform effort.

[5–32] First, the application procedure should apply to the prosecution as well as the defence to provide maximum protection from the inappropriate introduction of sexual experience evidence. Second, a definition of "sexual experience" should be introduced. The RCNI has recommended that "sexual experience" should be "broadly statutorily defined ... to include references to pregnancy, miscarriage, abortion, contraception and other indicia of sexual activity".[79] It is important that such a definition also clarifies that sexual experience includes both consensual and non-consensual sexual activity (i.e. sexual abuse).[80] Jurors may be unable to accept that a complainant could be subject to sexual assault more than once in a lifetime.[81] Alternatively, the defence

78 [2000] SCR 46.

79 Rape Crisis Network of Ireland, *supra* note 10, p 9.

80 Structured discretion schemes in Victoria and Scotland expressly state that the sexual activity referred to in the regime includes both consensual and non-consensual sexual activity: s 342 of the Criminal Procedure Act 2009 (Vic) and s 274(2) of the Criminal Procedure (Scotland) Act 1995 (as amended).

81 In reality, sexual re-victimisation is not an uncommon phenomenon. A significant number of participants in the *SAVI* study experienced re-victimisation. For women, experiencing penetrative sexual abuse in childhood was associated with a 16-fold increase in the risk of adult penetrative sexual abuse, and a five-fold increase in the

may seek to introduce such evidence in order to suggest that the complainant is prone to making false allegations or has a "victim mentality" which has resulted in her making mistaken allegations about the defendant.[82] Clarifying that "sexual activity" encompasses both consensual and non-consensual sexual experiences ensures that previous instances of sexual abuse cannot be used to prejudice a complainant's account and are only admitted where they are genuinely relevant to the case.[83]

The final improvements which should be included in a future reform effort relate to the application procedure, the criticisms of which have been outlined above. Some guidance for possible improvements in this area can also be gleaned from Canada. Section 276.1(2) of the Canadian Criminal Code provides that an application for the admission of sexual experience evidence should be made in writing to the court and set out (a) detailed particulars of the evidence that the accused wishes to adduce, and (b) the relevance of that evidence to an issue at trial. The defence is also required to provide a copy of the application to the prosecution.[84] The notice must be given seven days before the commencement of the trial. These application criteria should be adopted in Ireland. The requirement of a written application encourages the defence to take a considered approach to the application for admissibility. It discourages spurious requests as these will be much more obvious in a written form than perhaps would be the case with an oral application. The provision of detailed particulars of the information which the defendant wishes to introduce also gives the prosecution some warning of what is in store[85] and provides an opportunity to prepare a suitable response. Naturally, a judge must be able to accept a late application in limited circumstances where this is necessary to protect a defendant's fair trial rights and a provision to allow for this should be included in any prospective reform. **[5–33]**

With regard to the hearing of the application, although the current *in camera* approach should not be departed from, s 276 provides some ideas for improvements. Section 276(2)(3) provides that if the judge decides that the application to admit sexual experience evidence should be granted, then s/ **[5–34]**

risk of adult contact sexual abuse. For men, experiencing penetrative sexual abuse in childhood linked to a 16-fold increase in the risk of adult penetrative sexual abuse, and at least a 12-fold increase in the risk of adult contact sexual abuse: McGee et al, *supra* note 56, p 73.

82 Victoria Law Reform Commission, *Sexual Offences: Final Report* (Victoria Law Reform Commission, Melbourne, 2004), para 4.46.

83 For example, a previous experience of sexual violence at the hands of the defendant or a related individual might suggest a motive to fabricate the current allegation.

84 Criminal Code (Canada), s 276.1(2).

85 See Temkin, *supra* note 5, p 230.

he must provide written reasons for his decision. This written record must also provide the following information:

(a) where not all of the evidence is to be admitted, the part of the evidence that is to be admitted
(b) the factors that affected the determination; and
(c) where all or any part of the evidence is to be admitted, the manner in which that evidence is expected to be relevant to an issue at trial.

[5–35] In addition, s 276(4) provides that where evidence is admitted at trial, the judge shall instruct the jury as to the uses they may and may not make of that evidence. Requirements along these lines would be a welcome addition to the Irish regime. Requiring the trial judge to give reasons for granting or denying an application makes sure that these decisions are reasoned and not founded on spurious or knee-jerk reasoning. In turn, setting parameters for the use of sexual experience evidence ensures that a successful application is not tantamount to a *carte blanche* to use such evidence in any way counsel wish. If it is to be admitted, the uses to which it may be put will be strictly limited. Thus, the potential for unfairly prejudicing the complainant's credibility is minimised.

[5–36] The amendments to the application procedure which are suggested here would contribute to the success of the new regime for the admission of sexual experience evidence. These proposals improve upon the current application process by creating a much more structured procedure. Most notably, the introduction of notice periods and written applications introduces a level of formality which should ensure that these applications are taken seriously by lawyers. Similarly, requiring trial judges to issue detailed written decisions which justify and regulate the admission of such evidence encourages trial judges to be circumspect about the introduction of this evidence and not to grant applications lightly. Of course, the application procedure will only be successful if it is properly applied. Thus, training for the judiciary and legal professionals on appropriate application of the new regime would be essential, as would post-implementation monitoring in the form of empirical research which tracks the decisions on admissibility and the adherence to the new rules by both judges and legal practitioners.

Disclosure of Complainants' Personal Records

[5–37] Although, traditionally, the primary form of evidence which was adduced about a sexual offence complainant's character was sexual experience evidence, more recently, defence counsel have sought to admit evidence from personal records such as counselling or other therapeutic records, or social work or school reports. The trend for seeking access to this information may be linked to a number of developments, including the fact that greater numbers of victims now seek support from counsellors and therapists, as well as concerns that, with provisions such as s 3 of the 1981 Act, sexual experience evidence may not be as readily available at it was. Thus, this category of evidence has gained increased prominence. A discussion of the rules relating to character in sexual offence trials would not be complete without a consideration of the law in this area.

Current Irish Law

In criminal trials, the prosecution has a statutory duty to provide the defence with a book of evidence,[86] which contains the following information: **[5–38]**

> (a) a statement of the charges against the accused;
> (b) a copy of any sworn information in writing upon which the proceedings were initiated;
> (c) a list of the witnesses the prosecutor proposes to call at the trial;
> (d) a statement of the evidence that is expected to be given by each of them;
> (e) a copy of any document containing information which it is proposed to give in evidence by virtue of Part II of the Criminal Evidence Act 1992;
> (f) where appropriate, a copy of a certificate under section 6(1) of that Act;
> (g) a list of exhibits (if any).

Further, the prosecution also has a common law duty "... to make available all relevant evidence, parol or otherwise, in its possession, so that if the prosecution does not adduce such evidence, the defence may, if it wishes to do so".[87] This duty of disclosure is derived from the defendant's constitutional right to a fair trial.[88] **[5–39]**

The duty to disclose only applies to information which is in the hands of the prosecution. It is not applicable where material is held by individuals or organisations who are not a party to the trial. Where the defence in a sexual offence trial seeks access to a complainant's records which are in the possession of, for example, a counsellor or a social worker, there is no procedure to regulate disclosure. This differs to the situation in civil cases, where both the plaintiff and defendant can use the third-party discovery process to access documents held by third parties.[89] **[5–40]**

The unavailability of third-party discovery in criminal trials was confirmed **[5–41]**

---

86 Criminal Procedure Act 1967, s 4B (as amended by s 9 of the Criminal Justice Act 1999).

87 *People (DPP) v Tuite* (1983) 2 Frewen 175, 181, per McCarthy J.

88 In *People (DPP) v Tuite*, it was held that the duty to disclose arises out of the constitutional right to fair procedures: (1983) 2 Frewen 175.

89 Rules of Superior Courts 1986, Ord 31, r 29

by the Supreme Court in *DPP v Sweeney.*[90] The applicant was a defendant in a rape trial who sought an order for third party discovery against a rape crisis centre. Geoghegan J held that the Rules of Superior Courts 1986 (as amended by the Rules of the Superior Courts (No 2) (Discovery) 1999) which provide for non-party discovery in civil cases do not apply to criminal trials. Geoghegan J noted that "[i]t has always been part of the jurisprudence in relation to discovery and especially in relation to non-party discovery that the issues in the case are first defined" and "normally discovery will not be made until after the close of proceedings in a civil action".[91] This approach is not possible in a criminal trial. Geoghegan J observed that "[s]ubject to some modern statutory exceptions in relation to alibi evidence the defence is permitted to spring surprises and is perfectly entitled, pending the trial, to give no indication as to what issues might be raised".[92] As a result of these wholly different contexts, it was held that the Rules of Court which provide for third-party discovery can never have been intended to apply in criminal proceedings.[93]

[5–42] This reasoning was confirmed by the Supreme Court in *H(D) v Groarke*,[94] where a defendant in a sexual assault trial was seeking to have the *Sweeney* ruling overturned so that he could access the complainant's social work records. Keane CJ expressed himself to be satisfied that the decision in *Sweeney* was correct, again emphasising the lack of mutuality in criminal trials:

> "In a trial on indictment...the issue which the court has to determine is not defined until the accused has been arraigned and has pleaded to the counts laid against him. Even then, he is not required to do more than plead guilty or not guilty. There are some rare statutory exceptions to that, such as the requirement to notify the prosecution in advance of a proposed alibi. But in every other respect, while the prosecution must disclose comprehensively and in detail the case they propose to make against the accused, he is under no such obligation. Discovery, accordingly, in a trial on indictment would be a wholly one-sided process, which was certainly not what was envisaged by the procedure for inter partes and third party discovery provided under the Rules of Court."[95]

[5–43] It is thus clear that the civil procedure of non-party discovery is inherently unsuitable for use in criminal trials and cannot be used in this context. Successive cases have also clarified that the defence cannot use the subpoena

---

90 [2002] 1 ILRM 532.
91 *ibid*, 538.
92 *ibid*.
93 *ibid*.
94 [2002] 3 IR 522.
95 *ibid*, 531.

duces tecum procedure to access personal records which are held by third parties. This is a civil procedure which requires a witness to attend court to give evidence and to bring specified documents.[96] In principle, the defence could use this procedure to compel third-party record-holders to attend court, present the records and answer questions about their contents. In *F v DPP*,[97] Geoghegan J held that the subpoena duces tecum procedure cannot be treated as a mechanism for third party disclosure in criminal trials, stating that he was "quite satisfied" that availing of the deposition procedure is no solution to the current lacuna in the law.

There is thus a legal vacuum in this area with no existing procedure which can be adopted to allow for third-party disclosure of personal records. Further, it has been held that trial judges are not permitted to create their own ad hoc solutions to allow for disclosure. In *Health Service Executive v Judge White*,[98] a defendant in a case of unlawful killing sought access to certain HSE records on the basis that they were relevant to the charge. With no legal procedure to allow for such third-party disclosure and in an attempt to facilitate the request, the Circuit Court judge made an order requiring the DPP to obtain the documents from the HSE and to then forward them to the defence. In the High Court, Edwards J quashed the order, stating that it was a "novel" one which the trial judge was not justified in making. Edwards J conceded that trial judges have an inherent jurisdiction to make an order which is necessary to protect a defendant's rights but he emphasised that this jurisdiction should be exercised with "considerable restraint" and "only in exceptional circumstances". He pointed to the danger that in invoking its inherent jurisdiction a judge "may cross the line and that the process it is engaged in may amount de facto to legislation, or executive action, by the Court, thereby breaching the principle of separation of powers". Edwards J concluded that a solution to the problem of third-party disclosure should be provided by the legislature, not by ad hoc judicial remedies. This case was appealed to the Supreme Court but the disclosure issue was settled without a hearing due to the HSE making the documents available to the DPP to allow for disclosure to be made in the ordinary way. There is thus still a possibility that the Supreme Court might allow for such an order to stand in a future case. **[5–44]**

However, even if a judicial solution were to be permitted in future, there is still one further issue which will complicate decision-making in this area. A record-holder could refuse to disclose the records on the basis of privilege. Communications within certain relationships such as lawyers **[5–45]**

[96] Delany and McGrath, *Civil Procedure in the Superior Courts* (2nd ed, Thomson Round Hall, Dublin, 2005), p 482.
[97] [2008] IEHC 272.
[98] [2009] IEHC 242.

and their clients or journalists and their sources are privileged. Although there is no specific counsellor/client privilege in Irish law, a number of judgments have hinted that a claim of counsellor/client privilege might be successful. Sacerdotal privilege applies to communications between a priest and his parishioner.[99] In *ER v JR*,[100] Carroll J held that this privilege extended to a priest in his capacity as marriage counsellor. The fact that the marriage counsellor was a priest added weight to the relationship[101] and Carroll J did not state whether a lay marriage counsellor could rely on the same privilege. However, in *Johnston v Church of Scientology*,[102] drawing on *ER*, Geoghegan J stated that, given the extent to which counselling is availed of in modern society, "there may well be a privilege which the courts would uphold in some circumstances".[103] If such a privilege were to be recognised, it is important to remember that it would attach to the client and not the record-holder. It would fall to the complainant to claim privilege or to waive it. As O'Malley notes, this creates the potential for inappropriate disclosure, as while the privilege is held by the complainant, the request for access is made to the record-holder.[104] Disclosure could be made without the privilege properly being waived if the relevant individual or organisation disclosed without fully discussing this with the complainant. Should the complainant decide to claim privilege and a trial judge recognise it, a balancing exercise would then need to be carried out between the privilege and the defendant's right to a fair trial.[105] If such exercises were required in each case, disclosure decisions would be made on an ad hoc basis, making it very difficult to determine in advance whether disclosure would be available in a given case. This ambiguity could lead to unjust results for both defendants and complainants.

[5–46] There is significant ambiguity in this area. Some improvements been achieved with the creation of Memoranda of Understanding regarding disclosure between the Office of the DPP and a range of statutory and non-statutory agencies, including the HSE, the Child and Family Agency (Tusla), the Dublin Rape Crisis Centre, the Cork Sexual Violence Centre,

99 This privilege was recognised in *Cook v Carroll* [1945] IR 165 where a Roman Catholic priest was held not to be obliged to answer questions relating to confidential communications made between him and a parishioner.

100 [1981] ILRM 125.

101 The learned judge held that "advice given by a minister of religion has an added dimension which is not present between lay people": *ibid*, 126.

102 [2001] 1 IR 682.

103 *ibid*, 686.

104 O'Malley, *supra* note 15, p 378.

105 In *DPP v Cash*, Charleton J held that privileges in the law of evidence, whether state or diplomatic, are all now decided on a balancing test: [2007] IEHC 108, para 67. Presumably private privileges such as sacerdotal privilege or a counsellor/client privilege would also be covered by this line of reasoning.

OneinFour and Towards Healing.[106] The memoranda ensure "that disclosure is made only with the informed consent of the person to whom the material relates (usually, but not always the complainant)".[107] The record-holder "acknowledges that ownership of the information held by them vests in the patient or client, not the authority holding it".[108] The memoranda also outline the consequences of consent to disclosure and attempt "to assist non-parties in preparing themselves and their clients for the process [of disclosure] in good time, ensuring the early identification of potentially relevant material, allowing the necessary time for the identification and redaction of all non-relevant private or sensitive material".[109] Importantly, the Office of the DPP requires the defence to agree to certain conditions to minimise the potential for misuse of records. Such conditions include requiring that the material be kept in the possession of legal representatives at all times, that it be used only for the purposes of the trial and that the material is only accessed by the accused or witnesses under the supervision of legal representatives.[110] These memoranda are certainly useful and have offset some of the uncertainty in this area, but they are no substitute for a legal regime which provides all parties with a clear framework within which disclosure can operate. Fortunately, such reform has been included in the Criminal Law (Sexual Offences) Act 2017. However, before discussing these reforms, it is worth considering the problems posed by inappropriate introduction of personal records in sexual offence trials in order to fully comprehend the need for clear rules in this area.

Principled Objections to the Disclosure of Complainants' Personal Records at Trial

There are a number of reasons why disclosure of complainants' personal records and their introduction at trial is objectionable. First, most obviously, given the sensitive information which is contained in personal records, their release is a significant invasion of the complainant's privacy and complainants can experience considerable distress when such information is disclosed to the defence and potentially introduced at trial.[111] Further, unwarranted introduction of this evidence at trial may interfere with a [5–47]

---

106 Mulkerrins (Head of Policy and Research, Office of the DPP), contribution to Law Reform Commission Seminar on Disclosure and Discovery in Criminal Cases: Law Reform Commission, *Report of Seminar on Disclosure and Discovery in Criminal Cases* (Law Reform Commission, Dublin, 2014), p 7.

107 *ibid.*

108 *ibid.*

109 *ibid.*

110 *ibid.*

111 Leahy, "Regulating Disclosure of Complainants' Personal Records in Sexual Offence Trials" (2016) 4 *Criminal Law Review* 227, 228.

complainant's privacy rights under Art.40.3.1 of the Irish Constitution[112] and Art 8 of the European Convention on Human Rights (ECHR). Notably, in *X and Y v The Netherlands*,[113] the European Court of Human Rights held that States have a positive obligation to make sure that an individual's Art 8 privacy rights are protected.[114] However, constitutional and ECHR rights to privacy are not unqualified. They may be limited where another right is threatened such as the fair trial rights of the defendant (discussed below).[115] Thus, although complainants' right to privacy in their personal records must be respected and such evidence should not be adduced lightly, some provision for appropriate introduction of this information may be permissible if this is necessary to protect the rights of others and wider societal interests.

[5–48] Another problem created by the inappropriate introduction of personal records is similar to that raised by inappropriate use of sexual experience evidence, that is, the disproportionately prejudicial effect which this evidence can have on a complainant's credibility. Similar to the historic myth that "unchaste" women were prone to mendacity was a belief that women make false allegations of rape due to mental or psychological disorders. For example, Glanville Williams spoke of the danger of a "false allegation being made out of spite ... or for obscure psychological reasons".[116] Irrelevant details of a complainant's psychiatric or psychological well-being can greatly prejudice a complainant's credibility. Ellison notes that "jurors are likely to attach exaggerated significance to psychiatric evidence" and "this is likely to have an irrational, distorting influence on juror decision-making to the prejudice of the ... complainant and the fact-finding process".[117] Further Leahy highlights that even if personal records do not contain information about mental health issues, there is likely to be other information within them which could be used by the defence to improperly impugn a complainant's credibility. For example, social work or medical files may contain references to drug use or incidents with social workers which may be introduced to suggest that a complainant is not a worthy or reliable victim.[118]

---

[112] *Kennedy v Ireland* [1987] IR 587.

[113] (1986) EHRR 235.

[114] *ibid*, para 23. This right to privacy has been interpreted to include the right to protection of personal data such as medical records: *Z v Finland* (1998) 25 EHRR 371, para 95.

[115] Exercise of the constitutional right to privacy may be limited by the constitutional rights of others or by the requirements of the common good and the requirements of public order and morality: *Kennedy v Ireland* [1987] IR 587, 592. Similarly, Art 8(2) of the ECHR specifically provides that the right to privacy may be legitimately curtailed in certain instances, including where this is necessary for "the protection of the rights and freedoms of others".

[116] Williams, *Textbook of Criminal Law* (Stevens, London, 1978), pp 196–197.

[117] *ibid*, 36.

[118] Leahy, *supra* note 111, p 229

Inappropriate use of personal records in sexual offence trials also impacts upon record-holders. Disclosure applications can be time- and resource-intensive for those who must defend them. The organisations which usually hold personal records (e.g. counselling services offered by victims' groups, schools or the HSE) often operate under budget and staffing restraints. They should not have to expend valuable funds and staff energy defending applications for access to records unless this is absolutely necessary. The potential for records to be disclosed can also impact on the relationship between these professionals and their clients. To avoid being forced to reveal confidential information about their clients, record-holders may opt to minimise their note-taking or cease taking notes. This can impact negatively upon client care. **[5–49]**

There are also wider societal interests at stake when regulating disclosure of counselling records. Complainants may be deterred from reporting sexual offences if they fear that their personal records will be disclosed. Such fears are particularly likely where complainants have been heavily documented with, for example, social services. It is not in society's interest for sexual offending to go unreported as offenders will not be brought to justice and this may result in further victimisation. Society also has an interest in victims receiving counselling or access to medical and social services. This could be deterred if complainants feel that records of these interventions will be admissible in court.[119] The recovery of victims is an important social goal[120] and a permissive approach to the disclosure of counselling records which discourages victims from seeking the assistance they need to recover is contrary to this objective. **[5–50]**

The final concern which may be raised about the use of personal records in trials is purely pragmatic, that is, whether they are suitable for use as evidence in trials. As Temkin suggests in relation to counselling notes: **[5–51]**

> "A counsellor is only marginally concerned with the facts and the detail of what happened. The focus of counselling is the client's state of mind … As such the counsellor's notes should not be regarded as a reliable record of the matters at issue in a sexual assault trial. The counsellor is working at an entirely different level. The record contains the counsellor's perceptions coupled with a therapeutic analysis."[121]

---

[119] As Temkin cautions, society has an interest in facilitating victims attending counselling and thereby taking "positive and laudable steps to save themselves from the depression and other mental illnesses which so often ensue and which can prevent them from functioning in society or even bring them to suicide": Temkin, "Digging the Dirt: Disclosure of Records in Sexual Assault Cases" (2002) 61(1) *Cambridge Law Journal* 126, 131–132.

[120] *ibid*, 143.

[121] Temkin, *supra* note 119, 129–130.

[5–52] The unreliability of counselling records is compounded by the fact that complainants do not have the opportunity, as is the case with a police statement, to read the notes to ensure that they are an accurate reflection of their communications.[122] The same concerns are valid for medical files and records compiled by social workers or education authorities. Personal records are not created for use in criminal trials. Any revelations within these files should be treated with caution and their utility as evidence, save in exceptional circumstances, is questionable.

[5–53] Of course, weighed against all of these principled objections to the disclosure of personal records are the defendants' fair trial rights. As with sexual experience evidence, while personal records should not be disclosed where this is unwarranted or may create unfair prejudice, there may be circumstances where such disclosure is necessary to ensure a fair trial under Art 38.1 of the Constitution and Art 6 of the ECHR and to respect the principle of "equality of arms" between the prosecution and defence which was devised under the latter.[123] For example, counselling records may contain information about the unfolding of events or reveal prior inconsistent statements.[124] Alternatively, records could reveal that therapy has influenced the complainant's memory.[125] In situations like these, a rule which denied the defendant access to the records could create a real threat to the defendant's fair trial rights, thereby contravening due process safeguards. Consequently, a balanced approach to disclosure is needed to make sure that the rights of complainants and defendants are properly protected. The reforms introduced in the 2017 Act provide a suitable regime to scaffold decision-making in this difficult area.

Reform: The New Regime for the Regulation of Disclosure of Counselling Records

[5–54] The 2017 Act inserts a new s 19A into the Criminal Evidence Act 1992, introducing a procedure for the regulation of disclosure of counselling

---

122 Cossins, "Contempt or Confidentiality?" (1996) 21 *Alternative Law Journal* 223, 227.

123 As a result of the "equality of arms" principle, the defence entitlement to disclosure can only be curtailed in limited circumstances and where this is strictly necessary: *Rowe and Davis v United Kingdom* (2000) 30 EHRR 1, para 54; *Dowsett v UK* (2004) 38 EHRR 845. These cases related to inter partes disclosure but the principled commitment to defendants' rights would apply equally to third-party disclosure.

124 Gotell, "Colonization through Disclosure: Confidential Records, Sexual Assault Complainants and Canadian Law" (2001) 10(3) *Social & Legal Studies* 315, 321.

125 *ibid.* Concerns are sometimes raised about the phenomenon of "false memory syndrome" whereby a patient's memory can be distorted by the counselling experience, leading them to be confused about a chain of events or to incorrectly identify their attacker.

records in sexual offence trials. This section of the Act is not yet commenced but its commencement has been highlighted as a priority in the *National Strategy for Women and Girls 2017-2020*.[126] For the purposes of s 19A, a "counselling record" is defined as:

> "... any record, or part of a record, made by any means, by a competent person[127] in connection with the provision of counselling[128] to a person in respect of whom a sexual offence is alleged to have been committed ('the complainant'), which the prosecutor has had sight of, or about which the prosecutor has knowledge, and in relation to which there is a reasonable expectation of privacy."[129]

The regime applies to trials for sexual offences listed in the Schedule of the Sex Offenders Act 2001.[130] In a trial for any of these offences, the prosecution must notify the defendant if a "counselling record" exists but must not disclose the content of the record without obtaining leave of the court via the new disclosure regime.[131] If the defendant wishes to gain access to the records, a "disclosure application" must be made in writing to the court.[132] This application must "provide particulars identifying the record **[5–55]**

---

[126] Department of Justice and Equality, *National Strategy for Women and Girls 2017-2020* (Department of Justice and Equality, Dublin, 2017), objective 5.8.

[127] "Competent person" means a person who has undertaken training or study or has experience relevant to the process of counselling.

[128] "Counselling" means listening to and giving verbal or other support or encouragement to a person, or advising or providing therapy or other treatment to a person (whether or not for remuneration).

[129] Criminal Evidence Act 1992, s 19A(1) (to be inserted by s 39 of the Criminal Law (Sexual Offences) Act 2017).

[130] This includes: rape; sexual assault (whether the offence of which the person was convicted was known by that name or by the name "indecent assault upon a female person" or "indecent assault upon a male person"); aggravated sexual assault; rape under s 4; incest; an offence under the Criminal Law (Sexual Offences) Act 2006; an offence under s 3 (buggery of persons under 17 years of age) or s 4 (gross indecency with males under 17 years of age) of the Act of 1993; an offence under s 5 of the Act of 1993 (protection of mentally impaired persons); offences under the Child Trafficking and Pornography Act, 1998; an offence under the Criminal Law (Human Trafficking) Act 2008 in so far as the offence is committed for the purposes of the sexual exploitation of a person; an offence under the provisions of the Criminal Law (Sexual Offences) Act 2017 (i.e. s 3 (obtaining, providing etc. a child for purpose of sexual exploitation); s 4 (invitation etc. to sexual touching); s 5 (sexual activity in presence of child); s 6 (causing child to watch sexual activity); s 7 (meeting child for purpose of sexual exploitation); s 8 (use of information and communication technology to facilitate sexual exploitation of child); s 21 (sexual act with protected person); s 22 (offence against relevant person by person in authority). Inchoate offences related to any of the offences on the list of offences in the schedule are also included.

[131] Criminal Evidence Act 1992, s 19A(2) (to be inserted by s 39 of the Criminal Law (Sexual Offences) Act 2017).

[132] *ibid*, s 19A(3).

sought" and state "the reasons grounding the application, including grounds relied on to establish that the record is likely to be relevant to an issue at trial".[133] Where the accused intends to make a disclosure application, the record-holder, the complainant and any other person to whom the accused believes the record relates must be notified of the intention to make the application.[134] The notification periods are not set out in the legislation but will be prescribed under the Rules of Court.[135] Disclosure applications must be made before the trial begins but a trial judge may permit the making of an application after the commencement of the trial where this is in the interests of justice.[136] It is noteworthy that the disclosure regime also applies to the prosecution. Where a disclosure application is not made by the accused and the prosecutor believes that it is in the interests of justice that the record should be disclosed, the prosecutor may make a disclosure application in writing to the court.[137] Should the prosecution opt to make a disclosure application, there is also a notification obligation on them, requiring them to notify the record-holder, the complainant, the accused and any other person to whom the prosecutor believe the counselling record relates.[138] The court may also, at any time, order that a disclosure order made by the defence or the prosecution be notified to any person to whom it is believed the counselling record may relate.[139] The inclusion of the prosecution within the disclosure regime is significant. Applying the s 19A scheme to both the prosecution and the defence is sensible as the same concerns about unwarranted use of these records (i.e. invasion of privacy and potential prejudice) applies whether the record is used by the defence or the prosecution.

[5–56] Once a valid application is received by the court, a hearing must be held to determine whether the record will be disclosed.[140] The procedure surrounding this hearing is similar to the current procedure for hearings relating to the admissibility of sexual experience evidence. The record-holder must provide the record to the court for examination.[141] The record-holder, the complainant and any other person to whom the record relates will be entitled to appear and be heard at this hearing.[142] The hearing will be in camera with "all persons, other than officers of the court, persons directly concerned in the hearing and such other persons (if any) as the court may

133 *ibid*, s 19A(3).
134 *ibid*, s 19A(4).
135 *ibid*, s 19A(4).
136 *ibid*, s 19A(14).
137 *ibid*, s 19A(5).
138 *ibid*, s 19A(6).
139 *ibid*, s 19A(7).
140 *ibid*, s 19A(8).
141 *ibid*, s 19A(8).
142 *ibid*, s 19A(9).

determine … excluded from the court".[143] As with the procedure for hearings regarding the admissibility of sexual experience evidence, the complainant will be entitled to legal aid for the purposes of obtaining representation for this hearing.[144] The trial judge has discretion whether to order disclosure but s/he is provided with some guidance on the exercise of this discretion in the form of a list of factors to be taken into account when deciding whether disclosure is warranted. These factors are as follows:

> (a) the extent to which the record is necessary for the accused to defend the charges against him;
> (b) the probative value of the record;
> (c) the reasonable expectation of privacy with respect to the record;
> (d) the potential prejudice to the right to privacy of any person to whom the record relates;
> (e) the public interest in encouraging the reporting of sexual offences;
> (f) the public interest in encouraging complainants of sexual offences to seek counselling;
> (g) the effect of the determination on the integrity of the trial process;
> (h) the likelihood that disclosing, or requiring the disclosure of, the record will cause harm to the complainant including the nature and extent of that harm.[145]

This list of considerations makes sure that the trial judge considers all the relevant rights and interests—not only of the complainant and the defendant in the case at hand, but also of wider societal interests before making a determination about disclosure. Once the judge has concluded the hearing and considered all of these factors, s/he may order disclosure of the content of the counselling record to the accused and the prosecutor where it is in the interests of justice to do so.[146] The court must order disclosure of the content of the counselling record to the accused "where there would be a real risk of an unfair trial in the absence of such disclosure".[147] **[5–57]**

The trial judge must provide reasons for his/her decision to grant or refuse disclosure.[148] If disclosure is granted, "in the interests of justice and to protect the right to privacy of any person to whom the counselling record relates, the court may impose any condition it considers necessary on the disclosure of the record".[149] To minimise the potential for invasion of privacy or prejudice for the complainant, one or more of the following conditions may be included in an order for disclosure: **[5–58]**

---

143 *ibid*, s 19A(15).
144 *ibid*, s 19A(16) (amending s 27 of the Civil Legal Aid Act 1995).
145 *ibid*, s 19A(10).
146 *ibid*, s 19A(11)(a).
147 *ibid*, s 19A(11)(b).
148 *ibid*, s 19A(13).
149 *ibid*, s 19A12(a).

(i) that a part of the content of the counselling record be redacted,
(ii) that a copy of the counselling record and not the original be disclosed,
(iii) that the accused and any legal representative for the accused not disclose the content of the counselling record to any person without leave of the court,
(iv) that the counselling record be viewed only at the offices of the court,
(v) that no copies, or only a limited number of copies, of the counselling record, be made,
(vi) that information concerning the address, telephone number or place of employment of any person named in the counselling record be redacted from the record,
(vii) that the counselling record be returned to the person who owns or controls the said record,
(viii) that the counselling record is used solely for the purposes of the criminal proceedings for which the record has been disclosed.[150]

[5–59] Section 19A provides a solid basis for effective regulation of the disclosure of counselling records in Irish sexual offence trials, filling a significant lacuna in the current law. Importantly, the provisions are balanced, protecting complainants' interests without compromising defendants' fair-trial rights. It is regrettable that the scheme only applies to counselling records and was not extended to cover all personal records. The Canadian Criminal Code protects the latter which is defined as including:

> "...any form of record that contains personal information for which there is a reasonable expectation of privacy and includes, without limiting the generality of the foregoing, medical, psychiatric, therapeutic, counselling, education, employment, child welfare, adoption and social services records, personal journals and diaries, and records containing personal information the production or disclosure of which is protected by any other Act of Parliament or a provincial legislature, but does not include records made by persons responsible for the investigation or prosecution of the offence."[151]

[5–60] Although this definition is broad-ranging, it provides maximum protection for complainants. The Irish reform will only apply to counselling relationships, meaning that records like social work files (which have been the subject of judgments already) will continue to be dealt with via the Memoranda of Understanding between the Office of the DPP and the HSE. For records which fall outside of these memoranda, uncertainty will prevail.

[5–61] Originally, the Sexual Offences Bill provided a list of assertions which would not be sufficient on their own to establish that the record "is likely to be relevant to an issue at trial or to the competence of a complainant or witness to testify". These included an assertion that the record:

[150] *ibid*, s 19A(11).
[151] Canadian Criminal Code, s 278.1.

(a) exists;
(b) relates to counselling the complainant has received or is receiving;
(c) relates to the incident which is the subject matter of the proceedings;
(d) may disclose a prior inconsistent statement of the complainant or witness;
(e) may relate to the credibility of the complainant or witness;
(f) may relate to the reliability of the testimony of the complainant only for the reason that the complainant has received or is receiving counselling;
(g) may disclose allegations of sexual abuse of the complainant by a person other than the accused;
(h) relates to the sexual activity of the complainant with any person, including the accused;
(i) relates to the presence or absence of a recent complaint;
(j) relates to the complainant's sexual reputation;
(k) was made close in time to a complaint or to the incident that forms the subject matter of charge against the accused.[152]

Regrettably, this provision was not included in the Act. Including a legislative prohibition on "forbidden reasoning" which may play into stereotypes about sexual offences or rape myths would have sent out a clear message about the appropriate uses for counselling records in sexual offence trials and offset the potential for spurious applications. **[5–62]**

Since it is possible for complainants to waive the application of the new provisions and voluntarily disclose their counselling records,[153] it is important that sound policies exist to ensure that complainants who opt to waive the application of the scheme are giving fully informed consent. A best practice guideline on this could be produced by the Office of the DPP. A final concern with the new scheme is to ensure that it is effective and that judges do not take an overly permissive approach in the exercise of their discretion. In Canada, judicial interpretation of s 278 of the Canadian Criminal Code (a provision upon which s 19A is largely based) has not been entirely progressive.[154] In *R v Mills*,[155] it was held that the list of factors which the court should consider when making a decision on disclosure (the same list as provided in s 19A) were only to be "taken into account" and that an in-depth analysis of each factor was not necessary.[156] Gotell has suggested that this judgment "transforms [these criteria] into a 'checklist' of various factors" which "may come into play during a judge's deliberation"[157] rather **[5–63]**

[152] Criminal Law (Sexual Offences) Bill 2015,s 19A(4).
[153] Criminal Evidence Act,1992,s 19A(17) (to be inserted by s 39 of the Criminal Law (Sexual Offences) Act 2017).
[154] Leahy, *supra* note 111, p 239.
[155] *R v Mills* [1999] 3 SCR 668.
[156] *ibid* at 675 and 753, respectively.
[157] Gotell, "The Ideal Victim, The Hysterical Complainant, and the Disclosure of Confidential Records: The Implications of the Charter for Sexual Assault Law" (2002) 40(3) *Osgoode Hall Law Journal* 251, 270.

than a "list of considerations to frame the analysis of likely relevance".[158] To avoid such problems arising with the equivalent Irish provisions, a requirement of written decisions could be introduced. This would ensure that judge's decisions give due attention to each of the factors as a failure to consider specific factors would be very evident in a written decision.

[5–64] Overall, the s 19A regime holds significant promise for protecting complainants from unwarranted and prejudicial use of their counselling records in sexual offence trials. Of course, much will depend on its effective implementation. Hopefully, progressive judicial interpretation of the provisions will ensure maximum protection for complainants while still protecting defendants' rights. In this way, the new provisions will serve as an important new element in the rules relating to character in sexual offence trials, fitting neatly within the existing provisions on sexual experience evidence. Now, having discussed the special rules on character evidence relating to the complainant in sexual offence trials, it is necessary to consider the rules of evidence relating to the character of the defendant. Although these rules are not specific to sexual offence trials, it is important to understand their role in light of the "oath against oath" nature of these cases.

Introducing Evidence of the Defendant's Previous Bad Character

[5–65] As noted above, there are no special rules relating to the issue of admissibility of the defendants' prior criminal record in sexual offence trials. This may be somewhat surprising considering the particular relevance of character in such cases. Below is an examination of the general rules applicable to bad character evidence, which are relevant to consider in the context of sexual offence cases also.

Similar Fact Evidence

[5–66] Similar fact evidence, or perhaps more accurately misconduct evidence,[159] is evidence of the accused's character that may be become admissible as part of the prosecution's case. While the general rule of evidence is that only relevant

[158] *ibid.* Although, research conducted by Gotell on the application of the s 278 regime has demonstrated that judicial interpretation of s 278 has undermined its effectiveness, there is also evidence of progressive applications of the provisions. See: Gotell, "The Ideal Victim, The Hysterical Complainant, and the Disclosure of Confidential Records: The Implications of the Charter for Sexual Assault Law" (2002) 40 *Osgoode Hall Law Journal* 251 and "Tracking Decisions on Access to Sexual Assault Complainants' Confidential Records" (2008) 20(1) *Canadian Journal of Women and the Law* 128.

[159] This terminological distinction was made in *R v Lewis* [1982] 76 Cr App R 33, 35.

evidence is deemed admissible at trial, evidence of previous misconduct may sometimes be considered relevant if it constitutes background evidence or similar fact evidence. The parameters of admissibility of such evidence is narrowly construed and there is a general exclusionary rule applicable. The Court in the case of *R v Bond*[160] acknowledged this general exclusionary rule when it comes to previous misconduct:

> "...the facts proved must be strictly relevant to the particular charge and have no reference to any conduct of the [accused] unconnected with such charge; therefore it is not allowable to show...that the prisoner has a general disposition to commit the same kind of offence as that for which he stands indicted..."

This sentiment has been reinforced in recent case law in Ireland. In the case of *People (DPP) v Murphy*[161] the Special Criminal Court emphasised that previous convictions should not be unjustifiably taken into consideration at trial and any conviction which follows upon the improper introduction of previous convictions cannot be considered as safe.[162] **[5–67]**

The evidence to be introduced does not necessarily have to be of a previous conviction. Prior misconduct that has not resulted in a conviction can also be covered under the rules discussed below. Mere bad character, however, is insufficient to justify admissibility, and the evidence must demonstrate something more than this. In modern trials misconduct evidence often becomes an issue when applications are made to sever an indictment in circumstances where there is more than one complainant. The relevant issue then becomes one of determining whether the evidence of each complainant is cross-admissible. Of course, evidence of character does not simply pertain to bad character. Evidence of good character has historically been considered relevant at a criminal trial, both in establishing the credibility of the accused and his propensity to commit the crime in question. While this is still permissible in Irish courts, introducing one's good character at trial may open the accused up to cross examination on previous convictions if they exist. This will be discussed further below. **[5–68]**

The seminal case which laid the foundations for the general exclusionary rule is the case of *Makin v Attorney General for New South Wales*.[163] The case involved a husband and wife convicted of murdering a baby they had **[5–69]**

---

160 *R v Bond* [1906] 2 KB 389, 397.

161 *People (DPP) v Murphy* [2005] 2 IR 125.

162 In this case the Special Criminal Court, in convicting the accused, had stated that his prior convictions were corroborative of the confession he had made. Evidence of the prior convictions had not been introduced by the prosecution, nor had they arisen under s 1(f) the Criminal Justice (Evidence) Act 1924.

163 *Makin v Attorney General for New South Wales* [1894] AC 57.

taken in, and the misconduct evidence related to the fact that the bodies of other babies, who had similarly been adopted by the accused had been found in the backyards of other houses occupied by the couple. It is Lord Herschell's statement in this case that provides the clearest expression for the exclusionary rule. He did not think it was proper

> "for the prosecution to adduce evidence tending to show that the accused has been guilty of criminal acts other than those covered by the indictment, for the purpose of leading to the conclusion that the accused is a person likely from his criminal conduct or character to have committed the offence for which he is being tried."[164]

[5–70] The rationale for this rule lies in the fear that the jury will resort to a form of reasoning which would be unduly prejudicial to the accused in the face of all the facts. This reasoning which has sometimes been referred to as propensity reasoning[165] is based on the concept that, rather than attribute to the accused a clean slate and judge him on the facts of the case alone, the jury will infer guilt from the evidence of past misconduct. However, in order to remedy the potential harshness and impracticality of an absolute exclusionary rule Lord Herschell determined that:

> "[t]he mere fact that the evidence adduced tends to show the commission of other crimes does not render it inadmissible if it be relevant to an issue before the jury, and it may be so relevant if it bears upon the question whether the acts alleged to constitute the crime charged in the indictment were designed or accidental, or to rebut a defence which would otherwise be open to the accused."[166]

[5–71] Thus, the evidence can be admitted if relevant to and probative of an issue other than mere propensity, but is excluded it if it is proffered for the latter reason alone. In *Makin* the evidence was relevant as it rebutted a defence of accidental death, and was therefore admissible.

[5–72] The principles set down in Makin have been endorsed in the Irish context in

---

164 *ibid*, 65, per Lord Herschell CJ.

165 See Acorn, "Similar Fact Evidence and the Principle of Inductive Reasoning: Makin Sense" (1991) 11(1) *Oxford Journal of Legal Studies* 63, 94–95.

166 *Makin v Attorney General for New South Wales* [1894] AC 57, 65, per Lord Herschell.

cases such as *People (AG) v Kirwan*[167] and *Attorney General v Fleming*[168] which seemed to endorse the categorical approach to determining relevance and thus admissibility suggested in the *Makin* judgment. Later Courts became dissatisfied with this approach and instead focused upon the balancing exercise formulated in the case of *DPP v Boardman*.[169] In the case the appellant was a headmaster who had been convicted of offences of attempted buggery and incitement to commit buggery with two pupils. The count of buggery and one of the counts of incitement bore a number of similarities. The trial judge had allowed all the counts to be considered together as the evidence was mutually corroborative. The House of Lords affirmed this decision. The Court accepted the traditional exclusionary rule stating that the rationale,

> "... is not that the law regards such evidence as inherently irrelevant, but because it is believed that if it were generally admissible jurors would in many cases think that it was more relevant than it was, and that, as it is put, its prejudicial effect would outweigh its probative value."[170]

Lord Wilberforce then expressed the task for the Court: **[5–73]**

> "In each case it is necessary to estimate (i) whether and if so how strongly the evidence as to other facts tends to support, i.e. make more credible the evidence given as to the fact in question; and (ii) whether such evidence if given is likely to be prejudicial to the accused. Both these elements involve questions of degree."[171]

Thus, in order to be admitted, the similar fact evidence requires a strong degree of probative force. The task of determining the weight of the evidence inevitably falls to the judge. Lord Wilberforce also placed place heavy emphasis upon the "striking similarity" of the previous misconduct but the necessity of this remained questionable and was comprehensively rejected in the case of *DPP v P*.[172] The appellant was convicted of rape and incest of his two daughters. The Court of Appeal quashed the convictions on the grounds that the trial judge should have ordered separate trials. The House **[5–74]**

---

[167] *People (AG) v Kirwan* [1943] IR 279. In this case the accused was charged with murder and dismemberment of the body. Medical evidence was that only someone who had the relevant anatomical skill and knowledge could have dismembered the body in such a way. Evidence of three prison staff was admitted which revealed that the accused had such skill. This revealed to the jury that the accused had a criminal record but was considered incidental to the purpose of admitting the evidence.

[168] *Attorney General v Fleming* [1934] IR 166, where evidence of a prior attempt to poison was admitted at the trial for murder to show malice.

[169] *DPP v Boardman* [1975] AC 421.

[170] *ibid*, per Lord Cross.

[171] *ibid*, 896.

[172] *DPP v P* [1991] 2 AC 447.

of Lords allowed the prosecution's appeal and restored the convictions. On the issue of "striking similarity" the Court, per Lord Mackay determined that it is not appropriate to single out "striking similarity" as an essential element in every case, and that doing so would be to "restrict the operation of the principle in a way which gives too much effect to a particular manner of stating it."[173] The striking similarities in the various charges may indeed be a relevant factor, but confining the probative force of the evidence to such a factor would be inappropriate. The essential principle must always be that, in order to justify admitting the evidence, its probative force must be "sufficiently great to make it just to admit the evidence, notwithstanding that it is prejudicial to the accused in tending to show that he was guilty of another crime".[174]

[5–75] The Irish courts have also endorsed the balancing exercise as the authoritative approach to determining admissibility in this jurisdiction. Rather than adhere to the restrictive categorical approach premised upon specific categories of relevance, the trial judge is required to determine the probative value of the evidence and evaluate whether its probative value outweighs its prejudicial effect. In *DPP v Keogh*[175] the court expressly refused to admit the evidence in question stating that "evidence of character or of previous convictions shall not be given at a criminal trial except at the instigation of the accused." Kelly J considered the evidence was on the one hand probatively "vague and imprecise" and on the other hand highly prejudicial, since it was extremely difficult to rebut. In *People (DPP) v DO'S*[176] Hardiman J concluded that the misconduct evidence adduced was used deliberately and exclusively to establish the appellant's disposition and had little, if any, probative value. This case will be discussed in greater detail below. In *B v DPP*[177] Budd J cited *Boardman* with approval saying the "basic principle must be that the admission of similar fact evidence ... is exceptional and requires a strong degree of probative force."[178] In the case the evidence of sexual abuse against his daughters was cross-admissible in the accused's trial as the evidence was strikingly similar and of exceptional probative force. The judge in referring to the case of *DPP v P* also affirmed that the element of "striking similarity" was not essential in every case although it may be of strong probative force in some, particularly where the accused faces multiple accusations.[179]

---

173 *ibid*, 460, per Lord Mackay.

174 *ibid.*

175 *DPP v Keogh* [1998] 4 IR 416.

176 *People (DPP) v DO'S*, unreported, Court of Criminal Appeal, 28 July 2004.

177 *B v DPP* [1997] 3 IR 140.

178 *ibid* per Budd J, quoting Lord Wilberforce in *Boardman* (at 444).

179 Where there are multiple accusations Budd J felt that a trial judge must ensure that the jury considers and eliminates the possibility of collusion and must provide a careful warning to the jury in this regard (at 157–158). See also Maher, "Development in

In the case of *People v BK*[180] the applicant was convicted on several counts of attempted buggery and indecent assaults against a number of young boys in his care. He appealed on the basis that each count should have been tried separately. In allowing the appeal and quashing the convictions, the Court of Criminal Appeal determined that the test as to whether to sever the counts was whether each count could be admissible on the other and in doing so the Court would invoke the balancing test. The Court concluded that there were material differences in the evidence in relation to the boy in the dormitory and the alleged offences of the other two boys.[181] Thus the evidence was not cross-admissible and trying all the counts together had created unfair prejudice, resulting in an unsatisfactory trial. The alleged offences of the other two boys, in the caravan, were cross-admissible in relation to each other as they were alleged to have been committed in unusual but identical circumstances." Barron J thus felt the overall similarities "were sufficient to make a jury question as to whether the offence alleged on each count had been committed."[182] **[5–76]**

When various counts are tried together, as is often the case in sexual abuse cases, the possibility of collusion is something about which the Irish courts must be vigilant. In deciding whether to sever the indictments the trial judge must essentially consider whether the different counts are cross-admissible.[183] Moreover, to be successful in an application for severance the defence must show that the concerns for the accused's right to a fair trial outweigh the goals of joinder. The probative value of the evidence of multiple complainants must be determined and the court should be satisfied that collusion or unconscious influence of one witness by another has not occurred. Budd J in *B v DPP* expressed the sentiment of the Irish courts well when he stated: **[5–77]**

> "... the mere existence of multiple accusations of similar offences does not mean that the evidence will be admissible as it is still essential that there should be a sufficient degree of probative force to overcome the prejudicial effect of such evidence. Whether the accounts of each of several complainants are corroborative and also the risk of collusion, either by conspiracy or where one witness has been unconsciously influenced by another, may well be relevant factors at the trial. It seems that the underlying principle is that the

Bad Character Evidence: Undermining the Accused's Shield" (2007) 14(1) *Dublin University Law Journal* 57, 68.

180 *DPP v BK* [2000] 2 IR 199.

181 The court considered that to allow two counts relating to different boys to be tried together would be de facto to provide corroboration of the charges against him where there was none in law.

182 *DPP v BK* [2000] 2 IR 199, 210–11, per Barron J .

183 Often the view is that the fact that there are multiple counts is in itself probative and as long as the counts are cross-admissible then they may be tried together.

> probative value of multiple accusations may depend in part on their similarity, but also on the unlikelihood that the same person would find himself falsely accused on various occasions by different and independent individuals. The making of multiple accusations is a coincidence in itself, which has to be taken into account in deciding admissibility."[184]

[5–78] In *People (DPP) v McCurdy*[185] the Court of Criminal Appeal added that it is,

> "for the trial judge to determine, and instruct the jury, whether particular evidence is capable of being corroborative. It must then be for the jury...to decide, as a matter of fact, whether the evidence is actually corroborative in the circumstances of the particular case."

[5–79] The issue arose again in the case of *People (DPP) v LG*[186] The applicant had been convicted of rape and indecent assault of his sister between the years 1973 and 1978. He was also convicted of assaulting another sister sometime between 1974 and 1976. The Central Criminal Court refused him leave to appeal on the grounds that there should have been separate trials in respect of each complainant. Keane CJ noted that counsel for the accused accepted that it was within the discretion of the trial judge to decide whether or not to order separate trials. However, it was submitted that:

> "... in the present case the evidence in respect of the counts concerning the first complainant would not be evidence in respect of the count concerning the second complainant and *vice versa* ... in such circumstances, there was a danger that the jury would have regard to the cumulative effect of evidence in respect of offences of the same character. Alternatively, it was submitted that, if the counts were not severed, it was incumbent on the trial judge to give a clear direction to the jury that they should consider the counts in respect of the first complainant on the one hand and the count in respect of the second complainant on the other hand separately.....no such direction had been given in the present case."

[5–80] The Court determined that the evidence of the two complainants were cross-admissible and in this regard the trial judge was entitled to exercise his discretion to refuse the application for separate trials. However, Keane CJ found that

> "[t]he trial judge at no stage in the course of his charge expressly directed the jury that they should consider the evidence in support of the counts in respect of the two complainants separately and arrive at their conclusions in respect of each complainant's version of events separately."

---

184 *B v DPP* [1997] 3 IR 140, 157–8, per Budd J.
185 *People (DPP) v McCurdy* [2012] IECCA 76.
186 *People (DPP) v LG* [2003] 2 IR 517.

For this reason the Court treated the leave for appeal as the appeal and set aside the convictions. [5–81]

In the case of *The People (DPP) v TC*[187] the applicant was charged with 15 counts of rape and sexual assault in relation to three complainants, and was sentenced to a total of 14 years' imprisonment with the last year suspended. One of the grounds of appeal was that the trial judge had erred in law in failing to sever all the counts, thereby unduly prejudicing his defence. The Court of Criminal Appeal held that the issue of severance is a matter of judicial discretion in any particular case and in the circumstances they were satisfied with the decision of the trial judge in this regard.[188] [5–82]

In the case of *DPP v Mc Neill*,[189] the indictment contained eight counts of sexual abuse that had occurred over a number of years (of which the accused was convicted of seven). The Supreme Court had to consider whether background evidence of ongoing abuse allegedly inflicted by the appellant upon the complainant was admissible as being relevant to the jury's understanding of the case, albeit that the evidence was possibly prejudicial to the accused. The majority of the Court held that the evidence had been correctly disclosed and that background evidence could be admitted if it was relevant and necessary.[190] Moreover the Court, perhaps taking a somewhat liberal approach, felt that the absence of specific directions to the jury did not render the trial unsafe or unfair.[191] Thus it seems that if misconduct evidence is relevant in order to ensure the jury's comprehension of the counts in issue, this is also a valid reason for permitting the evidence. [5–83]

Cross-Examination of the Accused

The rules and principles governing cross-examination are different to similar fact evidence, largely due to the fact that the former is a creature of statute. The Criminal Law (Evidence) Act 1924 is the governing legislation that dictates the exclusion and admissibility of past conviction evidence under cross examination. It has been observed that "[f]or an accused, the strategic importance of the decision whether or not to take the stand cannot be [5–84]

[187] *People (DPP) v TC*, unreported, Court of Criminal Appeal, 23 June 2009.

[188] The convictions were quashed on another argument in relation to non-disclosure of a previous abuse of the complainant.

[189] *DPP v McNeill* [2011] IESC 11.

[190] This is arguably a lower standard than the high probative value required under the *Boardman* principle.

[191] Fennelly J dissented and commented that the test of helpfulness to the jury was much less strict than admissibility and relevancy and stressed that there must be a fair balance between realistic presentation of the prosecution case and the right of the accused to a fair trial.

overstated."[192] This is because testifying consequently invokes the right to cross-examine. The relevant section is s 1 of the Criminal Justice (Evidence) Act 1924 which provides as follows:

> "1.—Every person charged with an offence ... shall be a competent witness for the defence at every stage of the proceedings, whether the person so charged is charged solely or jointly with any other person: Provided as follows:—
> (*a*) a person so charged shall not be called as a witness in pursuance of this Act except upon his own application:
> (*b*) the failure of any person charged with an offence....to give evidence shall not be made the subject of any comment by the prosecution:......
> (*e*) a person charged and being a witness in pursuance of this Act may be asked any question in cross-examination notwithstanding that it would tend to criminate him as to the offence charged ...".

[5–85] Cross-examining an accused who testifies is not an unfettered process, however, whereby the prosecution can interrogate the individual in whatever manner and on whatever topic they please. First and foremost, the questioning must be relevant to a fact in issue.[193] This principle operates for all types of evidence sought to be admitted. In relation to evidence of bad character of the accused specifically there is a general exclusionary rule under s 1(f) of the Act:

> "(*f*) a person charged and called as a witness in pursuance of this Act shall not be asked, and if asked shall not be required to answer, any question tending to show that he has committed or been convicted of or been charged with any offence other than that wherewith he is then charged, or is of bad character ..."

[5–86] The primary effect of s 1(f) is to limit the scope of s 1(e), and act as a shield for the accused. Thus generally speaking cross examination may not cover issues that would be likely to expose the accused's bad character criminal. The rationale is primarily that past convictions are irrelevant and would be overtly prejudicial. Traditionally speaking the Irish Judiciary have maintained a protective stance towards upholding this shield. McWilliam J presented the view in *King v AG*[194] that,

> "one of the concepts of justice which the courts have always accepted is that evidence of character or of previous convictions shall not be given at a

---

[192] Heffernan, *Evidence: Cases and Materials* (Thomson Round Hall, Dublin, 2005), p 62.

[193] In *Maxwell v Director of Public Prosecutions* [1935] AC 309, Viscount Sankey emphasised that (on losing the shield) the accused could only be asked questions which were "relevant and admissible."

[194] *King v Attorney General* [1981] IR 233.

criminal trial except at the instigation of the accused, as that could prejudice the fair trial of the issue of the guilt or innocence of the accused."

In the case of *People (DPP) v Kelly*[195] the accused appealed his conviction for various offences relating to drug possession on the grounds that the prosecution had contravened s 1 (f) by cross-examining him in a way that suggested he had committed previous offences. The Court of Criminal Appeal found that the prosecution had used questioning on a specific amount of money to launch into a prolonged investigation of the character of the applicant. It was held that the overall purpose and tenor of the cross-examination was to establish a suspicion that the accused was dealing illegal drugs, and that in doing so the questioning infringed the provisions of s 1 (f). **[5–87]**

Losing the Shield

The proviso in s 1 (f) applies unless s 1(f) (i), (ii) or (iii) apply. In accordance with these subsections, an accused may be cross-examined on previous convictions where: **[5–88]**

> "(i) the proof that he has committed or been convicted of such other offence is admissible evidence to show that he is guilty of the offence wherewith he is then charged; or
> (ii) he has personally or by his advocate asked questions of the witnesses for the prosecution with a view to establish his own good character, or has given evidence of his good character, or the nature or conduct of the defence is such as to involve imputations on the character of the prosecutor or the witnesses for the prosecution; or
> (iii) he has given evidence against any other person charged with the same offence."

This section is amended by s 33 of the Criminal Procedure Act 2010, which inserts the following into s 1(f): **[5–89]**

> "(iiia) the person has personally or by the person's advocate asked questions of any witness for the purpose of making, or the conduct of the defence is such as to involve, imputations on the character of a person in respect of whom the offence was alleged to have been committed and who is deceased or is so incapacitated as to be unable to give evidence."

Section 33(b) of the 2010 Act also inserts a new provision, s 1A, to the effect that where the defence intends to make imputations on the character of a prosecution witness or a person in respect of whom the offence is alleged to have been committed and who is either deceased or so incapacitated, at **[5–90]**

---

[195] *People (DPP) v Kelly*, unreported, Court of Criminal Appeal, 21 March 2002.

least seven days' notice must be given to the prosecution of that intention.[196] This new section also provides that the accused may be called as a witness and be asked, and the prosecution may ask any other witness, questions that reveal the accused's past convictions or bad character,[197] or questions that show he is of good character.[198] This represents quite a change to the traditional approach of only allowing cross-examination as to character when the accused chooses to take the stand himself.

[5–91] The primary rationale behind the inclusion of bad character evidence lies in rebutting a favourable impression adduced by the defence. On the one hand introducing evidence of the individual's past record may create irreparable prejudice against him. On the other hand, an unyielding rule of exclusion might unwittingly permit the accused to abuse the shield, by giving the jury an unrealistically favourable image of himself. Under s 1(f)(i) an accused may be examined with regard to past offences where misconduct evidence has already been deemed admissible as evidence in chief. Cross-examination thus enables the prosecution to clarify issues raised earlier in the trial, by eliciting information directly from the accused.[199] Evidence adduced under this proviso may be admissible as proof of the accused's guilt, which distinguishes it from evidence adduced under the other provisos of s 1(f).

[5–92] Under s 1(f)(ii) an accused who seeks to admit evidence of his good character or seeks to cast imputations on the character of a witnesses for the prosecution, will lose the shield. The evidence must be elicited for the express purpose of demonstrating the accused's credibility and may not be adduced for the purpose of being probative of any other issue at trial. If the accused seeks to assert his good character or discredit the character of witnesses then the prosecution should be entitled to tender counter-evidence. The evidence cannot, however, be used to infer that the accused is guilty of the crime with which he is charged.[200] The shield is lost where the accused or his counsel seek to establish his good character, and since the 2010 amendments this applies to asking questions of "any witness"

---

[196] Alternatively, an application must be made to the Court citing the reasons why it is not possible to give the notice, and the defendant must be granted leave to do so.

[197] Criminal Procedure Act 2010, s 1(b)(i).

[198] *ibid*, s 1(b)(ii).

[199] If an accused chooses to testify then he automatically becomes open to cross-examination under s 1(f)(i) as this section is not dependent upon a loss of the shield arising from the conduct of the defence.

[200] In *Maxwell v DPP* [1935] AC 309, Viscount Sankey LC stated that "the question whether a man has been convicted, charged or acquitted ought not to be admitted, even if it goes to credibility, if there is any risk of the jury being misled into thinking that it goes not to credibility but to the probability of his having committed the offence of which he is charged": *ibid*, 321.

not just "witnesses for the prosecution."[201] Traditionally, evidence of good character which emerged during cross-examination of a defence witness by the prosecution, or which was volunteered by the witness, would not lead to loss of the shield. It seems this will remain the case unless s 1A applies.

With regard to the second limb of s 1(f)(ii), imputations on the character of a witness, the Irish courts have opted for a purposive approach in that the accused will not lose the shield if imputations made on the character of a witness are necessary for the proper conduct of a defence. The right to cross-examine prosecution witnesses is deeply engrained in our Constitution and falls within the parameters of the right to a fair trial. Counsel for the defence must be able to challenge the veracity of the State's case against the accused and cross-examination plays a vital role in this.[202] Vigorous cross-examination, aimed at exposing weaknesses, inaccuracies or even improper conduct, may often involve an imputation against a prosecution witness. If s 1(f) (ii) were to be invoked in all such circumstances this could severely inhibit the accused's ability to mount a defence and would thus impinge upon his right to a fair trial. In *DPP v McGrail*[203] the Court of Criminal Appeal, per Hederman J felt that the principles of fair procedure must apply. In the case, defence counsel for the applicant, had cross-examined the arresting Gardaí, who denied that they had invented the incriminating statements allegedly made by the accused, as well as other incriminating evidence. The trial judge held that this questioning had cast imputations on the character of the prosecution witnesses and permitted cross-examination of the accused as to his previous convictions. The Court of Criminal Appeal, in quashing the conviction and ordering a retrial, acknowledged that: **[5–93]**

> "[e]very criminal trial involves an imputation as to the character of someone. The mere fact that an accused is accused of a criminal offence ... is in effect an imputation against the character of the accused. If the accused, either by giving evidence or through his counsel's cross-examination of the witnesses

[201] In the case of *People (DPP) v Ferris*, unreported, Court of Criminal Appeal, 10 June 2002, the Court held that the accused should not have been cross-examined in relation to pornographic material found in his apartment. In the case it was a witness for the defence who asserted his good character, and not a witness for the prosecution as required under s 1(f)(ii). This case may now be considered in light of the amendments made under the Criminal Procedure Act 2010 (s. 33).

[202] The Criminal Law (Sexual Offences) Act 2017, aims to limit the scope of cross-examination by the accused of minors who give evidence in certain sexual offence cases. In announcing the Bill the then Minister for Justice stated that this was in order to "protect child victims of sexual offences from any additional trauma which may arise as a result of giving evidence..." Department of Justice and Equality "Minster Fitzgerald publishes the Criminal Law (Sexual Offences) Bill 2015" *Press Release*. Available at: http://www.justice.ie/en/JELR/Pages/PR15000487 (last accessed: 25 August 2017).

[203] *DPP v McGrail* [1990] 2 IR 38.

> for the prosecution, suggests to them that they are not to be believed, that is also an imputation as to their character in as much as it is suggested that they are telling an untruth ... A distinction must be drawn between questions and suggestions which are reasonably necessary to establish either the prosecution case or the defence case ... A procedure which inhibits an accused from challenging the veracity of the evidence against him at the risk of having his own previous character put in evidence is not a fair procedure. The gratuitous introduction of material by way of cross-examination or otherwise to show that the witness for the prosecution has a general bad character, divorced from the facts of the case at hearing, is a different matter."[204]

[5–94] Thus, in a criminal trial an accused is entitled to strenuously deny the charge against him and this even extends to imputations on the character of prosecution witnesses, so long as such is considered reasonably necessary for the defence to put in issue the truth of the evidence of a prosecution witness. When imputations reach beyond the facts of the particular case, the shield is lost, unless judicial discretion prohibits cross-examination in the interests of justice.

[5–95] In the context of a rape trial, imputations upon the complainant's character may be presented in challenge to the allegation of rape. Arguing that the complainant consented to the sexual encounter, in so far as it alleges that she is lying, is essentially an imputation on her character. However, it is accepted in Ireland that alleging consent does not lead to loss of the shield.[205] It would be impossible to for an accused to mount a defence if to simply deny the charge against them could lead to loss of the shield.[206] As the court in the case of *R v Sheean*[207] observed however, if the accused "goes out of his way to make an attack on the [complainant] based on matters outside the substance of the charge upon which he is being tried, it is otherwise."[208]

[5–96] The final circumstances under which the shield afforded by s 1(f)(iii) can be lost is where the accused testifies against a co-accused. The rationale behind this exception provision is centred on the gravity of the situation an accused finds himself in when his co-accused testifies against him. As a result, the trial judge retains no discretion to prevent cross-examination under this proviso. Cross-examination is permitted for the purpose of attesting to the accused's credibility. The provision only operates where the co-accused has

---

204 *ibid*, 48–51.

205 See the dicta of Hederman J in *People (DPP) v McGrail* [1990] 2 IR 38.

206 O'Malley notes that another explanation is that consent is not a defence to a rape charge per se. Rather it is the absence of consent which is the essential element of establishing the offence, and it is the prosecution who bear the burden of establishing this element. O'Malley, *supra* note 15, p 479.

207 *R v Sheean* (1908) 21 Cox CC 561, 562.

208 This was also reinforced by the Court of Criminal Appeal in *People (DPP) v McGrail* [1990] 2 IR 38.

been charged with the same offence and does not apply where a co-accused charged in the same proceedings but not jointly for the same offence gives evidence against his co-accused. In the case of *Murdoch v Taylor*[209] the House of Lords made it clear that the exception will only apply where an accused gives evidence which is adverse to his co-accused's defence, and not where the evidence merely inconveniences or contradicts the others defence.[210] Thus the incriminating evidence must be evidence probative of a fact in issue, leading the jury to use the information as proof of guilt

Judicial Discretion

It is for the trial judge to decide the circumstances which cause the accused to lose the shield under s 1(f). The question of whether he has raised the issue of his good character or made imputations, for example, depends very much on the nature of the evidence given and the circumstances of the case. Furthermore, even if the shield has technically been lost, the trial judge retains discretion as to whether to permit cross-examination of the accused on bad character.[211] In exercising his/her discretion the trial judge must consider the importance of a fair trial for both sides and must ultimately decide whether the evidence is of greater probative or prejudicial value. Improper examination of the past convictions of an accused would not be in the interests of justice, but neither would it be just to permit the accused to demolish the character and integrity of a witness (especially a victim) without any risk of compromise. If the latter case were allowed then the accused would be in a disproportionately more advantageous position than other witnesses. The case of *People (DPP) v Do*[212] is illustrative of the judicial adherence to principles of fairness and balance at trial. The case involved cross-examination of the accused tending towards establishing criminal disposition. The past behaviour alluded to however was not that for which the accused had been subject to conviction or even charged.[213] The cross-examination was instead on the basis that his involvement with a scouting movement was part of the "profile" of a sexual deviant.[214] Such **[5–97]**

---

209 *Murdoch v Taylor* [1965] AC 574.

210 An example of where the accused's testimony against his co-accused did not invoke the exception under this section is *R v Kirkpatrick* [1998] Crim LR 63. In that case the accused gave evidence that he had been asleep at the time of the offence, while his co-accused's defence was that he had intervened to prevent the commission of the offence. The court held that the testimony did not have the effect of supporting the prosecution's case and thus cross-examination was not permitted of the accused.

211 *R v Selvey* [1970] AC 304; *People (DPP) v McGrail* [1990] 2 IR 38.

212 *People (DPP) v Do* [2006] 2 ILRM 61.

213 Similar fact evidence was introduced as evidence in chief which consisted of two charges of sexual assault that had been severed from the indictment. The accused was later acquitted of these charges but the Supreme Court did not find it necessary to rule specifically on this aspect of the appeal.

214 The three justifications offered by the prosecution for the questioning were references

questioning the Supreme Court found to be entirely irrelevant and unmerited. In allowing the appeal and quashing the conviction, the Court unanimously decided that the jury had been improperly influenced by the prejudicial questioning and innuendos that had no admissible or evidential basis.

The Issue with Character: Jury Prejudice

[5–98] One of the perceived dangers of introducing evidence of previous bad character is that the jury may place undue weight upon the importance of such evidence.[215] It is considered important that the accused "starts his life afresh when he stands before a jury."[216] Studies have demonstrated that knowledge of the bad character of an accused can increase the likelihood of a conviction for the offence tried. Sally Lloyd-Bostock's study of mock juries in 2000 concluded that "evidence of previous convictions can have a prejudicial effect, especially where there is a recent previous conviction for a similar offence."[217] The study revealed a decrease in conviction where the previous offence was dissimilar in all instances except where the previous conviction was for indecent assault on a child. In the latter circumstances, Lloyd-Bostock observed that "a previous conviction for indecently assaulting a child ... produces a consistent and for some offences statistically significant increase in ratings of likelihood that he would commit dissimilar offences."[218] Other studies have also resulted in similar findings. A study conducted at Oxford[219] revealed that participants rated the accused more likely to have committed the crime where they were given evidence of a past similar offence. However, they regarded the accused as less likely to have committed the current offence where the past offence was not the same. While the usefulness of such mock jury studies is obviously limited, they nonetheless provide an important insight into the impact of bad character evidence. They also go some way towards reinforcing the important role of the trial judge in directing the jury as to the purpose of the evidence and possibly excluding the evidence even where the shield has technically been

---

to the appellant's involvement in scouting, reference that he was unmarried and references to his heterosexual orientation.

215 Jury prejudice is not always the issue however, as demonstrated in the case of *People (DPP) v Murphy* [2005] 2 IR 125 (above).

216 *People v Zackowitz* (1930) 172 NE 466, 466, per Cardozo CJ.

217 Lloyd-Bostock, "The Effects in Juries of Hearing about the Defendant's Previous Criminal Record: A Simulation Study" [2000] *Criminal Law Review* 734, 753.

218 *ibid*, 748–49.

219 Law Commission, Consultation Paper No 141, *Criminal Law – Evidence in Criminal Proceedings: Previous Misconduct of a Defendant* (Home Office, London, 1996).

lost.[220] Kennedy J put it in the case of *R v Bond*,[221] "nothing can so certainly be counted upon to make a prejudice against an accused upon his trial as the disclosure to the jury of other misconduct." While jury prejudice may indeed be an issue, O'Malley points out that the focus upon the jury, ignores the "awkward reality that in courts of summary jurisdiction ... judges ... will often, and inevitably, be very familiar with the criminal records of those appearing before them."[222] Where the judge is also the fact-finder, it is more difficult to ascertain how evidence of prior convictions will impact upon the decision in the case. Although there may be bias as a result of such knowledge, it would be impractical to prevent a judge who knows the criminal background of the accused from hearing a case.[223]

A Nexus between the Two Types of Character Evidence

It is interesting to note that despite the importance of character evidence to both complainants and defendants in sexual offence trials, in Ireland, there is no nexus between the introduction of the two types of evidence. Schemes have been established in other jurisdictions, Scotland for example[224], tying the two types of character evidence together in terms of relevance and admissibility. Creating such a link has been subject to some criticism and the practicable effect upon trial procedure has not been uncomplicated. Given the special nature of sexual offence trials, however, there is an argument to be made that linking these two types of evidence may be worth considering in this jurisdiction in the future. The scope of such a link would require careful consideration, being mindful of the need to avoid unduly prejudicing either party in a case. [5–99]

[220] Although the purpose of the evidence is to assess credibility, rather than establish the accused's guilt for the offence charged, it may be difficult for the jury to separate out these two rationales in their deliberations. Lane LCJ in the case of *R v Watts* [1983] 3 All ER 101, acknowledged this difficulty and referred to it as "intellectual acrobatics": *ibid*, 104.

[221] *R v Bond* [1906] 2 KB 389, 395-96.

[222] O'Malley, *supra* note 15, 467.

[223] See also the dicta of Smyth J in *DPP (Stratford) v O'Neill* [1998] 2 IR 383.

[224] See s 274 and s 275 of the Criminal Procedure (Scotland) Act 1995, as amended by the Sexual Offences (Procedure and Evidence) (Scotland) Act 2002.

Chapter Six

Corroboration and the Doctrine of Recent Complaint

Introduction

Carline and Easteal suggest that nowhere is the influence of myths regarding the credibility of sexual assault complainants "more explicit than with regards to corroboration warnings and recent complaint testimony".[1] These related but distinct rules form a cornerstone of the special rules of evidence which apply in sexual offence trials. Although both arguably continue to serve an important function in modern sexual offences law, they are rooted in historically prejudicial attitudes about sexual offence complainants. The original incarnation of the corroboration warning is related to the fear of false allegations and ancient suspicions about the veracity of sexual offence complainants, requiring trial judges to warn a jury about the dangers of convicting on a complainant's uncorroborated word. The doctrine of recent complaint has similar origins, hailing from the requirement that a complainant raise immediate "hue and cry" after an alleged attack if she was to be believed, permitting evidence of such swift complaints to support her testimony at trial. Of course, the modern incarnations of both rules are considerably more nuanced than their original forms but their shared origins make it logical to discuss them together in this chapter, which will describe in detail the law relating to both corroboration and recent complaint, as well as relevant contemporary critiques and reform proposals. [6–01]

Corroboration

Generally, all witnesses in criminal trials are deemed competent to testify to matters that are within their own knowledge. The evidence of one witness, if believed, is sufficient to support a guilty verdict. Nonetheless, in certain circumstances, the evidence of a lone witness may be seen as potentially unreliable and consequently, corroboration may be sought. Corroboration is evidence "which is independent of that evidence which requires corroboration and … which connects the accused or which tends [6–02]

1 Carline and Easteal, *Shades of Grey – Domestic and Sexual Violence Against Women: Law Reform and Society*, (Routledge: Oxon, 2014), p 170

to connect him with the offence in question".[2] Sexual offence complainants were one category of witness whose evidence was traditionally thought to require corroboration. The reasons for this were based on both the "oath against oath" nature of sexual offence trials[3] and a belief that allegations of sexual offences were easily made but difficult to disprove.[4] Because of these difficulties, a common law rule developed requiring the judge in a sexual offence trial to warn the jury of the dangers of convicting on the uncorroborated evidence of a complainant. The genesis of this special rule is explained well in *People (DPP) v Slavotic*[5]:

> "…in most if not all of the cases involving the commission of sexual offences, clearly a very great number of them, the issue of guilt or innocence of the accused has to be determined by reference to the evidence of two people, one of them the Complainant and one of them the accused person, and … typically … the events take place in secret or in private … That is the reason why historically the courts have developed the rule that in order that a person could be convicted of a sexual offence, the jury should be directed by the trial judge that it is dangerous for them to so convict unless there was corroboration, that is, that there should be independent evidence to connect the accused with the commission of the crime and that the particular crime had been committed."

[6–03] The mandatory corroboration warning rule was criticised by the Law Reform Commission (LRC) who noted that it was unduly restrictive and superfluous, and had the propensity to raise unnecessary doubts in the minds of jurors.[6] The LRC recommended that the corroboration warning should no longer be mandatory and that the decision whether to give a warning should be left to the discretion of the trial judge. This recommendation was enacted in s 7(1) of the Criminal Law (Rape) (Amendment) Act 1990, which provides that:

> "… where at the trial on indictment of a person charged with an offence of a sexual nature evidence is given by the person in relation to whom the offence is alleged to have been committed and, by reason only of the nature of the charge, there would, but for this section, be a requirement that the jury be given a warning about the danger of convicting the person on the uncorroborated evidence of that other person, it shall be for the judge to

---

2 Walsh, *Walsh on Criminal Procedure* (2nd ed, Round Hall, Dublin, 2016), p 1,276.

3 Due to the nature of sexual crimes, which usually occur in private settings, there are often no witnesses and little independent evidence. Therefore, the evidence in these cases usually boils down to one person's word against another's.

4 Hale noted that an accusation of a sexual offence is one which is "easily to be made and hard to be proved and harder to be defended by the party accused, tho' never so innocent": Hale, *Pleas of the Crown, Vol. 1*, p 633.

5 Unreported, Court of Criminal Appeal, 18 November 2002.

6 Law Reform Commission, *Report on Rape and Allied Offences* (Law Reform Commission, Dublin, 1990), para. 30

> decide in his discretion, having regard to all the evidence given, whether the jury should be given the warning ..."

Section 7 does not abolish the corroboration warning. It gives the trial judge discretion to decide, in light of the evidence, if a warning is warranted. To explain the operation of the corroboration warning in Ireland, it is necessary to discuss what constitutes corroboration and the interpretation of s 7 by the courts. **[6–04]**

What Constitutes Corroboration in a Sexual Offence Case?

In *R v Baskerville*,[7] corroboration was generally defined as: **[6–05]**

> "independent testimony which affects the accused by connecting or tending to connect him with the crime. In other words it must be evidence which implicates him, that is, which confirms in some material particular not only the evidence that the crime has been committed, but also that the prisoner committed it".[8]

Applying this definition to sexual offence cases, examples of corroboration would include medical evidence which verifies the existence of injuries consistent with the alleged sexual offence; police evidence (i.e. DNA evidence); and other witness evidence (e.g. evidence which places the accused and the complainant in a certain place at a certain time). Evidence of the complainant's distress in the immediate aftermath of the alleged incident may constitute corroboration but it is generally considered to be weak corroboration. O'Malley suggests that "[s]uch evidence will be more valuable when the distress was witnessed by a person who would have no apparent reason to lie and who can testify clearly as to the state in which he or she found the complainant".[9] Evidence that the complainant, at the first opportunity which presented itself, made a complaint which was consistent with her testimony will not amount to corroboration but may be admissible under the doctrine of recent complaint (discussed below).[10] **[6–06]**

When Should a Corroboration Warning Be Given?

When s 7 was first enacted, there was some resistance to its objectives, with judgments displaying a continued attachment to the traditional approach **[6–07]**

---

7 [1916] 2 KB 658.

8 *ibid*, 667.

9 O'Malley, *Sexual Offences* (2nd ed, Round Hall, Dublin, 2013), p 450.

10 Hanly notes that since such evidence is not independent of the complainant, permitting it to act as corroboration would essentially allow for self-corroboration: "Corroborating Rape Charges" (2001 11(4) *Irish Criminal Law Journal* 2, 3.

to corroboration. For example, in *People (DPP) v. Reid*,[11] the Court of Criminal Appeal held that, notwithstanding s 7, there would still be cases in which trial judges would consider it desirable to warn the jury about the dangers of convicting on the uncorroborated evidence of the complainant. Similarly, in *People (DPP) v Molloy*,[12] Flood J held that, while there was no statutory obligation on a trial judge to warn the jury of the dangers of convicting on the uncorroborated evidence of a complainant:

> "... where the charge is essentially supported by the evidence of the complainant alone without collateral forensic evidence or any other form of corroboration, it is prudent practice for the trial judge to warn the jury that unless they are *very very satisfied* with the testimony of the complainant ... they should be careful not to convict in the absence of corroborative evidence."[13] [Emphasis added].

[6–08] McGrath notes that these comments were, strictly speaking, obiter because the trial judge subsequently issued a warning following a requisition.[14] However, the statement seems "to indicate a firm view on the part of the Court as to the continued desirability of giving a corroboration warning, at least where there is no corroboration".[15]

[6–09] However, despite initial resistance to s 7, the courts subsequently indicated a greater commitment to honouring the objectives of the provision. The first significant judgment in this regard was *People (DPP) v JEM*[16] where Denham J endorsed the approach taken by the English courts in *R v Makanjuola*[17] towards the English equivalent of s 7.[18] In the latter case, Taylor LCJ stated that:

> "The circumstances and evidence in criminal cases are infinitely variable and it is impossible to categorise how a judge should deal with them. But it is clear that to carry on giving 'discretionary' warnings generally and in the same terms as were previously obligatory would be contrary to the policy

---

11 [1993] 2 IR 186.
12 Unreported, Court of Criminal Appeal, 28 July 1995.
13 Similar statements were made in *People (DPP) v PC* [2002] 2 IR 285 and *People (DPP) v O'Connor*, unreported, Court of Criminal Appeal, 29 July 2002.
14 McGrath, *Evidence* (2nd ed, Round Hall, Dublin, 2014), p 222.
15 *ibid*.
16 [2001] 4 IR 385.
17 [1995] 1 WLR 1348.
18 The English Criminal Justice and Public Order Act 1994, s 32, provides that:
> "(1) Any requirement whereby at a trial on indictment it is obligatory for the court to give the jury a warning about convicting the accused on the uncorroborated evidence of a person merely because that person is (a) an alleged accomplice of the accused, or; (b) where the offence charged is a sexual offence, the person in respect of whom it is alleged to have been committed is hereby abrogated."

> and purpose of the [1994] Act. Whether, as a matter of discretion, a judge should give any warning and if so its strength and terms must depend upon the content and manner of the witness's evidence, the circumstances of the case and the issues raised. The judge will often consider that no special warning is required at all. Where, however, the witness has been shown to be unreliable, he or she may consider it necessary to urge caution. In a more extreme case, if the witness is shown to have lied, to have made previous false complaints, or to bear the defendant some grudge, a stronger warning may be thought appropriate and the judge may suggest it would be wise to look for some supporting material before acting on the impugned witness's evidence. We stress that these observations are merely illustrative of some, not all, of the factors which judges may take into account in measuring where a witness stands in the scale of reliability and what response they should make at that level in their directions to the jury. We also stress that judges are not required to conform to any formula and this court would be slow to interfere with the exercise of discretion by a trial judge who has the advantage of assessing the manner of a witness's evidence as well as its content."

Denham J specifically endorsed this judgment as a guide to the interpretation of s 7.[19] Thus, a corroboration warning should be given by an Irish court only if there is an evidential basis for believing that the complainant's testimony is unreliable.[20] **[6–10]**

The approach in *JEM* was endorsed in *People (DPP) v Wallace*[21] where Keane C.J. stated that: **[6–11]**

> "the express legislative provision for the abolition of the mandatory warning…must not be circumvented by trial judges simply adopting a prudent or cautious approach of giving the warning in every case where there is no corroboration or where the evidence, might not amount, in the view of the trial judge, to corroboration. That would be to circumvent the clear policy of the legislature and that, of course, the courts are not entitled to do."

This was again confirmed in *People (DPP) v Slavotic*[22] where Fennelly J noted that a trial judge should not decide routinely to give a direction under s 7 in every case as to do so would "undermine the basis of the statutory charge".[23] A recent restatement of the law in relation to corroboration **[6–12]**

---

19 [2001] 4 IR 385, 402.

20 Hanly, *An Introduction to Irish Criminal Law* (3rd ed, Gill and MacMillan, Dublin, 2015), p 349.

21 Unreported, Court of Criminal Appeal, 30 April 2001.

22 Unreported, Court of Criminal Appeal, 18 November 2002.

23 Fennelly J again endorsed this line of reasoning in *People (DPP) v Ferris* (Unreported, Court of Criminal Appeal, 10 June 2002) when he quoted with approval the statements on corroboration made by Denham J in *JEM* and Keane CJ in *Wallace* and added that "the legislature is not only entitled to but has the function under the

warnings can be found in *DPP v RA (No 1)*[24] where Birmingham J, referring to earlier case-law, emphasised that "judges should not circumvent legislative policy by routinely giving the warning where, for instance it is a case without corroboration".[25] It is clear then that, in principle at least, the Irish judiciary are committed to honouring the legislative intent behind s 7 that corroboration warnings should only be given where they are justified on the basis of the evidence of the case and necessary to avoid potential injustice.

[6–13] When a trial judge is exercising his/her discretion on whether to give a corroboration warning, available jurisprudence suggests that a discussion with counsel is advisable. In *DPP v MK*,[26] McGuinness J noted that there had been no "preliminary discussion between counsel and the learned trial judge as to whether the judge intended to give a corroboration warning or, if so, what evidence amounted to corroboration" but that this was "not essential and the fact that it did not take place is not a ground of appeal".[27] However, McGuinness J suggested that "this practice is often helpful to the trial judge and consequently, on occasion to the jury, in that it leads to clarification as to what should come within the ambit of the established definition of corroboration".[28] In *DPP v D*,[29] MacMenamin J stated that:

> "it is not necessary for a trial judge to test out precisely a form of words that he or she intends to use, nonetheless, it is highly desirable that counsel should at least know the position as to how the judge's discretion will be expressed and the reasons therefore, prior to embarking on their closing speeches."[30]

[6–14] More recently, the Court of Appeal has issued a stronger endorsement of the value of discussions between a trial judge and counsel about the provision of a corroboration warning. In *DPP v RA (No 1)*,[31] Birmingham J emphasised that the Court of Appeal has "on a number of occasions indicated its view that it is desirable that [discussions between counsel and the judge before speeches or before the charge on the issue of corroboration] take place".[32] The learned judge noted that:

> "One reason why that is so, is that if the discussions take place in advance

---

constitution of evaluating changes in social and cultural circumstances, including sexual mores, and…giving them legislative form where warranted".

24 [2016] IECA 110.
25 *ibid*, para 15.
26 [2005] 3 IR 423.
27 *ibid*, 445.
28 *ibid*.
29 [2014] IECCA 20.
30 *ibid*, para 20.
31 [2016] IECA 110.
32 *ibid*, para 11.

of the speeches and charge, the judge may be more disposed to provide a warning whereas if the issue is raised only after the judge has concluded his charge it is possible that he may feel that to address the issue at that stage would be to do so in an unbalanced manner."[33]

Thus, it seems prudent that trial judges should have a discussion with counsel before exercising their discretion regarding the corroboration warning. However, as noted by O'Malley, there is no "inflexible rule" which mandates such discussions. In his view, "judges should not be left with their hands tied as a result of having undertaken to give or not to give a warning" and "[t]hey may quite properly change their minds having heard the closing speeches".[34] **[6–15]**

Some confusion also exists regarding the need for a reasoned judgment regarding the trial judge's decision on corroboration. Although the trial judge must have sufficient reason for giving a corroboration warning and, as discussed, should ideally discuss this with counsel, O'Malley notes that "Irish jurisprudence is less than consistent on the extent of a judge's obligation to explain his or her refusal to give a warning".[35] In *DPP v Dolan*,[36] there appeared to be a suggestion that a reasoned ruling was necessary, Kearns J stating that: **[6–16]**

"... during the course of a trial it cannot be expected that the trial judge will give an elaborate judgment on every legal issue which arises for his ruling, but every important ruling must at least disclose a decision judicially made, that is to say, one which is reasoned and based on legal principle."[37]

However, in *DPP v Ryan*,[38] Geoghegan J made clear that the Court of Criminal Appeal did not believe that the *Dolan* judgment "was laying down a universal rule that if the judge is asked to give the warning, he must always give a reasoned ruling".[39] This was due to the fact that "[i]n most instances, the arguments for and against a warning will be obvious to all concerned".[40] Similar reasoning was applied in *DPP v Gillespie*[41], where Mackin J stated that: **[6–17]**

"The Court does not accept that there is, in fact, any valid ground for suggesting that if the judge exercises the discretion by refusing to give a

---

33 *ibid.*
34 O'Malley, *supra* note 9, p 458.
35 *ibid.*
36 [2007] IECCA 30.
37 *ibid.* No paragraph numbers available in judgment.
38 [2010] IECCA 29.
39 *ibid*, para 18.
40 *ibid.*
41 [2009] IECCA 157.

warning, it must be by reference to detailed, specific and analytical reasons, mentioning the evidence in the case."

[6–18] More recently, in *DPP v C*,[42] Birmingham J stated that:

> "The dynamics of a jury trial often make the giving of an elaborate or analytical reasoned ruling impractical, though the Court would comment that where the accused claims to have identified a factual foundation making a warning desirable or indeed mandatory that it would be desirable for the judge when ruling to engage, even if briefly, with the arguments that have been advanced."[43]

[6–19] Thus, it would seem that reasoned rulings on a trial judge's decision regarding provision of the corroboration warning are generally not necessary,[44] but as *Dolan* and *C* suggest, there may be circumstances where some comment on a decision not to give a warning may be warranted. As noted in *DPP v D*,[45] it is unnecessary for a trial judge to deliver "an elaborate ruling" regarding corroboration but the decision made "must be one which is susceptible to analysis on the basis of whether it is, indeed a decision judicially made".[46] Where some comment is necessary to achieve this, a trial judge should provide it to avoid uncertainty and minimise the potential for appeals.

What Form of Wording Should Be Used for a Corroboration Warning?

[6–20] Section 7(2) provides that if the judge decides to give a corroboration warning, "it shall not be necessary to use any particular form of words to do so". There is no specific formula of words which must be used when providing a corroboration warning. In *People (DPP) v JEM*, Denham J cited Taylor CJ's guidance on this issue which provides that where a judge decides to give a warning, it will be appropriate to do so as part of the judge's review of the evidence and his/her comments as to how the jury should evaluate it rather than as a set-piece legal direction.[47] It was also emphasised that where some warning is required, it will be for the judge to decide the strength and terms of the warning. It does not have to be invested with

---

42 [2016] IECA 278.
43 *ibid*, para 30.
44 O'Malley suggests that while the judge's reasoning should be clear to the parties, "this will often have occurred naturally as a result of the exchanges between judge and counsel where there have been discussions about the need for a warning": O'Malley, *supra* note 9, p 459.
45 [2014] IECCA 20.
46 *ibid*, para 18.
47 [2001] 4 IR 385, 402.

"the whole florid regime" of the old corroboration rules.[48] Consequently, there is some flexibility regarding the form which a warning should take.

Nonetheless, in *People (DPP) v PJ*,[49] it was held that "once a trial judge has elected to give a warning it seems ... that the necessity remains for that warning to be clear and unmistakable".[50] Hanly suggests that if the trial judge decides to give a warning, s/he should still follow the elements of the old rule, that is, instruct the jury to seek corroborative evidence, define corroboration using *R v Baskerville*, and indicate what material, if any, is capable of constituting corroboration.[51] McGrath has also stated that the trial judge should be careful to warn the jury not to treat as corroboration evidence which they might mistakenly believe to have that quality.[52] This was confirmed in *People (DPP) v MK*,[53] where McGuiness J held that: **[6–21]**

> "It is essential that a clear definition of the principle of corroboration be given [to the jury] but it is also of great importance that it be clearly and unequivocally pointed out to the jury what, if any, of the evidence before them is capable of amounting to corroboration as defined."[54]

In *DPP v D*,[55] the Court also highlighted that it is important to clarify for the jury that they are still free to return a verdict of guilty even if there is no corroboration: **[6–22]**

> "A warning may, of course, also contain the addendum that, having borne the precautionary element in mind and having given due weight to it, if the evidence is nonetheless so clearly acceptable that the jury is satisfied beyond reasonable doubt on the guilt of the accused then they may act on it."[56]

Further, more recently, in *DPP v CC (No 2)*,[57] the importance of demonstrating to the jury the experience of the courts in relation to corroboration was emphasised: **[6–23]**

> "... all warnings given to juries are an attempt to give to a jury approaching a one off task something of the general experience of the courts. Thus whatever language is used, it is necessary to convey to a jury that the law

48 *ibid.*
49 [2003] 3 IR 550
50 *ibid*, 567.
51 Hanly, *supra* note 10, p 8.
52 McGrath, "Two steps forward, one step back: the corroboration warning in sexual cases" (1999) 9(1) *Irish Criminal Law Journal* 22, 29.
53 [2005] 3 IR 423.
54 *ibid*, 445.
55 [2014] IECCA 20.
56 *ibid*, para 17.
57 [2012] IECCA 86.

> considers it dangerous to convict in the absence of corroboration, because by definition these offences occur in private, or at least in circumstances of some furtiveness, and there have been occasions where evidence apparently plausible, has subsequently been shown to be untrue. Accordingly, over and above the degree of care and caution they would normally expect to exercise in coming to a verdict of guilt beyond any reasonable doubt, the jury should recognise that it is the law's experience that it is dangerous to convict on the uncorroborated evidence of a complainant, and should only do so when, having considered the warning, they nevertheless feel a very high degree of assurance that the evidence is true. Unless something of this nature is conveyed to the jury, there seems little benefit in giving a corroboration warning at all."[58]

[6–24] Consequently, although trial judges have leeway regarding the form of warning they give, there are some key requirements which must be satisfied. The warning must be clear, define "corroboration" and identify which evidence is and is not capable of amounting to corroboration. It is also important that the warning contain the type of addendum proposed in *D* to alert jurors that, even without corroboration, they may still convict. Without this, jurors may well be confused about the directions they are being given. Finally, some reference to the experience of the courts, as suggested in *CC*, may be helpful. However, extreme care is necessary in relaying this type of advice to avoid unfair prejudice for the complainant by returning to the old-style corroboration warnings about the dangers of convicting on the uncorroborated word of the complainant.

Appellate Oversight of the Operation of Section 7

[6–25] Appellate judgments have repeatedly highlighted that a trial judge's decision not to give a warning should not be lightly overturned. However, corroboration provides a fertile ground for appeal in sexual offence cases and the Court of Appeal will intervene where necessary. This was made clear in *DPP v Gentleman*,[59] where Keane CJ emphasised that while s 7 gives the judge a discretion whether to issue a corroboration warning:

> "... once the trial judge exercises it in a particular way, then an appellate court is entitled to consider whether, in all the circumstances, he gave the appropriate warning."[60]

[6–26] This view was re-iterated by Geoghegan J in *DPP v Ryan*,[61] where he held that although an appellate court would not normally interfere with discretion,

---

[58] *ibid*, para 35.
[59] [2003] 4 IR 22.
[60] *ibid*, 25.
[61] [2010] IECCA 29.

intervention will be justifiable where "on the facts of any particular case, a failure to give the warning was manifestly a wrong exercise of the discretion".[62] However, if defence counsel has "not pressed for the warning then its absence should not be entertained as a ground of appeal [unless there are] exceptional circumstances".[63] Most recently, in *DPP v RA (No 2)*,[64] the reluctance of the Court of Appeal to intervene in relation to corroboration warnings was re-iterated, with Birmingham J stating that "this Court should be slow to intervene interfering only when the decision was made on an incorrect legal basis or was clearly wrong in fact".[65]

Analysis of the Current Law and Proposals for Reform

It is fair to suggest that whilst the legislative intent behind s 7 has been met in principle, with clear judicial pronouncements about the need for caution in exercising the discretion to give a corroboration warning, in practice, corroboration warnings remain a fairly constant feature of sexual offence trials. As McGrath notes, "the traditional corroboration warning has proven very resilient and continues to be deployed by judges".[66] Of course, it is arguable that the continued resilience of the corroboration warning is inevitable in sexual offence cases, given their "oath against oath" nature. Lawyers interviewed for the purposes of a study on attrition in sexual assault cases which was conducted by Leane et al in 2001 outlined the following as situations in which a corroboration warning would typically be given: **[6–27]**

- Where the only evidence against the accused is the evidence of the complainant;
- Where there is no physical evidence;
- Where there are very young children involved;
- Where the case is very old;
- Where there is some unusual characteristic involved such as intoxication, mental illness or mental backwardness.[67]

Since many sexual offence cases will involve one of the foregoing circumstances, it appears that the giving of the warning will more often than not be justifiable and may indeed be necessary to protect the defendant from wrongful conviction. However, given the flexibility of the current law, there **[6–28]**

---

62 *ibid*, para 11.

63 *ibid*. It may seem counterintuitive that defence counsel would not seek a corroboration warning. Geoghegan J notes that "counsel for the defence might not always want a warning to be given as to corroboration where that would entail a much more detailed review of the evidence by the judge to the perceived detriment of the defence": *ibid*.

64 [2016] IECA 110.

65 *ibid*, para 25.

66 McGrath, *supra* note 14, p 225.

67 Leane, et al, *Attrition in Sexual Assault Offence Cases in Ireland: A Qualitative Analysis*, (Department of Justice, Equality and Law Reform, Dublin, 2001), p 93.

is also a danger that corroboration warnings may be given more often than is necessary and, as a result of a continued attachment to the former mandatory requirement. If the discretion to give a warning is exercised too liberally then the objectives of s 7 may be defeated and complainants run the risk of being unfairly prejudiced by unwarranted use of the corroboration warning.

[6–29] The discussion of the law above demonstrates that significant uncertainty surrounds the provision of corroboration warnings in sexual offence cases. It is difficult to predict when a corroboration warning will be warranted. Given the discretionary nature of the regime and the varying nature of sexual offence cases, some uncertainty is inevitable.[68] However, this uncertainty also suggests a lack of a uniform approach to corroboration which may result in unwarranted exercise of discretion to give a warning, leading to unfair prejudice for the complainant and potential confusion for jurors. The ideal format of such a warning is also unclear, creating space for inappropriately worded or confusing warnings which may unnecessarily confuse jurors.

[6–30] Ultimately, it would be beneficial to understand more about the operation of the corroboration warning in Irish sexual offence cases. To date, the only empirical evidence available on this issue is from the analysis of trial transcripts which was conducted for the *Rape & Justice in Ireland* study.[69] This research suggested that corroboration warnings are given only in a minority of cases but the number of trial transcripts which were surveyed was quite small and it is not safe to draw definitive conclusions on the basis of this evidence.[70] Moreover, the variety of circumstances in which a corroboration warning may be seen as warranted, coupled with the amount of case-law regarding the use of the warning, would seem to suggest that, contrary to the findings in this study, corroboration warnings could remain a regular feature of sexual offence trials. An empirical study which uncovers the frequency with which the warning is used, when it is typically provided, and the form of wording which is used when a warning is given, would be very beneficial to assess whether s 7 is achieving its objectives or not.[71] Mock jury research which studied the impact of the warning on juror deliberations would also be very useful in assessing the section and the need for reform.

68 Indeed, in *DPP v Ryan*, Geoghegan J stated that "[i]t would be wrong for this court to give any theoretical examples of cases where the discretion [to give a corroboration warning] could only be properly exercised in favour of a warning as each case depends entirely on its own particular and peculiar facts": [2010] IECCA 29, para 19.

69 Hanly, et al, *Rape & Justice in Ireland: A National Study of Survivor, Prosecutor and Court Responses to Rape* (The Liffey Press, Dublin, 2009).

70 *ibid*, 364. The study involved an analysis of 35 trial transcripts.

71 The RCNI has recommended that such research be conducted: RCNI, *Agenda for Justice I: Towards Ending Injustice for Survivors of Sexual Violence* (RCNI, Galway, 2005).

Should reform be considered in this jurisdiction, a suitable blueprint has been proposed by Leahy.[72] The recommended model would prohibit corroboration *warnings* whilst preserving the trial judge's entitlement to *comment* upon corroboration when directing the jury at the close of the trial. This change would have the symbolic effect of removing the final vestiges of the old-style corroboration warning with its potential negative connotations about the veracity of sexual offence complainants. At the same time, however, judges could comment on the lack of corroboration in a manner which is less potentially prejudicial (as it is not in a warning-style direction) but which still offsets any potential unfairness for defendants. Of course, the success of a reform like this would depend upon judicial commitment to its careful implementation. In particular, it would be important that judicial comment on corroboration was not delivered in a manner akin to the warning-type directions which are currently provided. Thus, careful oversight of the introduction of a provision like this would be necessary to ensure that it achieved its intended objective of removing the challenges of the corroboration warning from sexual offence trials, whilst still protecting defendants' rights. [6–31]

The Doctrine of Recent Complaint

The rule against narrative provides that: [6–32]

> "a witness may not repeat, or be asked about, a statement she made prior to the trial or hearing for the purpose of showing *consistency* with the version of events which she gives in her testimony; nor may a second witness give evidence of any statement made prior to the trial by the first witness which is consistent with the testimony given by the first witness in the trial."[73]

McGrath notes that one of primary justifications for excluding this type of "self-corroboration" is "the ease with which a witness who intended to give false evidence could bolster his or her credibility by repeating his or her version of events to a number of people and then calling them to the stand to show the consistency of his or her story".[74] The doctrine of recent [6–33]

[72] Leahy, "The corroboration warning in sexual offence trials: final vestige of the historic suspicion of sexual offence complainants or a necessary protection for defendants?" (2014) 18(1) *International Journal of Evidence and Proof* 41, 61. Leahy's proposals are modelled on reform recommendations made by McGrath: McGrath, *supra* note 52, p 45.

[73] Healy, *Irish Laws of Evidence* (Thomson Round Hall, Dublin, 2004), p 68. Heffernan comments that "[t]he primary purpose which the rule serves is preventing the manufacture of corroborative evidence by a deceitful witness who plants a story prior to trial and then repeats it in the witness box": Heffernan, *Evidence in Criminal Trials* (Bloomsbury Professional, Dublin, 2014), p 34.

[74] McGrath, *supra* note 14, p 139.

complaint provides an exception to this rule and allows for the introduction at trial of evidence of a complaint made by a sexual offence complainant in the aftermath of the incident. The purpose of this evidence is not to corroborate the complaint,[75] but to establish the complainant's consistency and credibility.[76] The rationale for the doctrine is based on the ancient principle of the common law that a sexual offence complainant should "raise hue and cry" by complaining about the rape as immediately as possible.[77] The idea that evidence of recent complaint can bolster the complainant's credibility is "... based on a view that it was the natural expression of a victim's feelings that reasonably soon after the offence she would complain to some person with whom she had a personal or confidential relationship".[78]

An Overview of the Admissibility of Recent Complaint in Sexual Offence[79] Trials

[6–34] For evidence of recent complaint to be admissible, the complaint must satisfy certain requirements, namely that: (1) it is consistent with the complainant's testimony at trial; (2) it was made voluntarily; and (3) it was made at the first reasonable opportunity after the alleged incident. In addition, the complaint must be proved by the person to whom the complainant made the complaint. If that person does not give evidence, the complainant will not be permitted to give evidence of complaints allegedly made by her.[80]

---

75 Evidence of recent complaint cannot provide corroboration because it is not independent of the complainant and so fails to satisfy the definition of corroboration which was given in *R v Baskerville* [1916] 2 KB 658.

76 Ring, "Trial and Error: Current Problems in the Trial of Sexual Offences: A Prosecutor's Perspective" (2003) 13(2) *Irish Criminal Law Journal* 3, 4.

77 McIntyre and McMullan, *Criminal Law* (Thomson Round Hall, Dublin, 2005), 122. The former importance of raising "hue and cry" is well illustrated in the following extract from Hale's *Pleas of the Crown:*

> "For instance, if the witness be of good fame, if she presently discovered the offence made pursuit after the offender, showed circumstances and signs of injury…these and the like are concurring evidences to give greater probability to her testimony, when proved by others as well as herself. But on the other side, if she concealed the injury for any considerable time after she had opportunity to complain…and she made no outcry when the fact was supposed to be done, when and where it is probable she might be heard by others; these and the like circumstances carry a strong presumption, that her testimony is false or feigned": *Pleas of the Crown*, Volume I, p 633.

78 *People (DPP) v MA* [2002] 2 IR 601, 608.

79 Although it is generally understood that the doctrine of recent complaint only applies in sexual offence trials, whether this includes all forms of sexual offences or not has never been clarified. In the absence of an express statement to the contrary, it assumed that it applies to all sexual offences.

80 McGrath, *supra* note 14, 140; *White v R* [1999] 1 Cr App R 153.

Consistency

With regard to the first requirement of consistency, McGrath notes that: **[6–35]**

> "[t]here is no precise test with regard to the degree of consistency that is required but it would appear that, if the complaint correlates in its main particulars with the testimony of the complainant as to the commission of the offence, it will not be excluded because of minor discrepancies".[81]

Indeed, O'Malley suggests that "the general consensus seems to be that evidence of the complaint should not be rendered inadmissible unless it is completely inconsistent with the complainant's evidence".[82] **[6–36]**

Voluntariness

The complaint must be shown to have been made voluntarily and not as a result of any inducements or exhortations.[83] The fact that the complaint was made in response to questioning will not render it inadmissible if the question merely anticipates a statement which the complainant was about to make.[84] Similarly, a complaint made in response to questioning will not be inadmissible if the questioning was merely assisting the complainant in saying what she wanted to say. In *People (DPP) v DR*,[85] the complainant told her husband about the alleged incident after he had questioned her about her remark that the defendant was "no gentleman". Barrington J held that the complaint was sufficiently voluntary to be admissible. It was "not a question of her husband interrogating her".[86] He "merely assisted her in saying something which she herself wished to say".[87] However, if the circumstances indicate that but for the questioning there would probably have been no voluntary complaint, the answer is inadmissible.[88] **[6–37]**

First Reasonable Opportunity

The final requirement for the complaint to be admissible is that it was made at the first reasonable opportunity after the commission of the offence.[89] Previously, the courts adopted a strict approach to this temporal requirement. For example, in *People (DPP) v Brophy*,[90] a complaint made **[6–38]**

---

81 McGrath, *supra* note 14, p 144.
82 O'Malley, *supra* note 9, p 509.
83 *People (DPP) v Brophy* [1992] ILRM 709, 716.
84 *R v Osborne* (1905) 1 KB 551, 556.
85 [1998] 2 IR 106.
86 *ibid*, 110.
87 *ibid*.
88 *R v Osborne* (1905) 1 KB 551, 556.
89 *People (DPP) v Brophy* [1992] ILRM 709, 716.
90 *ibid*.

just a few hours after the incident occurred was ruled to be inadmissible.[91] More recent cases have, however, demonstrated a tendency for the courts to embrace a more nuanced and realistic approach to this requirement. Traces of this new approach were first evident in *People (DPP) v Kiernan.*[92] The defendant brought the complainant to his house, gave her a quantity of alcohol which caused her to be intoxicated and had sex with her while she was so intoxicated. Afterwards, the complainant went downstairs and recounted the event to the defendant's girlfriend who did not believe her, suggesting that the complainant had imagined it as a result of her intoxication. The complainant then returned to her parents' house but did not tell any member of her family what had happened. The trial judge accepted the complainant's evidence that she was too frightened to tell her family and had decided to wait and tell her boyfriend as his brother was a social welfare officer who she felt would give her good advice. However, when she met her boyfriend on the morning following the incident (Saturday) she again made no complaint and did not tell him until the next day (Sunday). The Court of Criminal Appeal held that the complainant had "acted reasonably in delaying her complaint until she had an opportunity of doing so to [her boyfriend] on the Saturday". Had she done so, her complaint would have been admissible. However, because she had delayed until the following day her complaint was "not one made 'as speedily as could be expected'". While the complaint in this case was inadmissible, Foley argues that the judgment indicates that delay of itself does not invariably operate to bar the admissibility of a complaint.[93] Rather, it is an *unexplained* delay which will result in a complaint being deemed inadmissible.[94]

[6–39] A more liberal approach to the reasonableness requirement was again evident in *DR.*[95] In this case the complainant was allegedly raped by her sister's partner at her sister's home where the complainant and her husband were staying for the weekend. The incident took place on a Sunday evening but the complainant did not tell her husband until the following Monday when they were at home. It was held that the complainant could not have complained

91 The defendant shopkeeper took a 14-year-old customer to his house and indecently assaulted her. Afterwards, he dropped her to a shopping centre. Thereafter the complainant went to her mother's house where she stayed for some time and did not complain of the assault. It was only when she met her friends later that a complaint was made. She then recounted her alleged experience to her father. The Court of Criminal Appeal held that the complaint was inadmissible because it had not been made at the first reasonable opportunity.

92 Unreported, Court of Criminal Appeal, 11 March 1994.

93 Foley, "The Doctrine of Recent Complaint Revisited" (2001) 11(3) *Irish Criminal Law Journal* 20, 22.

94 In *Kiernan*, there was no apparent explanation for the complainant's delay from Saturday to Sunday.

95 [1998] 2 IR 106.

any earlier than she did. She could not complain whilst still at her sister's home as the defendant and her sister were the hosts and her husband "was a man who had a violent temper which he had difficulty in controlling".[96] The complainant feared that there may have been a violent confrontation between the two men if she complained whilst still in the house. Thus, her delay was held to have been reasonable and the complaint was properly admissible. It is clear from *Kiernan* and *DR*, that the "reasonableness" of a delay in complaining is now assessed in a nuanced manner. As McGrath notes:

> "In recent times, greater judicial awareness of the factors such as shame and guilt that may inhibit a complainant from making a complaint even to a trusted friend or close relative has led to an acceptance that a complainant may have made a complaint at the first reasonable opportunity even if there has been a significant lapse of time and the complainant has not availed of an opportunity to complain to a family member or friend."

In light of recent developments in the case-law (and no doubt more enlightened views on the part of the judiciary about sexual offence complainants), O'Malley suggests that "the elapse of a few days between the alleged offence and the first complaint will seldom render evidence of the complaint inadmissible provided it was made at the first reasonable opportunity".[97] As Heffernan points out, "reasonableness is not purely a matter of timing".[98] If the complainant does not come into contact with someone she trusted in the immediate aftermath of the incident, it is likely that the court will accept as reasonable her decision to delay her complaint until she found a suitable confidante. However, "where the victim met suitable persons during the period but failed to tell them about the alleged offences, the complaint will be ruled out".[99] The courts have demonstrated that where there are special circumstances for delay (e.g. where the victim has an intellectual disability or is a child or a victim of familial sexual abuse), a substantial delay may be regarded as reasonable so as to permit evidence of the complaint to be admitted.[100] **[6–40]**

Introducing Recent Complaint Evidence at Trial

Once a complaint is deemed admissible, both the fact of the complaint **[6–41]**

---

96 *ibid*, 109.
97 O'Malley, *supra* note 9, p 511.
98 Heffernan, *Evidence in Criminal Trials* (Bloomsbury Professional, Dublin, 2014), p 130.
99 *ibid*.
100 *DPP v T (J)* (1988) 3 Frewen 141.

and its particulars may be introduced at trial.[101] The witness can tell the court precisely what the complainant said at the time of the complaint. The defence is entitled to cross-examine the complainant to draw to the attention of the jury any elements of apparent or real inconsistency between those complaints and her testimony.[102] Importantly, it is incumbent upon the trial judge to explain to the jury the use to which evidence of recent complaint may be put in their deliberations, that is, that it is to be relied upon to demonstrate consistency of the complainant's testimony but not to corroborate it. The significance of this task was emphasised in *People (DPP) v MA*[103]:

> "Where evidence of a complaint made by a complainant to third parties in the absence of an accused is admitted in a trial of a sexual offence to establish the consistency of the complaint with the evidence of the complainant the purpose of the evidence should be explained to the jury and it should be made clear to it that such evidence is not evidence of the facts on which the complaint is based but may be considered by them as showing that the victim's conduct in so complaining was consistent with her testimony. It should also be explained to the jury that such evidence does not constitute corroboration, in the legal sense of that term, of the evidence of the complainant."[104]

Multiple Complaints

[6–42] In *People (DPP) v McDonagh*,[105] the Court of Criminal Appeal held that more than one complaint may be admissible under the doctrine of recent complaint as long as each complaint complies with the requirements for admissibility. According to O'Flaherty J:

> "... it is clear that evidence of more than one complaint may be given provided the conditions mentioned are complied with but, of course, a trial judge always has a discretion to limit the number of references there may be to complaints to ensure fairness in a trial. He is free to rule that many repetitions of the same form of complaint is unnecessary and might work an injustice. But it will always be in the discretion of the trial judge to rule on the matter as he thinks right."

[6–43] McGrath notes that caution is required in admitting evidence of multiple complaints:

> "... once the fact and particulars of a complaint are admitted, repetition of

[101] *R v Lillyman* [1896] 2 QB 167; *People (DPP) v McDonagh*, unreported, Court of Criminal Appeal, 27 July 1994.
[102] *People (DPP) v MA* [2002] 2 IR 601, 607.
[103] [2002] 2 IR 601.
[104] *ibid*, 611.
[105] Unreported, Court of Criminal Appeal, 27 July 1994.

> the complaint, especially if it is very similar in its terms, does not add much probative value to the complaint however, it gives rise to a risk of prejudice because of sheer weight of numbers. If a number of witnesses give evidence repeating the particulars of the same complaint, there is a substantial risk that the jury will not treat such evidence as going merely to the credibility of the complainant."[106]

The Practical Impact of the Doctrine of Recent Complaint

Unfortunately, there is no empirical evidence which can shed light on the impact of the use of the doctrine of recent complaint in Irish sexual offence trials. Instinctively, the doctrine appears to work to the advantage of sexual offence complainants. As Heffernan et al point out, the fact or existence of a fresh complaint tends to strengthen the inference that the complainant is consistent and truthful at trial.[107] Temkin notes that, particularly where consent is in issue, evidence of recent complaint will be important to demonstrate that the complainant's conduct was inconsistent with consent.[108] The doctrine provides a complainant with an important means of bolstering her credibility and, when one considers the inevitable lack of corroborating evidence in most sexual offence trials, it thus seems to represent a welcome element of the law. **[6–44]**

However, some commentators are ambivalent about the appropriateness of the recent complaint doctrine. In principle, there is a concern that a law that permits evidence of recent complaint to bolster the complainant's credibility inevitably carries the implication that failure to make a prompt complaint indicates that the complainant is lying.[109] For example, McColgan suggests that the doctrine merely suggests that sexual offence complainants do not benefit from the presumption of truthfulness which exists in respect of witnesses to other crimes.[110] Further, on a more practical level, there is a risk that this doctrine unfairly differentiates between complainants. The complainant who complained promptly is rewarded by having evidence of that complaint admitted at trial but the complainant who delays in reporting **[6–45]**

---

106 McGrath, *supra* note 14, p145.

107 Heffernan, et al, *Evidentiary Foundations: Irish Edition* (Tottel Publishing Ltd, Dublin, 2007), p 33.

108 Temkin, *Rape and the Legal Process* (2nd ed, Oxford University Press, Oxford, 2002), p 188.

109 Temkin, "Rape and Criminal Justice at the Millennium'" in Nicolson and Bibbings, (eds), *Feminist Perspectives on Criminal Law* (Cavendish Publishing, London, 2000), p 193. Hanly et al make a similar point noting that in admitting evidence of recent complaint to provide credibility for a complainant's story, the inverse is also implied, that is, that late complaints reflect poorly on credibility: Hanly et al, *supra* note 69, p 60.

110 McColgan, "Common Law and the Relevance of Sexual History Evidence" (1996) 16(2) *Oxford Journal of Legal Studies* 275, 277.

(a not-infrequent occurrence[111]) is not provided with this benefit. While the doctrine may work to the advantage of complainants in some cases, there is a risk that, on a broader level, it may be detrimental to the interests of sexual offence complainants and contribute to stereotypical views about appropriate victim behaviour in the aftermath of a sexual attack.

[6–46] Despite the potential negative connotations of the doctrine, critics are reluctant to recommend its abolition due to fears of "throwing the baby out with the bathwater", that is, in getting rid of the negative connotations of the rule (i.e. that a "real" victim would complain immediately), abolition would also eliminate an important means for complainants to bolster their credibility. Abolishing the doctrine would not eradicate the suspicion surrounding delayed complaints. Instead, it would deprive the complainant of the opportunity to adduce evidence which might support her credibility in a situation in which she continues to be viewed with disbelief and suspicion.[112] As Temkin suggests, abolition of the doctrine would represent "a further nail in the [complainant's] coffin" and "would serve only to place a further impediment in the way of prosecutions in rape cases".[113] As a result of concerns like these, it is arguable that the rules should be retained and the test for admissibility of complaints made more flexible. For example, the Rape Crisis Network of Ireland has proposed that the courts could admit evidence of a complainant's first complaint, whether it was "recent" or not.[114]

[6–47] Heffernan argues that the doctrine "has failed to keep pace with developments" and is "ripe for re-examination with a view to reform".[115] At the very least, it is worth interrogating the position of the doctrine in sexual offences law in the 21st century and considering whether its application might be extended. Should reform be considered in the future, a possible template may be found in s 120 of the English Criminal Justice Act 2003 which has extended the admissibility of recent complaint evidence to all offences. A reform like this would allow for the best of both worlds in relation to recent complaint. Complainants could continue to avail of the benefits of recent complaint evidence to bolster their testimony but without the negative connotations attached to the doctrine in its current form. Significantly, s 120 also allows for evidence of recent complaint to act not only to demonstrate consistency but also as evidence of the facts stated (i.e.

---

111 In Hanly et al's survey of 100 adult complainants who had reported to the gardaí, 18 percent waited a month or more before reporting. Among the reasons given for delay were shock, fear of others' reactions and fear of the defendant: Hanly et al, *supra* note 69, pp 156–157.

112 Temkin, *supra* note 108, p 191.

113 *ibid.*

114 Rape Crisis Network of Ireland, *Submission to the Balance in the Criminal Law Review Group*, (Rape Crisis Network of Ireland, Galway, 2007), p 7.

115 Heffernan, *supra* note 98, p 127.

a form of corroboration).[116] The requirement that complaints be timely to be admissible has also been abolished in English law.[117] These developments further strengthen the usefulness of the doctrine for complainants and remove some of the complexities of the traditional doctrine. Naturally, an extension of the law along these lines in Ireland would require careful consideration both with regard to any potential impact on defendants' rights, but also in regard to its suitability for incorporation into the trial of offences other than sexual offences. However, s 120 provides some food for thought regarding reform in this area and the benefit of even a partial extension of the law (e.g. removal of the temporal requirement) is worthy of consideration.

---

[116] Criminal Justice Act 2003 (UK), s 120(3).
[117] Coroners and Justice Act 2009, s 112.

Part Three

SENTENCING AND PUNISHMENT

Chapter Seven

Sentencing Sex Offenders

Introduction

The Power to Sentence: The Role of the Legislature and the Judiciary

Once a person has been convicted of an offence, the next step is sentencing. The sentencing process is a crucial stage in the criminal justice system, given that a breach of the substantive criminal law must result in the determination and application of an appropriate punishment.[1] Punishment is the means whereby the convicted offender is made to answer for their wrongdoing and violation of the social contract which binds society together.[2] An important feature of punishment is that it must be legally sanctioned.[3] As Easton and Piper have observed "[s]uffering consequent upon misdeeds is not punishment unless those who inflict it have authority over the offender."[4] Thus once the legislature creates an offence, it also prescribes the penalty which attaches to that offence. This may mean dictating a specified or fixed penalty, or setting a maximum or minimum penalty. Once the legislature has set out the range of penalties available then its task is complete and it has no further power to determine the individual sentence in a case. This is the realm of the sentencing judge.[5] So while the legislature prescribes that the **[7–01]**

1 The Law Reform Commission defined sentencing as "the judicial determination of a legal sanction to be imposed on a person found guilty of an offence." Law Reform Commission, *Report on Sentencing*, (Law Reform Commission, Dublin, 1996).

2 Social contract theory expounds the idea that society is bound together by a mutual agreement among citizens to abide by certain ideals of law and order. One example is Rousseau, *Of The Social Contract, Or Principles of Political Right* (*Du contrat social ou Principes du droit politique*) (1762; translated 1782 by Cole, Unforgotten Classics, 2013).

3 Hart prescribes the essential features of punishment as follows: the measures must involve pain or other consequences normally considered unpleasant; it must be for an offence against legal rules; it must be of an actual or supposed offender for his offences; it must be intentionally administered by a human being other than the offender; and it must be imposed and administered by an authority constituted by a legal system against which the offence is committed. Hart and Gardner, *Punishment and Responsibility: Essays in the Philosophy of Law* (2nd ed, Oxford University Press, Oxford, 2008).

4 Easton and Piper, *Sentencing and Punishment: The Quest for Justice* (3rd ed, Oxford University Press, Oxford, 2012), p 4.

5 This is due to the constitutional separation of powers between the legislature and

crime of rape in Ireland carries a maximum penalty of life imprisonment,[6] it is for the sentencing judge to determine the specific sentence for the individual offender in a case.

[7–02] Judicial discretion to determine the specific term in a case has generated much controversy, particularly in the context of sexual offence cases.[7] Perceptions that sentences are too lenient or do not properly take account of the harm suffered by the victims, presuppose that there is a fundamental flaw in our current sentencing system.[8] In fact sentencing judgments are usually assertive about the need to be mindful of the harm inflicted upon victims and society as a result of sexual violence. In *DPP v Walsh*,[9] Edwards J commented,

> "In assessing the harm done the court must consider the position of the victim, as well as the requirements of society in terms of the need to deprecate and deter future instances of the offending conduct."[10]

[7–03] The absence of sentencing guidelines generally, as well as those specifically applying to sexual offences, has also been an issue of contention. Ireland currently has an unstructured sentencing system that is not predicated upon the use of formal sentencing guidelines and within which judicial discretion may indeed carry with it the risk that offenders convicted of similar offences will receive significantly different sentences.[11] Individualised sentencing, however, has long been seen as the foundation of the Irish sentencing system and any radical reform of this approach has thus far been strongly resisted,

---

the judiciary. Sentencing belongs to the administration of justice role of the courts: *Deaton v AG* [1963] IR 170.

6 See further chapter two.

7 O'Malley argues that although it receives much attention, judicial discretion is actually the least discretionary aspect of the criminal justice system. While the legislature can choose the type of conduct to criminalise, victims may decide not to report crimes, prosecutors may decide not to proceed with the case, and juries may determine the outcome of a trial, judges can never refuse to sentence a person convicted of an offence. O'Malley, *Sentencing: Towards a Coherent System* (Round Hall, Dublin, 2011), p 2.

8 A study on rape sentencing in Ireland was completed by the Judicial Researchers' Office in 2012 and found that lenient punishments for rape are very rare and that such sentences are accounted for by the existence of exceptional factors. Ó Cathaoir, *Recent Rape Sentencing Analysis The WD Case and Beyond*, Judicial Researchers' Office, 22 November 2012.

9 *DPP v Walsh* [2017] IECA 187.

10 *ibid*, para 13.

11 Inconsistency in Irish sentencing has been highlighted in research. See for example Hamilton, "Sentencing in the District Court: 'Here be Dragons'" (2005) 15 *Irish Criminal Law Journal* 9; Maguire, "Consistency in Sentencing" (2010) 2 *Judicial Studies Institute Journal* 14.

particularly by the judiciary.[12] Indeed the principle of proportionality, valued at constitutional level, positively requires that sentences be individualised.[13] The Supreme Court in *People (DPP) v Tiernan*[14] felt that to issue guideline-type judgments would be inappropriate, having regard to the "fundamental necessity" for judges to impose a sentence which in their discretion appropriately meets all the particular circumstances of the case and the particular circumstances of the accused.[15] However, in recent years the Court of Criminal Appeal has become more willing to set out general principles as to the method for arriving at a proportionate sentence. In the case of *People (DPP) v Kelly*,[16] Hamilton J considered a two-tiered approach should be adopted, premised upon first looking at "the range of penalties and locates where on the range the particular case should lie" and then applying "the mitigating factors after having performed that exercise."[17] Guidance was also offered in the case *People (DPP) v Loving*[18] concerning the appropriate grading of sentences within an offence. In sentencing for possession of child pornography the Court paid particular attention to factors such as the accused's acceptance of responsibility, including his plea of guilty, previous character with particular reference to the offence in question, the sharing or distribution of images, the serious and numerousness of the images, the duration of the activity, as well as the application of the provisions of the Sex Offenders Act 2001.[19] Despite criticism of the current sentencing system,[20] judicial discretion continues to be a valued proponent of individualised sentencing, albeit in need of greater structure and predictability.[21] Discretion is not unfettered, however,

---

12 O'Malley argues that for sentencing to comply with the demands of justice it must remain discretionary, but that is not to say that reform is not necessary and indeed to comply with values such as "procedural fairness, equality and the rule of law, judicial sentencing must reform itself in order to produce consistency of approach, to reduce (if not eliminate) unwarranted disparity and to develop rational criteria for deciding on the nature and severity of appropriate sanctions." O'Malley, *supra* note 7, p 5. See also Maguire, "Consistency in Sentencing" (2010) 2 *Judicial Studies Institute Journal* 14.

13 This principle will be explained in further detail below.

14 *People (DPP) v Tiernan* [1988] IR 250; [1989] ILRM 149.

15 *ibid*, 254.

16 *People (DPP) v Kelly* [2005] 1 ILRM 19.

17 *ibid*, 22.

18 *People (DPP) v Loving* [2006] 3 IR 355.

19 The Court considered the offence to be at the lower levels of seriousness as so reduced the original sentence of five years' imprisonment (with two years suspended) to one year.

20 Frequent media rhetoric about inconsistency in sentencing has reinforced the assumption that the public want "a kind of revenge system of locking up offenders and throwing away the key." Charleton and Scott, "Throw Away the Key: Public and Judicial Approaches to Sentencing – Towards Reconciliation" *The Martin Tansey Memorial Lecture*, 10 April 2013.

21 The introduction of the Irish Sentencing Information System (ISIS) in 2006 is a

and judges are still restrained by statutory maximums and minimums, as well as prescribed fixed penalties and requirements to impose consecutive sentences for offence committed on bail.[22]

Custodial and Non-Custodial Sentences

[7–04] In considering the sentence to impose, judges have a range of options open to them.[23] Anything from sentencing under the Probation of Offenders Act 1907 to life imprisonment can be invoked as a means of appropriate punishment for the offence in question. It is fair to say that when it comes to sentencing the preoccupation often lies with whether or not a custodial sentence will be imposed upon the offender. Given that there are relatively few mandatory sentences or mandatory minimum sentences prescribed by statute, judicial discretion to consider non-custodial options is very broad. The most common non-custodial options are probation orders, fines and community service orders. Additional orders such as disqualification for driving offences or other ancillary orders, such as those under the Sex Offenders Act 2001, may also be imposed.

[7–05] Section 1(1) of the Probation of Offenders Act 1907 provides that a court of summary jurisdiction may dismiss the charge or discharge an offender conditionally, without imposing a conviction even where the court thinks that the charge is proved, if it considers the imposition of punishment to be inexpedient. Section 1(2) provides for a similar order in relation to indictable offences, although in these circumstances there must be a conviction registered against the offender. Conditional release requires the individual to enter into a recognisance arrangement and maintain good behaviour for the duration of the order. The court may also impose supervision as a condition of release, and require the individual to pay damages to the victim. The primary objective of sentencing an individual under this Act is rehabilitation and to reduce the risk of re-offending.

[7–06] Another option available to the courts is a community service order under the Criminal Justice (Community Service Order) Act 1983.[24] The essential feature of such orders is that they are an alternative to the imposition of a prison sentence.[25] The court must be satisfied that the offender is suitable for

---

welcome resource for Irish judges as well as academic researchers, which enables access to information regarding sentences that have been imposed for particular offences in previous cases.

22 Criminal Justice Act 2007, s 22.

23 The range of options is dependent upon the sentencing jurisdiction of the particular court.

24 This Act is amended by s 19 of the Fines (Payment and Recovery) Act 2014.

25 The minimum number of hours that can be imposed under the order is 40, and the maximum is 240: Criminal Justice (Community Service Order) Act 1983, s 3(3).

such an order and will take into account any comments or recommendations from the Probation Service in this regard. The offender must also agree to take part in the scheme before an order can be imposed.

The court may also impose a fine on conviction. While traditionally fines were considered appropriate for minor types of offences, s 10(3) of the Criminal Law Act 1997 permits the courts to impose a fine where a person is convicted on indictment. Unless the particular statute creating the offence sets out the scope of the fine, the sentencing judge has discretion to determine what amount they deem appropriate in the circumstances of the case.[26] Fines will be most suitable for minor offences to those falling in the middle of the scale of gravity. The more serious the crime, the more difficult it may be to justify the imposition of a non-custodial offence. Hefty fines are still possible however for serious offences, although perhaps not for those in the upper echelons of gravity. **[7–07]**

The most serious type of punishment available in Ireland is imprisonment, which can be imposed for most types of offences, apart from very minor ones. Whether or not an offender will be sentenced to a term of imprisonment and for how long will depend upon a number of variables, including the gravity of the particular offence, as well as a range of other factors that may influence the particular circumstances of the case. Violent offences against the person ordinarily attract custodial sentences and it would be difficult to argue with this. Such sentiment can be found in Irish cases dealing with rape. In the case of *People (DPP) v Tiernan*[27] the Supreme Court felt that, in consideration of the serious nature of the offence and the severe physical and emotional harm to the victim, rape must be punished with an immediate and substantial term of imprisonment, save in the most exceptional circumstances.[28] The Court stated: **[7–08]**

> "Whilst in every criminal case a judge must impose a sentence which in his opinion meets the particular circumstances of the case and of the accused person before him, it is not easy to imagine the circumstance which would justify departure from a substantial immediate custodial sentence for rape and I can only express the view that they would be wholly exceptional."[29]

---

[26] Judges must also have regard to the Fines Act 2010 (as amended by the Fines (Payment and Recovery) Act 2014).

[27] *People (DPP) v Tiernan* [1988] IR 250.

[28] This principle has been endorsed in subsequent Irish case law: see for example *People (DPP) v Keane* [2007] IECCA 113. In addition to an ordinary sentence upon conviction most sex offenders are also subject to the provisions of the Sex Offenders Act 2001, most notably notification orders under Part 2. See chapter eight.

[29] Per Finlay CJ in *DPP v Tiernan* [1988] IR 250, 53.

[7–09] When it comes to sexual offences, anything other than a custodial sentence often arouses public disapproval, particularly where the crime is serious. However, it may be that there is public underestimation of the severity of judicial sentencing in such cases. A 2012 study by the Judicial Researchers' Office into rape sentencing found that a sentence of less than three years is highly unusual in the context of rape even where the accused pleaded guilty at an early stage.[30] The average sentence handed down ranged between five and seven years. In 42 percent of the cases studied, offenders received between nine and 14 years, and 24 percent of the cases attracted sentences of 15 years to life imprisonment. There are Irish authorities which indicate that life sentences are rare. The Court of Criminal Appeal opined this view in the case of *People (DPP) v McC*[31]:

> "Even in relation to a fully fought out rape case, a life sentence would be rare. The kind of circumstances that might justify it would be if the rape had been accompanied by extreme violence or if, say there had been a gang rape and in addition there were previous rape convictions."

[7–10] This seems to align with research findings in the 2012 study, where a life sentence was imposed in three cases, due to factors involving serious child sexual abuse over a prolonged period against multiple victims, and previous serious aggravated sexual assault convictions. More recent figures indicate that the average sentence for rape is now 10 years, demonstrating a gradual increase in rape sentences over the past decade.[32]

[7–11] When a term of imprisonment is imposed, the courts reserve the ability to suspend the sentence, wholly or in part, for offences apart from those requiring a mandatory sentence.[33] Originally a common law power of the

---

[30] Ó Cathaoir, *supra* note 8.

[31] *People (DPP) v McC* [2003] 3 IR 609, 618.

[32] Gallagher, "Rape sentencing averaging 10 years after rise over last decade" *The Irish Times*, 23 May 2016.

[33] Plans to reform the law on sentencing are currently being considered by the Government. A Private Member's Bill, the Criminal Justice (Commission of Sexual Offences) (Amendment) Bill 2017, which was withdrawn due to procedural issues, is intended to form the basis for a Government Bill reflecting these proposals. See Department of Justice and Equality, "Government approves proposals to strengthen penalties for repeat sexual offenders and to amend existing incest laws", *Press Release*, 11 July 2017.The essence of the reform is to amend the Criminal Justice Act 2007 by extending s 25 (which provides for presumptive sentencing in the case of repeat offenders convicted of an offence listed under sch 2 of the Act) to include repeat sex offenders. The Irish Penal Reform Trust (IPRT) have expressed legitimate concerns about these proposals which may result in unintended negative consequences. See Irish Penal Reform Trust, "Sentencing Proposals: Sexual Offences" *News & Press Release*, 11 July 2017.

courts, s 99 of the Criminal Justice Act 2006 puts this upon statutory footing. The section provides:

> "Where a person is sentenced to a term of imprisonment (other than a mandatory term of imprisonment) by a court in respect of an offence, that court may make an order suspending the execution of the sentence in whole or in part, subject to the person entering into a recognisance to comply with the conditions of, or imposed in relation to, the order."

There is no limit on the length of the sentence that may be suspended, and **[7–12]** little by way of judicial guidance on this in the Irish context.[34] O'Malley has observed however that one principle derived from an English case, *R v O'Keefe*,[35] may be treated as applicable in the Irish context. That is, that a suspended sentence should only be imposed where "the court is convinced that a custodial sentence is warranted in the first place, and … the length of the sentence should never be increased merely because it is about to be suspended."[36]

Concurrent Sentences, Consecutive Sentences and the Principle of Totality

When an offender has been convicted of multiple offences, the sentencing **[7–13]** judge can decide whether to impose concurrent or consecutive prison sentences.[37] Sentences will often run simultaneously where a number of counts can be considered as part of one "transaction".[38] Although this so-called one transaction principle has been referred to in the Irish courts, it is by no means a steadfast rule. The essential question is whether concurrent sentences would adequately reflect the harm caused and the offender's blameworthiness.[39] In *DPP v R McC*[40] the Court of Criminal Appeal was asked to consider whether the sentencing judge had erred in principle in imposing eight concurrent life sentences in respect of the rape counts.[41] In delivering the judgment of the Court, Fennelly J, determined that:

34 Although the judgment in the case of *People (DPP) v Loving* [2006] 3 IR 355, may be instructive in the context of child pornography cases.

35 *R v O'Keefe* (1969) 53 Cr App R 91.

36 O'Malley, *The Criminal Process* (Round Hall, Dublin, 2009), p 910.

37 This is unless a statutory provision dictates that the sentence must run consecutively, such as in the context of bail: s 11 of the Criminal Justice Act 1984, as substituted by s 22 of the Criminal Justice Act 2007.

38 Conway, Daly and Schweppe, *Irish Criminal Justice: Theory, Process and Procedure* (Clarus Press, Dublin, 2010), p 170.

39 O'Malley, *Sexual Offences* (2nd ed, Round Hall, Dublin, 2013), p 621.

40 *DPP v R McC* [2005] IECCA 71.

41 The indictment contained 43 counts of rape, attempted rape, sexual assault and assault against six different female child victims.

> "The alternative to life imprisonment would, on the facts of this case, have been consecutive sentences for a determinate period. If the calculation of such cumulative sentences had totalled as much as thirty years, a figure suggested by the learned trial judge, the court would, in accordance with established principles, have been required to consider whether the totality of the sentences was disproportionate."

[7–14] The circumstances of the case were of such exceptional gravity, however, as to merit the imposition of the maximum penalty. This was upheld by the Supreme Court on appeal.[42] In *The People (DPP) v Stafford*[43] the Court of Criminal Appeal affirmed a sentence of nine years' imprisonment for rape and a concurrent sentence of four years for an offence under s 112 of the Road Traffic Act, 1961, as amended. Geoghegan J determined that the sentence was not unduly lenient, as argued by the DPP, as a further nine years' post-release supervision had also been imposed upon the offender.

[7–15] It may be that the principle of proportionality requires that consecutive sentences be imposed upon an offender. Consecutive sentences are often imposed in cases where there are a number of charges and/or multiple victims. In such circumstances, the totality principle will be taken into account in determining the appropriate sentence, though this will still usually result in the imposition of a severe sentence. The principle involves the court selecting an appropriate sentence for each offence, before then evaluating the cumulative length of sentence against the overall gravity of the offending. If the overall sentence is deemed unjust in light of the circumstances, then the sentence will be adjusted downwards in order to arrive at a more proportionate term of imprisonment. In *People (DPP) v McCarton*[44] a cumulative sentence of 20 years' imprisonment had been imposed for rape and other offences perpetrated against two women.[45] The Court of Criminal Appeal, taking into account the cumulative effect of the sentences, reduced the overall sentence to 18 years. In the case of *DPP v Melia*[46] a cumulative sentence of nine years' imprisonment, with one suspended, was increased to 12 years, in light of the offences perpetrated against four women within a matter of weeks, and the fact that the offender had a prior conviction for rape.[47]

---

42 *People (DPP) v McC and DC* [2008] 2 IR 92.

43 *The People (DPP) v Stafford* [2008] IECCA 15.

44 *People (DPP) v McCarton*, Ex tempore, Court of Criminal Appeal, May 19, 2005.

45 The Court had to impose consecutive sentences, as the second offence was committed while the offender was on bail for the first offence.

46 *DPP v Melia*, unreported, Court of Criminal Appeal, 29 November 1999.

47 See also *DPP v P.O'C* [2009] IECCA 116.

General Sentencing Principles and Policies

Before further discussing sentencing in the context of sexual offences, it is incumbent to first consider a number of important principles generally applicable to sentencing practices in the Irish courts. These include sentencing rationales, the important principle of proportionality and the factors which may fall to be considered by a sentencing judge in determining an individualised sentence in a case. **[7–16]**

The Principle of Proportionality

For Irish sentencing law, there is one dominating principle that runs concurrent to all the other aims of punishment. This principle states that "punishment should be appropriate not only to the offence committed but also to the particular offender."[48] The rationale underlying this principle is that of proportionate punishment. The doctrine of proportionality which stems back to the writings of Cesare Beccaria,[49] is based upon commonsense notions of fairness. Punishments are undeserved if minor offences are punished with severe sanctions and vice versa. The principle has attained constitutional status as affirmed in the case of *People (DPP) v C (W)* where Flood J, found that "the selection of the particular punishment to be imposed on an individual offender is subject to the constitutional principle of proportionality."[50] This is an extremely important principle which permits sentencing to be individualised on the basis of aggravating and mitigating factors, and which incorporates judicial discretion into the sentencing framework. **[7–17]**

Sentencing Rationales and Philosophy

Punishment is often considered to be the morally appropriate response to offending behaviour. It represents the formal expression of censure for the offender's actions and reinforces the public expression of condemnation for breaching the social contract.[51] Censure undoubtedly features in the punishment of violent and sexual offences. Such wrongdoing evokes strong feelings of distain, given the harm that can be inflicted upon the victim and society. Censure in such cases may be reflected in the severity of the sentence, or the fact of conviction itself may often serve as adequate censure, especially in the context of sensitive sexual abuse cases (such as those involving children). Even in such cases, however, the principle of **[7–18]**

48 *The State (Stanbridge) v McMahon* [1978] IR 314, 318, per Gannon J.

49 Beccaria, *On Crimes and Punishments* (Leghorn, false imprint Haarlem, 1764); Young, *Introduction on Crimes and Punishments* (Indianapolis, 1986).

50 *People (DPP) v C (W)* [1994] 1 ILRM 321, 324.

51 See Von Hirsch, *Censure and Sanctions* (Clarendon, Oxford, 1993).

proportionality will be invoked to determine the appropriate sentence in a given case.[52]

[7–19] While censure may to some extent serve as a viable justification for the imposition of punishment, punishment purely for the sake of punishment is rarely, if ever, considered appropriate. There must be a reason for imposing a criminal sanction upon an offender and accordingly a variety of rationales have been developed by the courts overtime in order to justify sentencing decisions. Although various rationales can be invoked in one particular case to justify a sentence, it is not proposed that they compete at the same time to provide justification for the same questions. Rather they are employed individually to provide answers to different questions such as; 'why punish?', 'how much punishment?', 'who do we punish?'[53] There are generally five key rationales of punishment. These are deterrence, both individual and general, incapacitation, rehabilitation and desert or retribution.

[7–20] Deterrence is focused upon the prevention of crime as the primary aim of punishment. The theory has two elements: individual deterrence, which seeks to deter the individual offender from reoffending in the future, and general deterrence, which serves as a warning to the public at large as to the consequences of offending. Both types of deterrence presuppose a rational actor who makes conscious decisions regarding offending behaviour, and can modify their behaviour under the threat of criminal sanctions.[54] The theory does not account for opportunistic criminal conduct, and as such may have little effect in deterring such conduct.

[7–21] Another rationale that can be invoked is the principle of incapacitation. A simplistic explanation of this rationale is that offenders are punished in order to physically prevent them from offending for the duration of their sentence. However, there are broader connotations inherent in this rationale which may challenge the principle of proportionality. The incapacitative approach is premised upon the notion of risk and public protection. It involves identifying offenders who are of particular danger to society and in view of the likelihood that they will harm again, invoking special protective measures.[55] As such it has been used to justify the imposition of disproportionately severe sentences, unwarranted by the gravity of the

[52] O'Malley has argued for an approach of "constructive censure whereby courts impose penalties that leave no doubt as to the gravity of the offending conduct but that will ... let the offender continue to live, or soon resume living, a productive life." O'Malley, *supra* note 39, p 530.

[53] See Hart, and Gardner, *supra* note 3.

[54] See O'Malley, *Sentencing Law and Practice* (2nd ed, Thomson Round Hall, Dublin, 2016).

[55] In the UK, a Dangerous Offenders Sentencing Scheme was introduced under the

offence and the personal circumstances of the individual offender. In the Irish context, the principle of proportionality and the constitutional prohibition upon punishing individuals for crimes not yet committed[56] means that while incapacitation may be considered in sentencing, it will usually only play a limited role in the determination of punishment.

Rehabilitation is another rationale often invoked in sentencing. The objective is the reform of the offender, so as to eliminate or reduce reoffending in the future. As such it may involve treatment such as therapy or counselling, cognitive-behavioural programmes, or the requirement to engage in an activity aimed at restraining reoffending behaviour. A key concern surrounding rehabilitation has been the effectiveness of reform interventions.[57] There is also concern that the sentence may be disproportionate (having regard to the offence and particular offender) given that there is little if any limitation placed upon the scope of the intervention. There is a public interest in rehabilitating offenders, however, which means it remains a desirable feature of sentencing policy. It is apparent that the Irish courts place great emphasis upon the rehabilitative approach[58] and often use it to justify the imposition of community sentences or reduced custodial sentences. **[7–22]**

Desert, or retributive theories, of punishment are premised upon the idea that offenders are moral agents who deserve censure in the form of punishment for their wrongdoing. The justification for state punishment is therefore premised upon a form of social justice which aims to express distain for the wrongdoing. This theory is favoured in many jurisdictions as the foundations of sentencing policy.[59] However, offenders do not sacrifice all their rights upon conviction, and have a right to be punished proportionately. Proportionality is thus the key principle of the desert rationale and is used to anchor the question of 'how much punishment?' in a given case. **[7–23]**

Criminal Justice Act 2003, as amended by the Legal Aid, Sentencing and Punishment of Offenders Act 2012, and the Criminal Justice and Courts Act 2015.

56 See *People (AG) v O'Callaghan* [1966] IR 501.

57 Ashworth, *supra* note 55, p 994; See also O'Malley, *supra* note 39, pp 524–526.

58 *People (DPP) v Eccles*, Ex tempore, Court of Criminal Appeal, 8 October 2005.

59 See Von Hirsch, *Doing Justice: The Choice of Punishments* (Hill and Wang, New York, 1976), (republished in 1986 by Boston: Northeastern University Press, 1986); Law Reform Commission, *Consultation Paper on Sentencing* (Law Reform Commission, Dublin, 1993). Kilcommins et al note that "just deserts has not subsumed other rationales to become the coordinating principle of sentencing practice in Ireland." : Kilcommins, O'Donnell, O'Sullivan and Vaughan, *Crime, Punishment and the Search for Order in Ireland* (Institute of Public Administration, Dublin, 2004), p 187.

Aggravating and Mitigating Factors

[7–24] The principle of proportionality dictates that the sentence must fit the crime and the offender who perpetrated that crime. Thus, achieving a proportionate sentence, requires consideration of individualised factors commonly referred to as aggravating and mitigating factors. Aggravating factors have the effect of increasing the penalty for an offence above what might have been imposed in the absence of such factors. The sentencing judge will generally begin by assessing the gravity of the particular offence, having regard to both the culpability of the offender and the harm caused by the offending behaviour. The severity of the offence will determine the starting point for ascertaining the appropriate sentence in the case. In *DPP v M.A.F.*[60] the offender appealed the severity of the custodial sentences handed down for rape and sexual assault, on the basis that the judge had erred in principle in over-assessing the seriousness of the offending behaviour and had failed to take sufficient account of the mitigating factors. In allowing the appeal and varying the sentence, the Court of Appeal, determined that the sentencing judge had located the case at the wrong point on the scale having regard to sentences imposed and upheld in other cases,[61] but rejected the argument that the sentencing judge had failed to take sufficient account of mitigating factors.

[7–25] Aggravating factors are also incorporated into this assessment of the appropriate punishment for the offence. There is no exhaustive list of such factors but aggravating factors which have featured commonly in case law include, the use of firearms or gratuitous violence in the commission of the offence, acts of sexual perversion in addition to a rape, or if excessive violence accompanied the rape act (apart from the violence of the act itself), and breach of trust between the victim and assailant. Under s 11(3) of the Criminal Justice Act 1984, as amended by s 10 of the Bail Act 1997, a court is obliged to consider the commission of an offence while on bail as an aggravating factor. Once the appropriate sentence for the offence has been selected, the judge will then assess any relevant mitigating factors. The Supreme Court in *People (DPP) v M*[62] stated:

> "Having assessed what is the appropriate sentence for a particular crime it is the duty of the court to consider then the particular circumstances of the convicted person. It is within this ambit that mitigating factors fall to be considered."[63]

---

[60] *DPP v MAF* [2016] IECA 14.

[61] The Court considered the appropriate point for the headline offence to be 13 years rather than the 15 years originally imposed, considering the psychological make-up of the particular appellant.

[62] *People (DPP) v M* [1994] 3 IR 306.

[63] *ibid*, 317 per Denham J.

The effect of mitigating factors can be to reduce the sentence as deemed appropriate by the sentencing judge. The most common mitigating factor considered is the guilty plea.[64] That, along with cooperation with the Gardaí, can signal remorse, saves the expenditure of a criminal trial, and spares the victim the ordeal of testifying. The stage of the proceedings at which the guilty plea arises is extremely important in determining the weight of this mitigating factor. While early admission of guilt can indicate genuine remorse, an admission late in the proceedings could be viewed as tactical and superficial. This factor has now been placed upon statutory footing under s 29 of the Criminal Justice Act 1999. Other factors that frequently arise in case law include the prospect of rehabilitation,[65] whether the individual is a first-time offender or has previous convictions, and the age of the offender. Such mitigating factors become extremely important in determining the appropriate punishment for the particular individual to be sentenced by the court. [7–26]

Sentencing Sex Offenders and the Role of Aggravating and Mitigating Factors

It has been noted above that there are no precise statutory or judicial guidelines established in Ireland which mandates a particular sentence in accordance with the range of circumstances in a particular case (apart from the few mandatory sentences that exist). Adherence to the principle of proportionality, requires that sentencing be individualised according to the offence and the offender who committed it. Consequently, sentences for similar offences can vary considerably depending upon the circumstances of the case and the aggravating and mitigating factors deemed relevant. This is also true when it comes to sentencing in sexual offence cases. Applying the principle of proportionality first requires an assessment of the appropriate sentence for the offence, considering the gravity of said offence. Sexual assault, for example, carries a maximum sentence of 10 years' imprisonment (14 where the victim is under 17 years of age), but behaviour within this category can vary on the scale of gravity from slight unwanted contact to violent assault. In addition, factors such as the age of the victim, the fact that the offender was in a position of trust, the numeracy of the incidents of assault and the age of the assailant and a guilty plea, may be incorporated to reconfigure the sentence so that it is deemed proportionate given all the circumstances. Similarly, the gravity of the crime of rape, which carries a maximum life sentence, can be further exacerbated by factors such as excessive violence accompanying the rape or gang rape, while mitigating factors such as ill health of the offender, an early expression of remorse and [7–27]

---

[64] *People (DPP) v Tiernan* [1988] IR 250; *People (DPP) v M* [1994] 2 ILRM 541.
[65] *People (AG) v O'Driscoll* (1972) 1 Frewen 351.

the lack of prior convictions can merit a more lenient sentence than might otherwise have been imposed. The harm sustained by the victim—not just physically but emotionally and psychologically also— may be of particular relevance in sentencing for sexual offences. In *The People (DPP) v WD*[66] the court, in concluding that a sentence at the upper end of the normal range would be appropriate, noted that:

> "[T]he victim impact statement indicates that the victim had difficulty sleeping at first and suffered panic attacks. Her concentration went as to her studies and she began to panic about all matters. She lost interest in study and almost dropped out and left her part time job. She suffered a big character change from being outgoing into being closed with family and friends. Now she is uncomfortable in the presence of men and wary while out particularly at night and looking over her shoulder."[67]

[7–28] The Court of Criminal Appeal in *People (DPP) v GK* also referred to the "serious harm" done to the victim in concluding that the particular aggravated sexual assault lay in "the mid to upper range of seriousness on the scale of gravity of such assaults."[68] Despite such judgments, sentences which are perceived not to properly reflect the harm sustained by the victims of sexual violence, have been the subject of much controversy in recent years.[69]

[7–29] The following section will now examine some of the key aggravating and mitigating factors that may be considered in determining the appropriate sentence for a sexual offence in a particular case.

The Guilty Plea

[7–30] A guilty plea is widely accepted as a mitigating factor which often justifies a reduction in the sentence imposed in a particular case. In a sexual offence case, an early admission of guilt can spare the victim the ordeal of testifying at trial and may indicate genuine remorse for the harm caused. As per s 29 of the Criminal Justice Act 1999, the court will take into account the point in time at which the admission was made, as more merit may be attributed to an early admission than one that takes place at a late stage in the criminal proceedings. The section does not preclude the imposition of the maximum

---

66 *The People (DPP) v WD* [2008] 1 IR 308.

67 *ibid*, 334.

68 *People (DPP) v GK* [2008] IECCA 110. The Court noted the victim's loss of security and permanent impairment of her enjoyment of life.

69 One example is the case of Anthony Lyons, which received much media attention and sparked significant public outrage over the sentence imposed by the trial judge despite the acknowledgement of the serious harm suffered by the victim. This sentence was ultimately appealed: *The People (DPP) v Lyons* [2014] IECCA 27.

sentence for the particular offence if the gravity of the circumstances dictate such, notwithstanding a guilty plea from the accused.[70] There are always "exceptional circumstances" which may warrant the maximum sentence. In *People (DPP) v R. McC*[71] the Supreme Court refused to interfere with several concurrent life sentences imposed by the trial judge and upheld by the Court of Criminal Appeal for offences of child sexual abuse. Despite the existence of mitigating factors, the Court acknowledged that the offences were of exceptional seriousness as to warrant the imposition of the maximum penalty. In relation to the plea of guilty the Court stated:

> "It would ... be an essential requirement when imposing a maximum sentence against a backdrop of a guilty plea that the court would identify those exceptional circumstances in such a way that would make it absolutely clear why the maximum sentence is warranted when there had been mitigating factors in the case. Such instances will of necessity be and confined to those cases where the offences represent the worst imaginable variation of the offence in question."[72]

Nonetheless an admission of guilt can be a significant mitigating factor as emphasised by the Supreme Court in the case of *People (DPP) v Tiernan*.[73] There the Court determined that inadequate credit had been given for the early plea of guilty, which had spared the victim the experience of testifying. Thus the original sentence of 21 years' imprisonment was reduced to 17 years. This sentence still reflected the gravity of the offence perpetrated again the victim.[74] **[7–31]**

The Supreme Court in *Tiernan* also determined that ordinarily the crime of rape will be punishable by a substantial custodial sentence unless there are "wholly exceptional" circumstances in a case that such is unwarranted and this principle has been endorsed in subsequent case law. In *People (DPP) v. Drought*[75] Charleton J stated: **[7–32]**

> "[a] suspended sentence can only be contemplated where the circumstances of the offence are such as to be so completely exceptional as to allow the

70 Criminal Justice Act 1999, s 29 (2). See also Editorial, "No jail term for man (25) who raped girlfriend while she slept" *The Irish Times*, 13 July 2015; O'Sullivan, "Tougher sentences in sex cases demanded", *Irish Independent*, 30 April 2014; Buckley, "Justice denied", *Irish Examiner*, 23 January 2013.

71 *People (DPP) v R McC* [2008] 2 IR 92

72 *ibid*, 105.

73 *People (DPP) v Tiernan* [1988] IR 250; [1989] ILRM 149.

74 See further discussion of this case below.

75 *People (DPP) v. Drought* [2007] IEHC 310.

court to approach sentencing for an offence of rape in a way that deviates so completely from the norm established by the case law."[76]

[7–33] In *DPP v NY*[77] the Court of Criminal Appeal held that the trial judge had erred in principle in assuming that he was automatically obliged to impose a custodial sentence for rape. The trial judge had imposed concurrent sentences of three years' imprisonment for each count with nine months suspended. The Court of Criminal Appeal upheld this sentence but suspended the remainder of the sentence, in consideration of the fact that the offender had already spent seven months in prison. The Court held that in imposing an appropriate sentence the court "must not deprive itself of the possibility of identifying the exceptional cases where a custodial sentence may not be warranted." The Court took into account that the offender had at all times admitted his guilt and saved the victim the trauma of a trial.

[7–34] In *People (DPP) v Kinsella*[78] an eight-year sentence with one year suspended had been imposed, in consideration of the guilty plea which had been entered once the trial began. The Court of Criminal Appeal held that the discount for the guilty plea was excessive in the circumstances and that the starting point of eight years was itself too low. Thus, it substituted a sentence of 10 years with six months suspended. In the case of *DPP v MF*[79] the accused pleaded guilty to the rape and sexual assault of four boys and was given an 18-year sentence with the final four suspended in consideration of his genuine expression of remorse. In *People (DPP) v DP*[80] however, the Court of Criminal Appeal upheld a life sentence handed down for a conviction of rape. The Court felt that the plea of guilty which only came two weeks before the trial, merited no consideration. The accused also had two prior extremely serious aggravated sexual assault convictions.

[7–35] While usually a guilty plea will merit some mitigation of sentence, save in exceptionally rare circumstances, the accused should not be penalised for exercising his constitutional right to a trial in due course of law.[81] Fighting the case should not be treated as an aggravating factor in sentencing as such would arguably be regarded as an error of principle.[82]

---

76 See the judgment of Charleton J for a useful analysis of gradients of punishment for sexual offence cases.

77 *DPP v NY* [2002] 4 IR 309.

78 *People (DPP) v Kinsella* [2012] IECCA 73.

79 Case reported in *The Irish Times*, 19 July 2011.

80 *People (DPP) v DP* [2009] IECCA 149.

81 See *People (DPP) v Daly* [20011] IECCA 104; [2012] 1 IR 476

82 O'Malley, *supra* note 39, p 561.

The Presence or Absence of Previous Convictions

Another factor which frequently arises in the context of sentencing decisions is whether or not the accused has previous criminal convictions. The impact of good character or bad character upon the sentencing process has been well documented in case law in this jurisdiction. **[7–36]**

First Time Offenders

The absence of previous convictions is ordinarily treated as a strong mitigating factor in favour of the accused. It indicates to the court that the accused has never been in trouble with law before and is unlikely to reoffend and consequentially merits a sentence to reflect the likelihood of rehabilitation.[83] This along with considerations such as the accused coming from a good background, being in stable employment, and supporting a family, may be used to justify a lesser sentence than might otherwise have been imposed. This is not an uncomplicated matter in the context of sexual offence cases. The absence of previous convictions alone may not necessarily represent an accurate portrayal of the character of the accused (consider cases of historic sexual abuse). It may be argued that as such, character-based mitigation ought not to be considered by the courts, but it would be difficult to sustain such an argument in the long run. It is incumbent on the courts to seek to provide the offender with an opportunity for reform and as such it seems this factor will continue to be important for a sentencing judge. The weight accorded to this factor will, however, depend upon the circumstances of the particular case, and the gravity of the offence charged.[84] In the case of *DPP v Keane*[85] the trial judge considered the mitigating factors and questioned **[7–37]**

> "... whether or not I would be comfortable if I imprison this particular accused who is a young man with no previous convictions whose attitude was that he thought what he did was out of character, what he was alleged to have done was out of character, but if the DNA established that he had done it he would not resile from his responsibilities in the matter."

In view of the fact that the accused had no previous convictions and was unlikely to offend again, a three-year sentence was imposed but suspended for a period of five years. On appeal the Court of Criminal Appeal paid due attention to the absence of previous convictions but considered the **[7–38]**

---

83 It has also been noted that imprisonment is a harsh punishment which should be a penalty of last resort, especially for first time offenders: *People (DPP) v Kelly* [2005] 2 IR 321. Inevitably however, there are crimes so serious that imprisonment cannot be avoided even if it is a first offence.

84 *People (DPP) v KG* [2008] IECCA 110; *People (DPP) v Loving* [2006] 3 IR 355.

85 *DPP v Keane* [2007] IECCA 119.

appropriate sentence to be one of 10 years' imprisonment, with three years suspended, and also imposed a one year post-release supervision order upon the offender.

Repeat Offenders

[7–39] There is clearly a disparity in the way in which first-time offenders and repeat offenders are treated in sentencing. In *DPP v P. O'C* the Court of Criminal Appeal commented that "[t]he previous convictions and sentences are relevant to the appropriate sentence to be imposed on the [offender]."[86] While the absence of previous convictions may indicate good character and an unlikelihood of reoffending, the existence of previous convictions will usually result in a more serious penalty than if there had been none. In the case of *DPP v O.R.*[87] the Court of Appeal held that,

> "... a previous record, even if not aggravating, and depending on how bad it is will result in the progressive loss of the substantial mitigation that would otherwise be available to an accused who was of previous good character."[88]

[7–40] Previous convictions may indicate to the court a propensity for criminal behaviour, particularly if similar to the current offence. Indeed, in cases of sexual offence, more weight will normally be attributed to prior convictions for a sexual offence than for a dissimilar offence. A previous conviction for, say, a road traffic offence or a theft offence, will have little value in a case of rape and as such may have minimal if any practical effect upon the sentence for such an offence. In *DPP v M.M*[89] the Court of Appeal, per Mahon J, noted that the appellant did have previous convictions but they were of a very different nature to the offences of sexual assault and buggery in this case and as such were not considered relevant.

[7–41] In *People (DPP) v S (P)*[90] the appellant was convicted of sexual offences committed against two boys and sentenced to multiple life sentences and some determinate sentences. He had multiple convictions for similar sexual offences and the trial judge had indicated that in the absence of the previous convictions 10 years would have been an appropriate sentence to impose. The appellant argued that disproportionate weight had been placed upon his previous convictions. The Court of Criminal Appeal, in reducing the sentence to 15 years' imprisonment and a 10-year post-release supervision order felt that,

86 *DPP v PO'C* [2009] IECCA 116.
87 *DPP v O.R.* [2017] IECA 61.
88 *ibid*, para 25, per Edwards J.
89 *DPP v M.M.* [2016] IECA 282.
90 *People (DPP) v S (P)* [2009] IECCA 1.

> "... in relation to the previous offence the applicant has already been punished and should not on the occasion of sentencing for the present offences be punished again for those former offences."

The Court of Criminal Appeal also determined however that "the nature of the previous offending indicates that the offender represents a continuing danger to the public" and that "[t]his is a relevant factor in sentencing." A similar sentiment was expressed in the case of *People (DPP) v KG*[91] where the Court of Criminal Appeal held that prior convictions, **[7–42]**

> "... are relevant not just in terms of their absence in mitigation of sentence but also in terms of assessing an appropriate sentence in terms of the seriousness of the offence, which sentence will be proportionately more severe than would be the case were these circumstances absent."

The trial judge had relied on the case of *DPP v Melia*,[92] where a sentence of nine years' imprisonment for multiple sex offences was appealed on grounds of undue leniency. The Court of Criminal Appeal increased the sentence to 12 years having regard to the gravity of the offences and the offender's previous rape conviction. In doing so the Court commented that a previous conviction was relevant to the seriousness of the offence rather than as a factor relevant to mitigation of sentence. In *KG* the Court also considered that "previous convictions are relevant not in relation to mitigation of sentence but in aggravation of the offence." The Court felt that the trial judge was entitled to take into account the two previous convictions for rape, but substituted the life sentence imposed, for the aggravated sexual assault, with a sentence of 16 years' imprisonment with the last three years suspended, in addition to a 10-year post-release supervision order. The Court also felt that the trial judge had not erred in his failure to regard the guilty plea as a mitigating factor given the late stage in the proceedings at which it was entered. **[7–43]**

As noted above, the impact of prior convictions will largely depend upon the nature and relevance of those convictions to the current case. In *DPP v Walsh*[93] the Court of Appeal accepted that the trial judge had erred in failing to give any additional discount for the fact that the appellant was of substantially previous good character. The appellant did have a number of prior convictions, but these were entirely dissimilar in that they were mostly road traffic offences. The Court suspended a further year of the headline sentence of seven years' imprisonment in order to reflect that while, **[7–44]**

---

91 *People (DPP) v KG* [2008] IECCA 110.

92 *DPP v Melia*, unreported, Court of Criminal Appeal, 29 November 1999.

93 *DPP v Walsh* [2017] IECA 187.

> "...the mitigation to which he would have been entitled on account of previous good character might have been lost by him on account of his previous convictions they were neither so numerous nor so serious as to have justified the total loss of that discount."[94]

[7–45] The Court of Appeal has spoken out about the need to rehabilitate sex offenders and the challenge this presents, particularly where the individual has demonstrated a pattern of repeated sexual misconduct. In the case of *DPP v J.P.*[95] the appellant had pleaded guilty to sexual assaulting a vulnerable young boy just hours after his release from serving a six-year sentence for a previous sexual assault. The sentencing judge had imposed a 12-year sentence of imprisonment with the final two years suspended, but Court of Appeal increased the suspension period to three years on condition that the offender seek out psychological counselling in prison and complete all treatment offered. The post-release supervision period was also extended to two years. Mahon J acknowledged the worrying fact that the appellant had prior convictions for sexually assaulting boys and young men and that the 12-year sentence was "entirely appropriate" with reference to such past behaviour. However, the Court also determined that insufficient weight was attached to the prospect and need for rehabilitation which is essential if the public is to be protected, thus warranting the alteration to the original sentence imposed.

Invasion of the Victim's Home

[7–46] The invasion of the victim's home in order to perpetrate a crime is considered to be an aggravating factor in sentencing, given the inviolability of the dwelling protected under the Irish Constitution (Art 40.5). A case illustrative in this matter is *People (DPP) v Keane.*[96] The accused had entered the victim's home without her knowledge and raped her as she slept. Additional aggravating factors in the case were the fact that the victim suffered from a hearing impairment and that her three children were asleep in the house at the time. Although the accused argued that he did not recall the events of the evening due to his having consumed a large quantity of alcohol and drugs, he was convicted of rape. In relation to invasion of the home the trial judge stated that it was "... necessary to come down clearly from this Court that people cannot wander around the bedrooms and behave in this predatory fashion" given that it was "...not only a violation of the victim herself ... but also the sense of security which citizens feel they have for themselves and their children in the safety of their home." Despite this the court imposed a fully suspended sentence which was appealed by the DPP. The Court of

---

94 *ibid* per Edwards J, accepting the appellant's submission.
95 *DPP v JP* [2015] IECA 266.
96 People *(DPP) v Keane* [2007] IECCA 119.

Criminal Appeal held that the trial judge had erred in principle in imposing the suspended sentence as there were no exceptional circumstances which justified the departure from the principle that a custodial sentence should be imposed for rape. The Court pointed to the range of aggravating factors relating to the effect of the rape on the victim to which the trial judge had not given appropriate consideration, including the violation of her and her children's sense of security, that she moved out of the house in which the rape occurred and now slept with two guard dogs in her room.

In the case of *DPP v Meyer Hustveit*[97] the Court of Appeal dealt with a review on grounds of undue leniency of a sentence imposed in the Central Criminal Court. The sentencing judge had imposed a seven-year sentence for rape and a concurrent sentence of two years' imprisonment for sexual assault, upon the man (named after the victim dropped her right to anonymity). These sentences were wholly suspended, with McCarthy J acknowledging that there would have been no case but for the confessions of the offender. He also acknowledged the guilty plea entered, absence of previous convictions, cooperation with the Gardaí and a favourable reference from his employer. The crimes had been perpetrated against the victim while she was asleep and admitted to her when she confronted the offender at a later date. The victim expressed to the court her distress that someone she had trusted "violated me in the sanctity of sleep and rest" and she had "lost everything you can claim to have or be. Above all, I've lost my sense of identity and self worth."[98] The Court of Criminal Appeal acknowledged the mitigating factors that "certainly justified and indeed required the imposition of a sentence that would be appreciably less than would be normal in the case of multiple rapes and sexual assaults." However the Court did not agree that "the case was so wholly exceptional as to permit an entirely non custodial disposal."[99] The repeated offending over a significant period of time, which had impacted upon the victim "in a serious, indeed profound way"[100] warranted a 15-month sentence of imprisonment to be imposed. **[7–47]**

Extreme Circumstances in the Case

The harm sustained by victims in cases of rape and serious sexual assault is considered the act perpetrated against them. This in itself is sufficient to place such offending behaviour high on the scale of gravity. However, the courts can also consider additional aggravating factors accompanying **[7–48]**

---

[97] *DPP v Meyer Hustveit* [2016] IECA 271.

[98] Brennan and Conlon, "Face of man who raped girlfriend while she slept", *Irish Independent*, 13 July 2015.

[99] *DPP v Meyer Hustveit* [2016] IECA 271, para 29, per Bermingham J.

[100] *ibid*, para 11, per Bermingham J.

the act itself, which can justify the imposition of a more severe sentence. Excessive violence accompanying a rape or sexual assault, rape by multiple assailants, or rape of multiple victims can all aggravate the circumstances of a case to warrant a harsher punishment.

[7–49] Gang rape is viewed by the courts as particularly egregious given the increased trauma and risk of serious injury occurring to the victim. As a result, it usually ranks highly on the scale of seriousness. The case of *People (DPP) v Tiernan*[101] is illustrative. In this case the victim had been raped and buggered by three men, who dragged her out of her car, gagged her and sat on her face as she was raped. Her boyfriend had been locked in the boot of the car so as to prevent him coming to her aid. As a result of the attack, the victim was deeply traumatised and suffered from a serious nervous disorder which lasted for at least six months and rendered her for that period unfit to work. Given the savage nature of the attack, the assailants were sentenced to 17 years, 14 years and 12 years based upon their roles in the attack and relevant personal circumstances.[102] The appellant in the case, Tiernan, also had a number of previous convictions, for crimes involving violence and indecency. The court considered this to be "particularly relevant as an aggravating circumstance to a conviction for rape".[103]

[7–50] The extreme violence perpetrated against the victim, apart from the violence of the act itself, can be seen to exacerbate the degradation of the victim in such cases and will be considered an aggravating factor in sentencing. The use of a weapon or threats of additional violence during the assault for example will be viewed seriously by the courts. In the case of *People (DPP) v Crowley*[104] a sentence of six and a half years was imposed despite the early admission and a plea of guilty. The victim in the case was, however, only 14 years old and the offender had use gratuitous violence, including threats to kill her, in order to commit the offence. In the case of *People (DPP) v Horgan*[105] the respondent was convicted of the manslaughter (on retrial) and rape of a woman he had attacked and strangled in a public park. The Court of Criminal Appeal, in imposing a 12-year sentence on each count, stated that

101 *People (DPP) v Tiernan* [1988] IR 250; [1989] ILRM 149.

102 Tiernan had his sentence reduced from 21 years to 17 years as a result of his guilty plea which spared the victim the ordeal of testifying. One of the other assailants had his 21-year sentence reduced to 12 years given that he was 19 years old at the time of the attack and acting under the influence of an older person. The third assailant was sentenced to 14 years as his involvement was considered to fall between that of the other two.

103 *ibid*, 254.

104 Reported in *The Irish Times*, 25 July 2006.

105 *People (DPP) v Horgan* [2007] IECCA 29.

> "there are strong public policy considerations which demand that a rape accompanied by violence which carries an appreciable risk of death, must be seen as being in a most serious category and must attract a sentence at the higher range."[106]

In *People (DPP) v Moore*[107] the Court of Criminal Appeal imposed a sentence of 10 years for rape and assault causing harm, where considerable violence had been used to perpetrate the attack upon the victim, and due to the fact that the offender had only recently been released from prison following his conviction for a previous rape. In *People (DPP) v W (TC)*[108] the assailant was sentenced to four years imprisonment, with two years suspended, for sexually assaulting the 13-year-old child of his partner who was minding his own three-year-old child at the time. The assault which occurred in the presence of the three-year-old child, was described as aggressive and included threats to kill the victim. The Court of Criminal Appeal increased the sentence to six years, with the last two years suspended, for what was described as an offence being in thee "upper reaches" of gravity. Mitigating factors, particularly the guilty plea were also relevant however, in reaching the sentence. In *People (DPP) v Smith*[109] a sentence of eight years was imposed upon an offender who dragged a 60-year-old woman, on her way home from bingo, off the road, sexually assaulted her and threatened to kill her. This sentence was imposed notwithstanding the guilty plea entered by the assailant. **[7–51]**

A 12-year sentence, with the last four suspended was imposed upon a man who forcefully entered the home of an intellectually disabled 58-year-old woman and violently sexually assaulted her.[110] The assault had been accompanied by extreme violence during which the man had grabbed the victim by her throat punched her in the head and burned her with a cigarette. In imposing the sentence, Hunt J observed the significant impact of the assault upon the victim and her considerable loss of independence. The court also noted that the man had pleaded guilty to the aggravated sexual assault and had no previous convictions. **[7–52]**

Offending against multiple victims is also considered to be an aggravating factor in sentencing. Where this is the case the court has discretion to impose concurrent or consecutive sentences for the multiple counts. Although the court may choose to exercise its discretion to impose concurrent sentences **[7–53]**

---

106 A higher sentence would have been warranted if not for the age of the offender, who was only 16 years old at the time of the attack, and his plea of guilty to the manslaughter charge.

107 *People (DPP) v Moore*, unreported, Court of Criminal Appeal, 20 December 2005.

108 *People (DPP) v W (TC)* [2010] IECCA 95

109 Case reported in *The Irish Times*, 14 March 2012.

110 Case reported in *The Irish Times*, 6 July 2015.

for offences perpetrated against multiple victims, often the longest sentence will be imposed in view of this aggravating factor.[111]

Age and Related Factors

[7–54] Age can become a relevant factor in sentencing deliberations both in relation to the victim and the offender. Age is a relevant personal circumstance of the offender and as such may often be considered in mitigation of the sentence. An offender who is young may benefit from a desire to facilitate rehabilitation, particularly where it is a first offence. An elderly offender may similarly benefit from a desire to alleviate the harsh impact a prison environment may have on such an offender. Age and infirmity is not a barrier to prosecution, nor will it automatically omit the imposition of a custodial sentence for a serious offence. However age and infirmity can justify a significant degree of leniency, particularly where the offender does not have a long remaining life span. In such circumstances, the principle of proportionality operates to permit old age to be treated as a mitigating factor. In *People (DPP) v H*[112] the Court of Criminal Appeal was of the opinion that the

> "age and health of the offender should be looked at. If the offender is so elderly, or so unwell, then prison will be a special burden to bear, the sentence should reflect how a particular term may punish him as much [as] a longer term for a younger offender in reasonable health."

[7–55] In *People (DPP) v JM*[113] the defendant, who was convicted of a series of sexual assaults on pupils in the past, was 84 years old and in poor mental and physical health, and thus the court imposed a sentence of three years' imprisonment instead of the eight years which would have otherwise been appropriate. On appeal, it was subsequently held that the sentencing court had erred in failing to suspend the sentence considering the age and health of the defendant. In 2013, 72-year-old Patrick O'Brien was convicted of the rape and sexual abuse of his daughter over a 10-year period. Carney J, presiding over the case, described it as one of the most serious cases of serial rape of a daughter and imposed a 12-year sentence with nine years suspended, taking into account the offender's health problems. On appeal, the sentence was held to be "unduly lenient" and a new sentence of 12 years with three years suspended was imposed. The Court stated that despite the serious ill health and advancing age of the offender, it would nonetheless not be impossible for him to tolerate imprisonment.

[111] *People (DPP) v S (P)* [2009] IECCA 1.
[112] *People (DPP) v H* [2007] IEHC 335.
[113] *People (DPP) v JM*, unreported, Court of Criminal Appeal, 22 February 2002.

The age of the victim at the time of the commission of the offence enhances their vulnerability and this becomes relevant as an aggravating factor in sentencing. In 2016 a man was jailed for 13 years for the vaginal and anal rape of a 73-year-old woman in her home.[114] The commission of the offence following the break-in of her home added to the seriousness, with McCarthy J commenting, **[7–56]**

> "One runs short of words to describe the seriousness of some of the offences that come before the court, particularly offences of a sexual nature ... She was violated in the vilest manner in her own home."

A five-year post-release supervision order was also imposed upon the offender. A sexual offence perpetrated against a child will also be viewed more harshly, and such cases may also involve a breach of trust where the offender is a parent or someone in a close relationship with the child. In 2016 a Cork man was convicted for sexually assaulted his friend's 11-year-old daughter.[115] Imposing a three-year custodial sentence, with the last year suspended, Ryan J determined that the young age of the victim, the lasting impact the offences had on her, the fact the offender was a close family friend and the breach of trust involved, were all aggravating factors warranting a custodial sentence. In mitigation of the sentence was the fact that the man had no previous convictions. **[7–57]**

Compensating the Victim

Providing financial compensation to a victim can be viewed as a positive step in seeking to make amends. Under s 6 of the Criminal Justice Act 1993 a court may on conviction, **[7–58]**

> "... of any person of an offence...instead of or in addition to dealing with him in any other way, may, unless it sees reason to the contrary, make...an order...requiring him to pay compensation in respect of any personal injury or loss resulting from that offence...to any person...who has suffered such injury or loss."

Although this section does not appear to be used extensively in relation to serious offences, the statute clearly envisions that a compensation order may be made where considered appropriate and a trial judge can exercise their discretion in this regard even in serious cases. In considering the payment of compensation the court will take the means of the offender into account.[116] **[7–59]**

---

[114] Editorial, "Man sentenced to 13 years for raping elderly woman", *The Irish Times*, 25 July 2016.

[115] Editorial, "Man jailed for sexually assaulting his friend's daughter during sleepover", *Independent*, 6 May 2016.

[116] The Court of Criminal Appeal in the case of *The People (DPP) v Lyons* [2014]

It is also possible for the offender to make an offer of compensation to the victim, independent of the statutory provision. A genuine offer of compensation can indicate that the offender is remorseful of the crime and the harm inflicted upon the victim. In *People (DPP) v Gray*[117] the Court of Criminal Appeal regarded as reasonable, the sentence imposed by the trial judge which took into account the significant compensation paid by the offender to the victim. Thus, it is a factor which a judge may take into account at sentencing, but this does not necessarily mean it will operate as a mitigating factor or may only be considered a marginal factor in mitigation.[118] In *People (DPP) v McLaughlin*[119] the Court of Criminal Appeal rejected the suggestion that compensation should lead to a suspended sentence, or be considered an "exceptional factor" as per the *Tiernan* judgment. The Court of Criminal Appeal again dealt with the issue in the case of *The People (DPP) v Lyons*.[120] The accused was convicted of the sexual assault of a woman for which the trial judge had imposed a sentence of six years' imprisonment with five and a half years suspended.[121] The offender was also ordered to pay €75,000 compensation to his victim, under s 6 of the 1993 Act, and was placed on the sex offenders register in accordance with the provisions of the Sex Offenders Act 2001. In referring to his decision to make the compensation order, Hogan J commented:

> "... I want to mark the seriousness of this offence by the defendant giving something back, not just to society against whom he has offended, but giving some back directly to the lady that he has offended against and has offended against in mind and in body."

[7–60] He also commented on "the long abiding psychological trauma" suffered by the victim and that the offence had involved "violence of a seriously frightening nature." However, the learned judge also noted that the offender had "expressed remorse, has been hitherto of good character, is well regarded and is unlikely to reoffend." The DPP appealed against the leniency of the sentence arguing that while the judge had referred to the lasting effect of the attack on the victim, the sentence did not reflect the harm sustained. Having due regard to the aggravating and mitigating factors in the case, the Court of Criminal Appeal substituted a sentence of six years with four

---

IECCA 27, remarked that this should not be misconstrued as creating one rule for the wealthy and one rule for the poor.

117 *People (DPP) v Gray* [2010] IECCA 119.

118 See the judgment of Murray J in *The People (DPP) v Lyons* [2014] IECCA 27.

119 *People (DPP) v McLaughlin* [2005] 3 IR 198.

120 *The People (DPP) v Lyons* [2014] IECCA 27.

121 Despite admitting to the offence, the accused pleaded not guilty, arguing that he had been overcome with an "irresistible urge" due to a concoction of alcohol and medication. This defence was rejected by the jury.

suspended,[122] along with a 12 months post-release supervision order, in addition to keeping the offender on the sex offenders register for 10 years. In analysing the use of the compensation order, Murray J commented that "where serious indictable offences are concerned it would seem that, in principle, if a compensation order is being made it should be made only in addition to the appropriate sentence, including imprisonment, that meets the gravity of the case."[123] The Court felt the trial judge had not erred in exercising his discretion by making the compensation order but, in the circumstances of the case, it was not considered to be a mitigating factor.

Miscellaneous Factors

The factors examined above by no means represent an exhaustive list of all the factors that can be considered by a sentencing judge. Additional factors may present themselves under the circumstances of a particular case and be deemed relevant either in aggravation or mitigation of the punishment to be imposed. Another factor that the courts have dealt with is that of premeditation, which although not specific to sexual offence cases, can be deemed a relevant aggravating factor. The Court in *People (DPP) v Tiernan*[124] acknowledged premeditation to be an aggravating factor. Planning to perpetrate a criminal offence and cause harm to another is viewed more harshly than an impulsive reaction committed in the spur of the moment. How this factor will aggravate a sentence will also be influenced by the degree of the premeditation involved. In the case of *People (DPP) v Murray*,[125] the offender pleaded guilty to assault and attempted rape, and confessed that he had prepared a rape kit, which contained items such as rope, vaseline, a dog lead and duct tape, with the intention of attacking the first young woman who came along. Mr Justice Carney imposed a 12-year sentence with the final three years suspended, acknowledging the "planned" nature of the attack. He also imposed an eight-year post-release supervision order upon the offender. **[7–61]**

Intoxication is another factor that may be considered by the court, although it is not clear whether it will be considered in aggravation or mitigation of the sentence. It may also have no appreciable impact whatsoever. Generally speaking, offender intoxication will not justify a more lenient sentence for the offence, although substance addiction may be considered in assessing the totality of the circumstances of the offender and the reasons for perpetrating **[7–62]**

[122] The Court, per Murray J, commented that "this Court may and should take cognisance of the fact that imprisonment is a particularly hard punishment for any convicted person in a position similar in age and previous good character to the respondent."

[123] *ibid*, per Murray J.

[124] *People (DPP) v Tiernan* [1988] IR 250

[125] *People (DPP) v Murray*, CCC, 15 October 2010.

the crime. In assessing rehabilitative prospects the sentencing judge may refer to the addiction of the offender or any attempts made on his part to address the addiction.[126] Offender intoxication is an issue which has arisen in sexual offence cases in this jurisdiction. In the case of *The People (DPP) v Lyons*[127] the offender claimed that the alcohol he had consumed on the evening of the offence, when mixed with the medication he was taking for a cough and respiratory congestion, may have contributed to his behaviour on the night. In considering the medical evidence presented in support of this claim Murray J determined that,

> "The Court is not convinced that it has been established on that evidence that "voluntary intoxication", as described, is a probable or even reasonably possible explanation for his conduct in committing the assault. It certainly appears to be an event that was totally out of character with the known history in every respect, of the respondent, but nonetheless one, of course, for which he bears criminal responsibility."

[7–63] Alcohol consumption by the victim also features in sexual offence cases in this jurisdiction. Studies have revealed that a high portion of complainants are intoxicated at the time of the commission of the offence.[128] As such this can often create problems for proceeding with prosecution, giving evidence and securing convictions.[129] Where a conviction has been secured, however, the matter of intoxication can arise in consideration of the appropriate sentence. A victim who is intoxicated at the time of the offence is clearly in a vulnerable position and taking advantage of the victim's helplessness while in such a state is treated as an aggravating factor. In *People (DPP) v Drought*,[130] the accused was convicted of rape in what the Court described as a "horrible predatory attack on a young woman who was drunk". The victim had been found wandering in a state of dishevelment and distress in the aftermath of the crime and suffered psychologically as a result. Charleton J commented that the offender had been "very much aided in overpowering her by the effects of the alcohol which she had drunk." The nature of the attack was such as to warrant a substantial custodial sentence, but the court felt consideration also had to be given for mitigating factors, such as the lack of previous convictions, the fact that the offender was only 18 years old at the time, and that there must be a "real attempt by the court to look to rehabilitation rather than simple punishment." Thus, a sentence of seven

---

126 See comments by Edwards J in *DPP v Walsh* [2017] IECA 187.

127 *The People (DPP) v Lyons* [2014] IECCA 27.

128 Hanly, Healy and Scriver, *Rape & justice in Ireland: A National Study of Survivor, Prosecutor and Court Responses to Rape* (The Liffey Press, Dublin, 2009).

129 See Leahy, ''Bad Laws or Bad Attitudes? Assessing the Impact of Societal Attitudes upon the Conviction Rate for Rape in Ireland'' (2014) 14 (1) *Irish Journal of Applied Social Studies* 18, 29.

130 [2007] IEHC 31.

years' imprisonment was imposed with the last 18 months suspended on condition of good behaviour and availing of counselling in prison.

The Role of the Victim at Sentencing Stage

Traditionally, the participation of the victim in a criminal trial was limited to their role as a prosecution witness. However, as O'Malley notes, "[a] recurring theme in campaigns for rape law reform from the 1970s onwards and in the broader victims' movement ... was the need to rebalance the criminal justice system in order to cater for the needs and views of victims."[131] One of the ways in which the criminal justice system has sought to accommodate the voice of the victim, is by making provision for victim impact statements in sentencing hearings. Such statements, usually provided to sentencing judges prior to the sentencing of the offender, affords victims an opportunity to be able to express how the crime has affected them. The relevant statutory provision providing for victim impact statements in Ireland is the Criminal Justice Act 1993, as amended by the Criminal Procedure Act 2010. The legislation allows for victim impact statements in relation to sexual offences, offences involving violence or the threat of violence, offences under the Non-Fatal Offences against the Person Act 1997 and related inchoate offences.[132] Section 5(2)(a) of the 1993 Act, as amended, states that: **[7–64]**

> "When imposing sentence on a person for an offence to which this section applied, a court shall take into account, and may, where necessary, receive evidence or submissions concerning, any effect (whether long-term or otherwise) of the offence on the person in respect of whom the offence was committed."

While a sentencing court is obliged to hear a victim impact statement, it is clear that the impact of such a statement upon the sentence imposed is limited. The provision is intended to allow the victim to express "any effect" the offence has had upon them, and thus statements are restricted to this statutory purpose. This has been emphasised in case law on the issue. **[7–65]**

In *People (DPP) v MC*[133] Flood J stressed that "[s]ection 5 cannot, and does not, purport to make any change to the manner in which a court is obliged to carry out its constitutional duty to independently select an appropriate **[7–66]**

---

[131] O'Malley, *supra* note 39, p 710.

[132] Although generally victim impact statements are given in court, provision is also made for such statements to be given via live television link in certain circumstances: s 5A and s 5B of the Criminal Justice Act 1993 as inserted by s 5 and s 6 of the Criminal Procedure Act 2010.

[133] *People (DPP) v MC*, unreported, Court of Criminal Appeal, 16 June 1995.

sentence for a particular accused."[134] This has sparked concerns that a victim's expectations may be raised by the provision of a victim impact statement only to be left disappointed and distressed if the sentence is less than they had hoped for.

[7–67] The Irish courts have also taken a guarded approach against victim impact statements being used as a platform for making fresh allegations against the offender at sentencing stage. In *People (DPP) v O'Donoghue*[135] the Court of Criminal Appeal made clear that any departure from the statement furnished to the court involving unfounded or scurrilous allegations against an accused, may warrant mitigation of the sentence to be imposed.[136]

[7–68] Another issue which has arisen by giving a voice to victims at sentencing is whether and how a victim's plea for leniency should be considered. In general the courts are tasked with determining the appropriate sentence, impartially and objectively, notwithstanding that victims are permitted to express their views regarding the sentence. If courts were required to follow victims' recommendations as to the severity of leniency of a particular sentence, this would undoubtedly detract from the important principle of proportionality, as well as leading to greater inconsistency in sentencing. Nonetheless, it seems that where a victim expresses forgiveness, this is a factor to at least be taken into account, though it is not to be the determinative factor in sentencing. In *People (DPP) v O'D (R)*[137] the Court of Criminal Appeal stated:

> "[t]he trial court is under an obligation to administer justice rather than mercy but very often the reasons given for a plea of mercy are reasons which are relevant to the assessment of a just sentence."

[7–69] In *People (DPP) v MS*[138] the victim of a rape indicated to the court that she would not object to a reduction in the offender's sentence so long as he did not interfere with her or her children. Denham J suggested that while the impact of the offence on the victim was not determinant of the court's decision in terms of the sentence, it is an important factor. In *People (DPP)*

---

[134] This was again reinforced by Finnegan J in the case of *DPP v GK* [2008] IECCA 110 where he stated that the court "does not participate in an exercise in vengeance or seek to retaliate against the applicant on behalf of the victim."

[135] *People (DPP) v O'Donoghue* [2007] 2 IR 336

[136] In the case the mother of the deceased victim had mentioned matters which were not part of the prosecution's case against the offender and which were considered to be highly prejudicial. The sentencing judge ignored the statements in determining a sentence which was later upheld by the Court of Criminal Appeal. See also the case of *People v Magee*, unreported, Court of Criminal Appeal, 29 July 1997.

[137] *People (DPP) v O'D (R)* [2004] 4 IR 361, 364.

[138] *People (DPP) v MS* [2000] 2 IR 592

v McCormack[139] the victim of a sexual assault and attempted rape told the sentencing judge that she did not want the offender to go to jail as she felt that he was very young and would not offend again. The judge considered himself bound in imposing a sentence of imprisonment for the crime, but the Court of Criminal Appeal felt that the express wishes of the victim ought to have been taken into account. After all, the sentence "to be imposed is not the appropriate sentence for the crime, but the appropriate sentence for the crime because it has been committed by that accused."[140] In *People (DPP) v Vardoshilli*,[141] the rape victim indicated that she did not want to see the offender spend a long time in prison, out of consideration for his wife and family. The Court of Criminal Appeal took this into consideration in suspending the last two years of a 10-year sentence.

139 *People (DPP) v McCormack* [2000] 4 IR 356

140 *ibid*, 359, per Barron J.

141 *People (DPP) v Vardoshilli*, Ex tempore, Court of Criminal Appeal, 9 February 2009.

CHAPTER EIGHT

Post-Release Provisions

Introduction

Earlier chapters of this book have documented the substantive legislative provisions that exist in relation to sexual offences and the sentences that those offences may carry. Recording the potential consequences of a conviction for a sexual offence would, however, be incomplete without discussing the entire range of penalties that can be imposed upon an offender. This chapter aims to explain the ancillary orders that may attach to a conviction for a sexual offence, namely through documenting the provisions of the Sex Offenders Act 2001 and the implementation thereof. **[8–01]**

Policy makers have traditionally tread a cautious line in formulating policies dealing with sexual crimes, mindful of the need to safeguard vulnerable persons while at the same time giving due respect for the rights of an accused. To some extent once the accused has been found guilty of the crime in question, the balance reshuffles and the issue becomes one of determining the appropriate sentence and ensuring effective management of the offender for the duration of their sentence. Policy provisions tend towards taking a dual approach of intervention and protectionism. Imprisonment becomes the way of providing for public safety and security, while at the same time the Prison Service must safeguard prisoners' rights and provide for their safety during incarceration. However, effective management of the offender does not simply end once the sentence does. The scope of the penal system extends beyond prison and the carceral system[1] and into the social sphere where protectionism becomes the pervasive objective. Deterrence and prevention are important goals of the criminal law and it is evident that any proposed sentence imposed must be forward thinking and reflect the need for these goals to be incorporated beyond the duration of the prison sentence. Thinking about effective management of sex offenders has moved beyond the original structures of the prison walls and into the aftermath of prisoners' release. Policies that provide for post-release supervision and monitoring have been developed and become an essential element of contemporary crime management. **[8–02]**

---

1 Foucault, *Discipline and Punish; The Birth of the Prison*, translated by Sheridan, (Penguin Books, London, 1977).

[8–03] Before moving on to examine the Irish provisions is it first imperative to note the developments elsewhere that pre-date the developments in the Irish law, and which to some extent have been influential in effecting change in Ireland. Towards the latter half of the 20th century public concern regarding dangerous and mobile sex offenders provoked a novel approach to dealing with such offenders on release. In countries such as the US and the UK, post-prison release arrangements were enacted in order to reduce the threat of re-offending by those convicted of sexual offending.[2] In the US, policies have been enacted providing for indefinite incarceration periods for sex offenders, obligation to notify the police of information relating to these offences, and disclosure of information regarding them to the community.[3] The UK has also enacted a range of civil orders which at one time ranged from a notification order ("register"[4]), sexual offences prevention order, a foreign travel order and a risk of sexual harm order.[5] These have now been consolidated into two orders under the Anti-Social Behaviour, Crime and Policing Act 2014—the Sexual Risk Order and the Sexual Harm Prevention Order.[6]

The Sex Offenders Act 2001

[8–04] The Sex Offenders Act 2001 was initiated in Ireland following suit from provisions in the UK and elsewhere. The provision of notification requirements for released sex offenders (the so-called "register") in the UK initiated the idea of having a sex-offender register in this jurisdiction.[7] In 1998 the government published a discussion document entitled '*The Law*

2 Zgoba, Miner, Levenson, Knight, Letourneau and Thornton, "The Adam Walsh Act: An Examination of Sex Offender Risk Classification Systems" (2015) 28 (8) *Sexual Abuse: A Journal of Research and Treatment* 722-740; Hebenton and Thomas, "Sexual Offenders in the Community: Reflections on Problems of Law, Community and Risk Management in the USA, England and Wales" in O'Malley, (ed), *Crime and the Risk Society* (Aldershot, 1998), pp 168–201.

3 The policies and requirements vary from State to State. See Terry, "Sex offender laws in the United States: smart policy or disproportionate sanctions?' (2015) 39 (2) *International Journal of Comparative and Applied Criminal Justice* 113-127; Delson, "Using Global Positioning Systems (GPS) for Sex Offender Management" (2006) 18 *Association for the Treatment of Sexual Abusers Forum*, pp 24–30.

4 The term register refers to the documentation of information about sex offenders who are obligated to adhere to requirements under the Act.

5 Sex Offenders Act 1997, Pt 1; Sexual Offences Act 2003, Pt 2. See Thomas, *Sex Crime: Sex Offending and Society* (2nd ed, Willan Publishing, Devon, 2005).

6 Inserting s 103A–K and s 122A–K into the Sexual Offences Act 2003. Thomas, *Policing Sexual Offences and Sex Offenders* (Palgrave Macmillan, London, 2016); Thomas and Thompson, "New civil orders to contain sexually harmful behaviour in the community" (2014) 12 (3) *British Journal of Criminology*, pp 19–33.

7 Thomas, "Protecting the Public: Some Observations on the Sex Offenders Bill 2000" (2000) 10(2) *Irish Criminal Law Journal* 12.

on Sexual Offences – A Discussion Paper,'[8] in which the registration and supervision of released sex offenders was posited as a positive proposal that would greatly contribute to protecting the public and reducing the risk of re-offending. Given that the Gardaí would manage and maintain the register it was believed that it would improve the quality of information already in their possession and would assist them in "keeping an eye on persons as part of their normal policing role"[9] In commending the idea to be placed upon statutory footing, the report acknowledged that the register was but one element of the management of the released offender and that management involved both increasing personal control through treatment and maintenance programmes, and increasing external control though surveillance and supervision.[10] According to the then Minister for Justice, Mr John O'Donoghue, the rationale for the register under the 2000 Bill mirrored that of introducing the UK register, i.e. that it *could* prevent crimes and *might* act as a deterrent.[11] In Dáil debates the view was expressed that the provisions in the Bill would target those who "prey on the vulnerable" and would send the message that such individuals would be dealt with swiftly and uncompromisingly.[12] This emphasis upon the predatory sex offender may be partly why it was recommended in the Bill that its provisions would not apply to offenders not more than three years older that the victim/other party to the offence who was aged between 15 and 17 at the time of the offence.[13] According to Mr O'Donoghue this was to distinguish between consensual sexual activity taking place between young people of broadly similar age on the one hand, and cases involving an abuse of authority or trust on the other.[14] Furthermore the intention was to find a balanced approach and the Minister considered that the principle of proportionality must be applied as between the sentence and the notification period that would be invoked as a result of this sentence, and that furthermore power must be given to discharge a potentially indefinite notification period.[15]The necessity of having multi-agency approach was emphasised in the Dáil debates, and sentiment expressed that the Gardaí, the Probation and Welfare

8 Department of Justice and Equality, *The Law on Sexual Offences – A Discussion Paper* (The Stationary Office, Dublin, 1998).

9 *ibid*, para. 10.7.3.

10 *ibid*, para. 10.2.2

11 Department of Justice and Equality, *Press Release*, January 2000.

12 See for example the speech of Mr Crawford at the Second Stage of the Bill 520 *Dáil Debates*, 1 June 2000.

13 See the speech of Ms Hanafin (then Minister for the Department of Justice and Equality), 166 *Seanad Debates*, 30 May 2001.

14 Mr O'Donoghue speaking at the Committee Stage of the Sex offenders Bill 2000, Select Committee on Justice, Equality, Defence and Women's Rights, 10 October 2000.

15 See comments by Ms Hanafin to the same effect: 166 *Seanad Debates*, 30 May 2001.

Service and the Health Boards should undertake continuous risk assessment of those subject to notification requirements.[16]

Notification Orders

[8–05] Although the term "register" is not actually used in the 2001 Act, Pt 2 of the Act makes provision for notification requirements for released sex offenders. When a person is convicted of a sexual offence under the Act, a Certificate of Conviction issues from the relevant court to the Sex Offender Management and Intelligence Unit[17] and the convicted sex offender is recorded on the PULSE (Police Using Leading Systems Effectively) system. The Sex Offender Management & Intelligence Unit has responsibility for maintaining records of all persons in the State with obligations under the provisions of the Sex Offenders Act 2001 and a Garda Inspector is nominated in each division to oversee the implementation these provisions. The obligation under Pt 2 of the Act is for an offender convicted of a sex offence in this jurisdiction or elsewhere[18] to notify the Gardaí of certain information including name, address and date of birth within seven days from the date of the conviction or if imprisoned then seven days from release.[19] After this initial obligation is satisfied, there is an obligation to notify the Gardaí of a change of address and/or name, within a seven-day period and furthermore to notify any intention to stay outside the given address for a continuous period of seven days or more.[20] Where there was no intention to be outside

16 See 520 *Dáil Debates*, 1 June 2000.

17 The Sex Offender Management and Intelligence Unit is part of the Garda National Protective Services Bureau (GNPSB) which was established in March 2015 as part of a victim-centred approach in carrying out the functions of the organisations responsible for dealing with sexual offences and sex offender management. The Bureau, which replaces the Domestic Violence Sexual Assault Investigation Unit, is comprised of the following Units: Sexual Crime Management Unit; Paedophile Investigation Unit; Sex Offender Management & Intelligence Unit; SORAM Multi-Agency Office (including personnel from the Probation Service, Child & Family Agency and Local Authority Housing); Human Trafficking Investigation & Co-ordination Unit; Missing Persons Unit; Domestic Violence Unit; Child Protection Unit; ViClas (Violent Crime Linkage Analysis System); Victim Services Offices. Annual Report of An Garda Síochána 2015.

18 Those convicted of a sex offence outside the State are subject to the requirements regardless of whether they were resident in the State the time (Clause 12). Provision is made however for a defence of honestly believing that one was not subject to the requirements because the offence was not one that would have merited the obligations if committed within the State.

19 Sex Offenders Act 2001, s 10. Under s 9 of the 2001 Act, the governor of the prison where the person is being held must notify them in writing before their release that they are subject to part two of the Act and must also notify the Commissioner of the Gardaí that the person will be released at least 10 days before this happens.

20 The "qualifying period" means a period of seven days or two or more periods in 12 months which together amount to seven days.

the address for this period of time, the individual has a further seven days within which to notify the Gardaí. No such obligation arises where the individual returns before the expiration of seven days.[21]

The sexual offences which trigger the notification requirements are defined in s 3 and the Schedule to the Act.[22] The list of offences include rape, rape contrary to s 4, sexual assault, aggravated sexual assault, incest, sexual offences against mentally impaired persons, an offence contrary to the Criminal Law (Sexual Offences) Act 2006, an offence under s 2 of the Criminal Law (Sexual Offences) (Amendment) Act 2007, an offence under the Criminal Law (Human Trafficking) Act 2008, sexual offences committed outside Ireland contrary to the Sexual Offences (Jurisdiction) Act 1996 and certain inchoate offences including (but not limited to) aiding, abetting or inciting any of the offences above.[23] The obligations apply to all offenders convicted of a sexual offence within the meaning of the Act after the commencement of the Act and to those convicted before if the sentence has not yet been passed or is still current and in force.[24] Persons convicted in other jurisdictions may also be subject to the requirements, if the act constituting the offence in the other jurisdiction would also be capable of constituting an offence under the 2001 Act.[25] **[8–06]**

There is however an exception as to the effect of the registration on offenders who are not more than three years older than their victim or the other party to the offence. Pursuant to s 3 and paras 2, 5, 6, 18, 19 and 20 of the Schedule, it is not a sexual offence for the purpose of the Act if the victim or other party was 17 years or older at the time of the offence and the offender was not sentenced to a term of incarceration in respect of the offence. Pursuant to s 3 and paras 8, 11, 12, 18, 19 and 20 of the Schedule, it is not an offence for the purpose of the Act if the victim or other party was aged between 15 and 17 at the time and the offender not more than three years older. However, the 2001 Act has been amended by s 7(5)(b) of the Criminal Law (Sexual Offences) Act 2006, which replaces paragraph 7 of the Schedule (defilement of a girl under 15) with an offence under the 2006 Act. Paragraph 8 of the Schedule (defilement of a girl between 15 and 17) has been deleted. As a result of this change, the extent to which a young person convicted of that offence is currently exempt from the notification requirements is unclear. **[8–07]**

---

21 Sex Offenders Act 2001, s 10.

22 See further the Schedule to the Sex Offenders Act 2001.

23 See also various provisions of the Criminal Law (Sexual Offences) Act 2017 (e.g. s 10).

24 Sex Offenders Act 2001, s 7. This includes a person temporarily released under ss 2–3 of the Criminal Justice Act 1960 (s 7(b) (ii)).

25 Sex Offenders Act 2001, s 13.

[8–08] Section 8 of the Act sets out the time periods for which the notification requirements will apply and provides for an ascending (or descending) scale based upon the length of the original sentence imposed. At the two ends of the scale a non-custodial sentence for adult offenders attracts an obligation to notify for five years, while any term of imprisonment imposed that is greater than two years can create an obligation to notify for life. The periods in between are: 10 years notification if the original sentence was greater than six months but two years or less, seven years for a sentence of six months or less and five years for a fully suspended sentence.[26] The periods of notification listed in the section are halved where the offender is, at the time of sentencing, under the age of 18.[27] Furthermore s 8 (5) provides as follows:

> "(5) If a sentence of imprisonment for any term is imposed on the person referred to in *subsection (1)* in respect of the offence concerned and the operation of a part of that term is suspended—
>
> *a*) the part of that term the operation of which is not suspended shall be regarded as the term of imprisonment imposed on that person for the purpose of *subsection (3)* (but, if the operation of the first-mentioned part of that term is revived by the court, whichever of *paragraphs (a), (b)* and (*c*) of *subsection (3)* is appropriate shall apply without regard to this paragraph),
>
> *b*) the preceding paragraph extends to a case in which that suspension is provided for subsequent to the imposition of the sentence."

[8–09] If a person is or has been sentenced in respect of two or more sexual offences and the sentences imposed are consecutive then the sentence imposed in respect of each of the offences were or had been a sentence equal to the aggregate of those sentences. If the sentences imposed are partly concurrent then the sentence imposed in respect of each of the offences were or had been a sentence equal to the aggregate of those sentences after making such deduction as is necessary to ensure that no period of time is counted more than once.[28]

[8–10] Failure to comply with the notification requirements is an offence under s 12 of the Act. The person may be guilt on summary conviction, punishable with a class A fine, up to 12 months' imprisonment, or both. A person may be guilty on indictment, punishable with a fine of €10,000, up to five years' imprisonment, or both.[29] The power of arrest was introduced under the

---

[26] *ibid*, s 8(3).

[27] *ibid*, s 8(4).

[28] *ibid*, s 8(6).

[29] Sex Offenders Act 2001, s 12(3), as substituted by s 13(b) of the Criminal Law (Human Trafficking) Act 2008.

Criminal Law (Human Trafficking) Act 2008 in relation to offenders who do not comply with their obligations under the Sex Offenders Act 2001.

Significantly the obligations may be discharged in certain circumstances. Where a person is subject to registration for an indefinite duration (where a potential lifetime obligation may be imposed), they may petition the Circuit Court after 10 years has passed to remove the obligation which the court may do if the "interests of the common good would no longer be served" by the requirement continuing.[30] This provides an essential balance to what might otherwise have been a disproportionately onerous obligation for many offenders. In the case of *R (F (A Child)) v Secretary of State for the Home Department*[31] the UK Supreme Court criticised the absence of a review provision in the equivalent English legislation and declared it incompatible with Art 8 of the European Convention on Human Rights. Although some interference with privacy rights is permissible, a lifetime obligation to notify where the person posed little risk, amounted to a disproportionate interference with those rights. **[8–11]**

Sex Offender Orders

The Sex Offender Order is a civil order that the Gardaí can apply for if concerned about the behaviour of someone who has been convicted of sex offences in the past.[32] Concern that the register did not apply retrospectively is the most likely rationale for this order, although it is not fully retrospective in effect, insofar as it only applies to high-risk sex offenders. Essentially the idea is "to ensure the inclusion in the register of past offenders who still pose a threat."[33] The intention of the order to target dangerous offenders was also emphasised by the five-year minimum period for the order. Despite query as to why the court (according to the provision) should be able to impose a longer period if necessary but not a shorter period, it was felt that a five-year minimum was proportionate considering the offenders to whom this order would be applied. **[8–12]**

Under Pt 3 of the 2001 Act, a member of An Garda Síochána not below the rank of Chief Superintendent can apply to the Circuit Court for a sex offender order where an individual has been acting in a manner that gives reasonable grounds for believing an order is necessary to protect the public. The order can be imposed on any individual who has been convicted before **[8–13]**

---

30 Sex Offenders Act 2001, s 11, s 11(2) and s 11 (5).

31 *R (F (A Child)) v Secretary of State for the Home Department* [2010] UKSC 17.

32 Sex Offenders Act 2001, s 15

33 Mr O'Donoghue, Committee Stage of the Sex offenders Bill 2000, 10 October 2000. Mr Callely speaking in the Dàil debates referred to the order as "an important safety net." 520 *Dáil Debates*, 1 June 2000.

or after the commencement of the Act either within the State or outside the State (so long as the act would also constitute a sexual offence under the 2001 Act).[34] The Court may impose the order if it is considered necessary to protect the public from serious harm, which is defined as death or serious personal injury whether physical or psychological.[35] The Court is given a very wide discretion regarding the terms of the order, but usually imposes a prohibition on the individual from acting in a suspicious manner or requires the offender to stay away from certain areas or individuals. There are some constitutional restraints however, particularly in the context of the right to privacy and liberty, which will limit the scope of judicial discretion if the terms are too vague or disproportionate. The order lasts for a period of five years, or longer if the court considers it necessary,[36] and there is an obligation during this period to notify the Gardaí pursuant to Pt 2 of the Act.[37] To some extent the effect of the provision is that it applies the registration requirements retrospectively, in some limited circumstances. However, as it is assumed that such orders would only be sought and granted where the past sex-offender poses a substantial or high risk, their scope is more limited than the register. Of significance also is the fact that any order made can be subsequently discharged, on application, if the court is satisfied that the protection of the public no longer warrants continuing the order, or if the effect of continuing the order would be to cause an injustice. As the order made is considered civil in nature the standard of proof required is that applicable to civil proceedings, i.e. on the balance of probabilities.[38] This is so, even though contravention of an order made leads to criminal sanctions. Under s 22 the penalty under summary conviction is a fine and/or imprisonment of up to 12 months. The penalty under indictment is more severe with a maximum of five years capable of being imposed.

Post-Release Supervision Orders

[8–14] In Ireland prior to the 2001 Act there was no means by which released offenders could be mandatorily supervised in the community after completion of their prison term, unless the original sentence imposed was one of life imprisonment.[39] This was considered to be problematic for a number of reasons. For one, many sex offenders serve long prison sentences and adjusting to life after release may be difficult in the absence of support and external monitoring. Moreover, any treatment sustained in prison might be more difficult to implement on the outside and supervision could assist in

34 Sex Offenders Act 2001, s 16(2).
35 *ibid*, s 6(5).
36 *ibid*, s 16(6).
37 *ibid*, s 16(7).
38 *ibid*, s 21(1).
39 Department of Justice and Equality, *supra* note 8, para. 10.8.3.

an individual's endeavour to reform themselves in the aftermath of prison. It could also be the means whereby offenders who did not receive treatment in prison would receive the necessary support on the outside. Furthermore, supervision could assist in the monitoring of offenders post-release. The 1998 Discussion Paper therefore perceived two aims of supervising sex offenders in the community: "to help the offender maintain internal control over his offending behaviour and to provide external monitoring of his behaviour and activities."[40] This twofold aim was also stated by the Minister for Justice at the time, to be the purpose for including this provision in the Act.[41] It was also noted that many paedophiles in particular seem to pose a long-term threat and thus long-term supervision would be appropriate for such individuals.[42]

To remedy the perceived shortfall in the law, Pt 5 of the 2001 Act empowers a court to impose a period of supervision on sex offenders in the aftermath of their prison sentence. To a large extent the purpose of the order is to protect the public from serious risk of harm, but the provision also expresses a commitment to rehabilitation and therefore a balanced approach was clearly the intent of the order. It is the sentencing court that considers whether a period of post-release supervision is necessary for the offender. In considering the appropriate custodial sentence the court may not be influenced by the element of supervision (so as to award a lesser custodial sentence), but the aggregate period of the custodial sentence and the period of supervision may not exceed the maximum term of imprisonment available for the particular sexual offence.[43] Pursuant to s 28(2), the court, before a supervision order can be imposed, must consider four material elements: **[8–15]**

> "(a) the need for a period, after the offender has been released into the community, during which his or her conduct is supervised by a responsible person
> (b) the need to protect the public from serious harm from the offender,
> (c) the need to prevent the commission by the offender of further sexual offences, and
> (d) the need to rehabilitate or further rehabilitate the offender."[44]

The court has considerable discretion with regards to the terms of the order and conditions included within the supervision period may include requiring the individual to stay away from certain areas and/or requiring **[8–16]**

[40] *ibid*, para 10.8.1.

[41] Mr O'Donoghue, Committee Stage of the Sex offenders Bill 2000, 10 October 2000.

[42] Department of Justice and Equality, *supra* note 8, para 10.8.6.

[43] Sex Offenders Act 2001, s 29(2).

[44] Sex Offenders Act 2001, s 28. The court may hear any relevant evidence in this regard.

him to receive treatment or counselling.[45] The provision is amended by s 51 of the Criminal Law (Sexual Offences) Act 2017, which allows the court, upon application from probation officer not more than one month before the date of the offender's intended release from prison or any time during the supervision period, to amend any condition or include further conditions if considered necessary.

[8–17] Since the Probation Service are responsible for enforcing compliance with the order, the court is likely to be influenced by their advice with regard to the form or terms of the order. It is important however that any condition imposed must be necessary for public protection. It is an offence, under s 33, to fail to comply with the conditions of an order made, punishable with a fine and/or imprisonment of up to 12 months on summary conviction. Proceedings for this offence may be brought and prosecuted by a probation officer.[46] Any supervision order made may be subsequently discharged by a court, on application by either the offender himself or a probation officer, where it would be in the interests of justice to do so and it is no longer required for the protection of the public.[47]

Obligation to Disclose in Employment Applications

[8–18] The 2000 Sex Offenders Bill introduced the idea of obligating all convicted sex offenders to disclose their convictions to prospective employers and proposed to make it an offence to default on this obligation. The then Minister made clear though that disclosure would not necessarily exclude the person from employment and that it would be "a matter for the prospective employer ... on being informed of the conviction, to decide if it is relevant to the work or position concerned."[48] Some did express concern that the scope of the provision was too narrow and should cover access to vulnerable adults in addition to children.[49] Although this recommendation was not implemented, one extension that was made was to include protection for mentally impaired persons within the provision.

[8–19] The proposal became law under Pt 4 of the 2001 Act. The Act makes it an offence to apply for or accept employment which would give the sex offender unsupervised access to children or mentally impaired persons, without first so informing the employer.[50] The individual must make such

45 Sex Offenders Act 2001, s 30.

46 Sex Offenders Act 2001, s 33(4) as inserted by s 13 of the Criminal Law (Human Trafficking) Act 2008.

47 Sex Offenders Act 2001, s 32.

48 Mr O'Donoghue, 538 *Dáil Debates*, 22 June 2001.

49 Mr Callely, 520 *Dáil Debates*, 1 June 2000.

50 Sex Offenders Act 2001, s 26. The Act does not provide for such obligations if the employment involves unsupervised access to vulnerable adults (apart from the

a disclosure at the time of applying for the position, or, if later, as soon as he becomes aware that the position involves unsupervised access to children. The penalty for non-disclosure is a fine and/or imprisonment of up to 12 months on summary conviction, and a maximum fine of up to €12,697 and/or up to five years' imprisonment on indictment. Once the individual informs the employer, then it seems he has met his obligations under the Act and the assumption then is that the application would fall. The employer in such situations is in a somewhat precarious position. First, in the absence of disclosure they have no way of determining if an applicant has past convictions for sexual offences unless the position is one covered by existing vetting procedures.[51] Secondly, the Act does not anticipate the prospect of an employer hiring an offender despite being aware of his past sexual convictions. In the UK it is a criminal offence under the Criminal Justice and Court Services Act 2000 to knowingly employ an applicant who is disqualified from working with children.[52] There is no such specification under Irish legislation, although there remains the possibility of the employer being liable in the event of any offending against children committed in the course of employment. The obligation to notify operates de facto for life, and applies to those convicted of a sex offence within the meaning of the Act either before or after the commencement of the provisions. Thus this particular provision has retrospective effect. The obligation applies to all convicted sex offenders and is not limited to those who have been convicted of a sex offence against children. The provisions of the Criminal Justice (Spent Convictions and Certain Disclosures) Act 2016, which allows for non-disclosure of spent convictions in certain circumstance, do not apply to a conviction for a sexual offence.

Community Notification

An issue that was been raised prior to the enactment of the Sex Offenders Act 2001 is whether the public should or should not have access to the information gathered in relation to released offenders. In the US, although

---

mentally impaired). In the UK it is an offence to apply for employment where the person is on the Department of Education's list of persons excluded from employment in schools, or on the Department of Health's Consultancy Service Index or where the individual is subject to a "disqualification order."

51 Current vetting procedures relate to recruitment of staff for children's residential centres or positions with health boards that will allow individuals access to children or vulnerable adults. Private employers or voluntary organisations do not have access to these vetting procedures.

52 Criminal Justice and Court Services Act 2000, s 35(2). The Probation Service will also pass information to the Employment Service on anyone they are supervising who has convictions for sexual offences and should not be offered certain work. Home Office, *Disclosure to the Employment Service of Restrictions that should be placed on the Employment of Potentially Dangerous Offenders* (Home Office, Probation Unit, London, 1999).

the form varies from state to state, there is a public right of access under Megan's Law.[53] The enactment of this law followed the Jacob Wetterling Crimes against Children and Sexually Violent Offender Registration Act 1994 which established a national sex offender registry in the US Most statutes permit public posting of name, conviction, photograph, and often a home and work address.[54] Some states notify the public only about high risk sex offenders, while other states employ broad notification practices and disseminate information about all registered sex offenders.[55] In the UK there has traditionally been no widespread public access to information about sex offenders, but rather "limited disclosure to third parties" allowable under the Multi-Agency Public Protection Arrangements (MAPPA) procedures.[56] Cases following this approach emphasised the careful balance to be drawn with regard to fundamental rights issues. In the case of *R v Chief Constable of North Wales ex p. A.B.*[57] the Court of Appeal stressed that disclosure should only be in exceptional cases, and that blanket disclosure is highly undesirable and unlawful, having regard to the right to privacy under Art 8 ECHR.[58] As a result of increased pressure to strengthen the use of controlled disclosure under the MAPPA procedures, Sarah's law[59] was piloted in the UK in 2009, and has since been rolled out nationwide. This law, though much more limited than Megan's law in the US, allows a parent, carer, guardian or concerned adult to apply to the local police for information about specified persons who have unsupervised access in relation to specified

53 Named after seven-year-old Megan Kanka, who was sexually abused and murdered by a paedophile living on her street in New Jersey. Such community disclosure has been challenged and upheld: *Connecticut Department of Public Safety v Doe* (2003) 538 US 84.

54 The approach is not universal uncontrolled disclosure. Many states restrict which offender records can be browsed online and can differ in the types of information which are included on the sex offender registry website. Zgoba and Ragbir, "Sex Offender Registration and Notification Act (SORNA)" (2016) *Sexual Violence* 33-49; Fitch, *Megan's Law: Does it protect children? (2)* (NSPCC, London, 2006).

55 Leveson, Brannon, Fortney, and Baker, "Public Perceptions About Sex Offenders and Community Protection Policies" (2007) 7 (1) *Analyses of Social Issues and Public Policy* 1, 2.

56 Kemshall, Dominey and Hilder, "Public Disclosure: Sex Offenders' Perceptions of the Pilot Scheme in England." (2011) *Journal of Sexual Aggression* 1.

57 *R v Chief Constable of North Wales ex p. A.B.* [1998] 3 All ER 310.

58 In the case of *R v Devon County Council, ex p. L* [1991] 2 FLR social workers, suspecting L of paedophile offences, went to the homes of his female partners who had children to warn them of their suspicions. The disclosure was legitimate, because it was limited to specific individuals where there was a reasonably apprehended specific risk to specific children. Hence it was a "legitimate aim" under Art 8(2) ECHR.

59 The scheme is named after eight-year-old Sarah Payne who was abducted and murdered by a sex offender in 2000.

children.[60] The police retain discretion as to whether it is necessary and reasonable to release the information sought.

In Ireland at present the public do not generally have access to information pertaining to convicted sex offenders. The idea of introducing a Megan's law-type scheme permitting such disclosure has repeatedly been rejected in this jurisdiction. An Garda Síochána's policy on the investigation of sexual crime expressly provides that they are not at liberty to disclose any such information as to do so would affect ability of the Gardaí to effectively provide for public safety. This does not mean, however, that information about sex offenders can never be shared. The Sex Offenders Act 2001 does not expressly address disclosure, but it is currently an administrative issue in this jurisdiction. The Gardaí, who are responsible for maintaining the information and monitoring sex offenders subject to the 2001 Act, may release appropriate information to the public, including parents, in exceptional circumstances.[61] If the Gardaí have reason to believe a particular high-risk sex offender poses a real and immediate danger, they are free to tell individuals who need to know. Disclosure in such circumstances is considered to be reasonable and necessary. **[8–20]**

Steps have been taken to introduce reform of the current approach to disclosure in recent times. The first such reform was introduced in the form of a private members' bill, the Child Sex Offenders (Information and Monitoring) Bill 2012, which aimed to establish an ICSO Scheme (Information on Child Sex Offenders), modelled on Sarah's Law in the UK The scheme aimed to enable parents and guardians to enquire whether persons coming into contact with their child or vulnerable adult have been convicted of a sexual offence or otherwise pose a danger.[62] Further provisions provided for a similar entitlement for persons in authority in schools and clubs. While the general scheme of the Bill was initially well received it was acknowledged that the specific provisions raised issues both of a constitutional nature and under the European Convention on Human **[8–21]**

---

60 See O'Sullivan, Hoggett, Kemshall and McCartan, "Understandings, implications and alternative approaches to the use of the sex offenders register in the UK" (2016) 13 *Irish Probation Journal* 84-101; Kemshall and Wood, *Child Sex Offender Review (CSOR): Public Disclosure Pilots, A Process Evaluation* (Home Office, London 2010).

61 A press release from the Department of Justice at the time stated that disclosure of information on registered sex offenders would only be made "in the most exceptional circumstances in order to prevent an immediate risk of crime or to alert members of the public to an apprehended danger and then only on a strict need to know basis." Department of Justice and Equality, "O'Donoghue publishes Bill to protect the public from sex offenders and to provide for separate legal representation for victims of rape" *Press Release*, 12 January 2000.

62 The idea of this and subsequent proposals is to place the current administrative issue of disclosure upon a statutory footing.

Rights.[63] The Bill was sidelined in favour of government-led legislation. It was initially intended that this reform would become part of the Criminal Law (Sexual Offences) Act 2017. The initial drafting of this Act contained a number of provisions for reform of the law in relation to management of released sex offenders, including amendment of the Sex Offenders Act 2001 by the insertion of a provision explicitly dealing with disclosure of information relating to an offender on the "sex offenders register". It also provided that disclosure (of the offender's name, address and level of risk) would be authorised by a member of the Garda Síochána not below the rank of Inspector only where such disclosure is unlikely to result in public disorder, physical harm, damage to property or intimidation of or threats to any person. It further proposed to change the number of days to comply with notification orders under the 2001 Act from seven days to three days, and providing the Gardaí with fingerprints, palm prints and photographs upon request. Although these proposed amendments are omitted under the enacted legislation, the intention to incorporate these changes into a reform of the Sex Offenders Act 2001 remains. The most recent proposal comes in the form of the Sex Offenders (Amendment) Bill, which is likely to include some of the recommendations for reform discussed above, in addition to proposed electronic monitoring of released sex offenders.

Implementation of the Act

[8–22] Since the implementation of the 2001 Act, the number of released sex offenders subject to the notification provisions of the Act, has risen steadily. In 2008 it was reported that 1,075 sex offenders were being monitored including several high-risk sex offenders who had arrived in the State.[64] The most recently available figures in October 2017 set this number at 1575. The implementation of the provisions has also seen a rise in those supervised under Pt 5 of the Act. In 2007, a total of 158 sex offenders were supervised by the Probation Service including on post release supervision orders.[65] This figure rose to 211 in 2013[66] and by the end of 2016 there were 375 sex offenders supervised by the Probation Service in the community.[67] While figures are scant on the total number of sex offender orders that have been applied for under Pt 3 of the Act, it seems as though only a handful have been granted since its inception.[68] In 2015 it was reported that only three such orders had been obtained since the enactment of the

63 http://www.merrionstreet.ie/index.php/2013/10/shatter-statement-on-child-sex-offenders-information-and-monitoring-bill-2012-2/.
64 Annual Report of An Garda Síochána 2008.
65 The Probation Service, *Annual Report* (The Probation Service, Dublin, 2007).
66 The Probation Service, *Annual Report* (The Probation Service, Dublin, 2013).
67 The Probation Service, *Annual Report* (The Probation Service, Dublin, 2016).
68 It seems that the Courts are taking a cautious approach when dealing with applications

provision.[69] Conditions utilised by the courts in the granting of supervision orders and sex offender orders, have ranged from refraining from use of social media, to making a mobile phone available for Garda inspection, to the requirement to notify the Gardaí before travelling on public transport. While figures for breaches of the orders are not readily available, it seems that the courts are dealing with these breaches in an effective manner, consistent with the legislative requirements.[70] Sentencing under the 2001 Act has become a routine part of the modus operandi of the courts in sexual offence cases, with the post-release supervision order in particular, being habitually utilised by the judiciary. Cases such as *People (DPP) v S (P)*,[71] where a 10-year post release supervision order was given, *People (DPP) v K (G)*[72] where another 10-year supervision order was handed down, and the case of *DPP v M.A.F.*[73] where the order lasted 18 months, demonstrate how post-release supervision has become a normalised part of sentencing sex offenders usually adherent to a custodial decree.

Since the enactment of the 2001 Act, the information on released sex offenders now contained within the PULSE system can be passed on to agencies in other jurisdictions as a way of identifying and managing risk. In November 2006, a Memorandum of Understanding placed the informal sharing of information between An Gardaí Siochana and the UK police forces on a formal footing. Pursuant to this Memorandum, when a convicted sex offender, who is subject to Pt 2 of the 2001 Act, travels between these two jurisdictions, information may be passed in the interests of public safety, regarding any risks posed, to the destination state. The Probation Service also have a "Protocol" for the sharing of information on the management of sex offenders with the Probation Board for Northern Ireland. This mutual information sharing arrangement facilitates the effective case management of sex offenders between jurisdictions by enabling exchange of relevant information on a structured basis.[74] **[8–23]**

for such orders: Editorial, "Order to stop sex offender contacting children online refused" *The Irish Times*, 1 August 2014.

69 Degan, "Sex offender ordered not to have Tinder, Facebook profiles" *The Irish Times*, 13 February 2015.

70 See for example Farsaci, "Sex offender breached court order by using public transport without notifying gardaí" *Irish Independent*, 4 July 2017.

71 *People (DPP) v S (P)* [2009] IECCA 1.

72 *People (DPP) v K (G)* [2008] IECCA 110.

73 *DPP v M.A.F.* [2016] IECA 14.

74 See generally Department of Justice and Equality (2009) *op. cit.* See also Thomas, *The Registration and Monitoring of Sex offenders: A comparative study* (Routledge, 2011).

Effect of the Provisions: Are They Punitive?

[8–24] One question arising out of the post-release provisions documented above is whether or not they constitute a form of punishment. It is asserted in political spheres that post-release requirements are regulatory in nature and are not to be considered punishment per se. This has not however displaced concern that their effect upon offenders is punitive to some degree. If the measures are to be regarded as civil then it does not mean that the consequences arising from the imposition of such measures are not still punitive. Moreover, irrespective of whether the measures are classed as regulatory or as punishment, they still impose a significant restriction upon the individual in the aftermath of imprisonment.

[8–25] In examining the nature of post-release provisions, the various orders can be broken down into two sub-categories: those that are imposed in addition to ordinary punishment and those that derive automatically from the conviction itself. Notification requirements fall into the latter category. The constitutionality of the notification requirements under the Sex Offenders Act 2001 has been challenged and upheld in the case of *Enright v Ireland.*[75] The High Court found that the requirements could not be considered punitive or part of the punishment. In deciding the matter Finlay-Geoghegan J in the High Court determined that in order for the requirements to be considered part of the punishment, they must be punitive in intent and effect. The learned judge found the provision of the 2001 Act to be for the benefit of the public and that there was no punitive intention on the part of the Oireachtas. The element of risk was a significant factor in the case, with the court relying heavily on and ultimately siding with expert evidence that the risk posed by sex offenders demanded measures to manage this risk. Furthermore these measures were not found to constitute disproportionate interference with the constitutional rights of offenders under Arts 38.1 and 40.3 of the Constitution given that the Act was there to protect the constitutional rights of other citizens.[76] The decision was supported by the Central Criminal Court in the case of *People (DPP) v Cawley*, where it was said that "notification requirements … are undoubtedly a consequence of the offences but could hardly be properly said to be a penalty."[77] Thus the Courts in these cases not only denied that notification could be a punishment, but went further in suggesting that the public safety intent behind the provisions eliminated any punitive element. This conclusion may be difficult to comprehend, given that measures can be classed as civil but still have punitive consequences.[78]

---

[75] *Enright v Ireland* [2003] 2 IR 321.

[76] The court applied the tests developed in *Tuohy v Courtney* [1994] 3 IR 1 and *Heaney v Ireland* [1994] 3 IR 593 and found that the test of proportionality was passed.

[77] *People (DPP) v Cawley* [2003] 4 IR 321, 335.

[78] Ashworth, Gardner, Morgan, Smith, Von Hirsch and Wasik, "Neighbouring on the

There is something of a confliction between these cases and subsequent decisions on the Sex Offenders Act 2001. Subsequent cases do not seem to rule out the prospect of the requirements being punitive despite having a protective aim. In the case of *DPP v NY* Fennelly J held that if an individual poses low risk, the application of the Act "constitutes a real and substantial punishment" and therefore the court could have regard to this when sentencing.[79] This view was endorsed by the Supreme Court in the case of *CC v Ireland* who felt that the register could be regarded as being punitive in nature.[80] Hardiman J in this case considered that enrolment on the register was a very "formalised stigma" and had no hesitation in regarding the compulsory enrolment as a punitive consequence of conviction.[81] **[8–26]**

The case of *GD v Ireland* also held that enrolment on the register was "in itself a punishment."[82] It has also been considered that the requirements though they may not be a primary punishment could be considered as a "secondary" punishment following from ordinary conviction and sentence and thus may be considered for the 'totality' of the sentence. Thus in the case of *P.H. v Ireland*, Clarke J, in attempting to analyse the conflicting judgments, said that "the provisions of the 2001 Act were amongst the "relevant circumstances" which should be taken into account when imposing sentence."[83] Rather than being part of the punishment the requirements were an additional burden which "must be weighed in the balance." Hence, while not endorsed as punishment per se, the burden imposed under the Sex Offenders Act 2001 may be considered by a court when imposing the ordinary sentence for the offence.[84] **[8–27]**

In 2015 the High Court dealt with another challenge to the provisions of the 2001 Act in the case of *J.F. v Ireland.*[85] The plaintiff challenged the constitutionality of various provisions of the Act specifically s 8(3)(a), s 11(2) and s 12. In 2004 the plaintiff had, at the age of 20, pleaded guilty to rape (committed as a minor) and was sentenced to 30 months' imprisonment. He also became mandatorily obliged under Pt 2 of the 2001 Act, requiring **[8–28]**

Oppressive: The Government's Anti-Social Behaviour Order Proposals" (1998) 16 *Criminal Justice* 7.

79 *DPP v NY* [2002] 4 IR 309.

80 *CC v Ireland* [2006] 4 IR 1.

81 The case concerned the constitutional compatibility of offences of strict liability, the issue of notification requirements being considered in this context.

82 *GD v Ireland*, unreported, Court of Criminal Appeal, 13 July 2004.

83 *P.H. v Ireland*, unreported, High Court, 16 February 2006, para.7.7.

84 The courts in sexual offence cases do consider many of the adverse consequences arising from a conviction outside the formal punishment, such as loss of employment etc. The courts also strive to impose a sentence that will be fair and promote the rehabilitation of the offender.

85 *J.F. v Ireland & anor* [2015] IEHC 468.

him to notify the Gardaí of particular information including any change in address, for an indefinite period of duration. In dismissing the legal challenge, the Court affirmed the reasoning in the *Enright* case, that "the requirements are not penal in nature but rather constitute an additional burden placed upon a convicted person in the interests of the common good and for the purpose of protecting society at large."[86] Significantly the Court determined that the application of the provisions, in requiring those who committed offences while aged under 18 to abide by the same requirements to notify the Gardaí as those required by adults is not disproportionate or contrary to Arts 38 and 40 of the Constitution. Binchy J acknowledged that the application of the Act in this particular case may appear harsh, but went on to determine that,

> "Even if the Oireachtas did not contemplate the possibility that a person would be so young at the time of commission of an offence, and that it would take so long to secure a conviction in relation to the same offence, these are not in my view grounds for the Court to set aside sections 8 or 11 because to do so would amount to no more than the Court saying that it disagreed with the policy set by the Oireachtas rather than a determination of some manifest and objective disproportionally in those sections. For those reasons in my view the provisions of Part 2 of the Act, as they apply to minors, meet the test posed by Costello J in *Heaney v. Ireland* and McMenamin J. in McNally and for the same reasons set out by Finlay Geoghegan J. in Enright."[87]

[8–29] In relation to s 12 the plaintiff contended that this was a strict liability offence and as such offended the presumption of innocence, in addition to being incompatible with Arts 38 and 40 of the Constitution.[88] In rejecting this argument the Court observed that while the onus (to establish a "reasonable excuse") was placed upon the plaintiff, this operated as a defence, allowing the accused the opportunity to explain why he did not comply with his obligations under Pt 2 of the Act.[89] Binchy J further dismissed the claim that the wording of the relevant provisions of the Act was impermissibly vague.

[8–30] In other jurisdictions, equivalent provisions for managing sex offenders have also been upheld. In England in the case of *R v Durham Police, ex parte R*, the House of Lords decided that notification requirements were not punitive

---

[86] *ibid*, para 53, per Binchy.

[87] *ibid*, para 54. The Court noted that the plaintiff can apply for removal from the order after a period of 10 years pursuant to the Act.

[88] Sex Offenders Act 2001, s 12 made it an offence to fail to notify change of address if that failure was "without reasonable excuse", the onus being on the accused to provide a reasonable excuse.

[89] The Court further determined that there was no issue of offending the privilege against self-incrimination, given that the burden of proof imposed on the accused is evidential and not legal in nature.

but rather preventative.[90] The Court relied heavily on the international case of *Ibbotson v United Kingdom*.[91] The European Commission on Human Rights accepted in that case that the purpose of the requirements under the Criminal Justice Act 1997 was prevention, and did not amount to punishment within the meaning of Art 7. This decision was confirmed in the case of *Adamson v United Kingdom* where the European Court of Human Rights felt that the fact that though the individual may feel as though he is being punished, depersonalised and inhibited in trying to start a new life, this was "not sufficient to establish the registration requirement has a punitive nature or purpose under Art.7."[92]

Even if the provisions under the 2001 Act are not formally regarded as punishment, there is still an impact upon the offender's fundamental rights, particularly the right to privacy.[93] When measures such as notification orders are invoked the right to personal and family privacy is encroached upon and it is necessary to consider whether this is for a legitimate aim. It is observed that sexual violence is a human rights violation in itself and consideration must also be given to such.[94] In order to effectively protect the rights and freedoms of others, states are entitled to employ measures to prevent and detect sexual offences. Legitimate curtailment of the right to privacy is justified as proportionate and necessary to the goals of public safety. Nonetheless, restrictions on rights of privacy, liberty and other personal freedoms can only be justified to the extent that such interference is necessary to reduce the risk of harm to others. Measures such as notification orders can constitute a disproportionate interference with the rights of the offender who has already served his punishment if they no longer serve a valid goal.[95] **[8–31]**

Acknowledging the protective intent of the 2001 provisions, should not necessarily preclude that the effect of the provisions is also potentially punitive. Thomas has noted that "what starts life as a preventative, regulatory **[8–32]**

---

90 *R v Durham Police* [2005] UKHL 21. The House of Lords controversially considered that imposing the requirements pursuant to a caution was not the determination of a criminal charge and thus not incompatible with Art 6 of the ECHR. The American Courts have refused to recognise the punitive nature of registration and community notification: *Smith v Doe* (2003) 538 US 84.

91 *Ibbotson v UK* (1998) 27 EHRR 332.

92 *Adamson v UK* (1999) 28 EHRR 209.

93 The right to privacy is protected under the Constitution and also Art 8 of the European Convention on Human Rights.

94 O'Malley, *Sexual Offences* (2nd ed, Round Hall, Dublin, 2013), p 23.

95 In *R (on the application of F and Another) v Secretary of State for the Home Department* [2010] UKSC 17, the UK Supreme Court held that indefinite registration without the right of review amounted to a disproportionate interference with privacy rights under Art 8 of the ECHR.

measure can easily become a more punitive measure in its own right."[96] Prevention and deterrent rationales are often legitimately drawn-on as grounds for imposing punishment. To this end it may also be acknowledged that failure to comply with the orders leads to the imposition of criminal sanctions for a breach.[97] In relation to sex offender orders for example, the behaviour that gives rise to such an order may not be criminal but default of the obligations imposed leads to a conviction penalty of up to five years' imprisonment.

Support and Rehabilitation

[8–33] A notable element of the measures enacted under the Sex Offenders Act 2001 is that the element of rehabilitation has been given fresh consideration and merit. It was stated prior to the introduction of the 2001 Act that "a co-ordinated approach" was needed to sex offending and emphasis was placed upon the need for treatment in prison.[98] It was further stated to be "more beneficial to society if effective treatment is provided for people in prison rather than putting them on a sex offenders register and allowing them out on the streets."[99] In April 2009 the Irish Prison Service announced a new policy for the management of sex offenders in custody, which through therapeutic interventions, aims to reduce the risk of re-offending in the future.[100] The then Minister for Justice Dermot Ahern, announcing the new policy, said that it is designed "to ensure, as far as possible, that higher risk sex offenders will not simply serve out their sentences without engaging with the relevant services."[101] Initiatives are aimed at increasing the range and availability of therapeutic services in prison and promoting prisoner engagement with the

---

96 Thomas, "When Public Protection Becomes Punishment? The U.K. Use of Civil Measures to Contain the Sex Offender" (2004) 10 *European Journal on Criminal Policy and Research* 337, at 337. See also O'Malley, "Sentencing Recidivist Sex Offenders: A Challenge for Proportionality" in *Criminal Law and Procedure: Current Issues and Emerging Trends* (Bacik, and Heffernan ed, First Law, Dublin, 2009).

97 The fact that breaches will take place unless the individual can prove "reasonable excuse" invokes, as Rogan remarks, "a danger of establishing a 'shadow legal system' where individuals are accused of criminal activity on pain of punishment but without the traditional protections of the criminal law, short circuiting the protections of Article 38.1 in the process." Rogan, "Extending the Reach of the State into the Post-Sentence period: Section 26 of the Criminal Justice Act 2007" 15(1) *Dublin University Law Journal* 233.

98 See for example Ms Sullivan speaking at the Committee Stage of the Sex offenders Bill 2000, 10 October 2000.

99 *ibid.*

100 Irish Prison Service, *Sex Offender Management Policy: Reducing Re-offending, Enhancing Public Safety* (Irish Prison Service, Dublin 2009).

101 Department of Justice and Equality, "Ahern Announces New Policy for Managing Sex Offenders in Prison-Sex Offender Management Policy-Reducing Re-offending, Enhancing Public Safety", press release, 22 April 2009.

relevant services in an endeavour to support the rehabilitation of a greater number of sex offenders in custody than was possible under pre-existing interventions. A key element of this is the recognition that sex offenders comprise a diverse group with a range of needs and levels of risk. Thus, any interventions pursued aim to be informed by individual assessments and based on integrated sentence plans.[102] A strong multi-agency approach is also a key focus in managing offenders in the community once they are released from custody. The Prison Service, the Gardaí and the Probation Service, continue to work together, along with other relevant agencies in order to assess risk, monitor and assist offenders in the community. Promoting positive change in offenders, encouraging ties with family and society, as well as identifying those who pose a high risk of reoffending is a key objective of collaboration between these agencies.[103]

Acknowledging the deep and lasting impact of sexual offending upon individual victims and society as a whole, criminal justice systems are striving to find more effective ways of managing offenders and reducing the risk of reoffending. When it comes to sex offenders, there is a profound lack of trust in the ability of such offenders to reform and be integrated into law-abiding society. Public concern surrounding sex offending is justified given the harm sustained by such offending. However, the assumption that all sex offenders pose a high risk of reoffending is unsubstantiated by data available in this area. Research has shown that the rate of re-offending for sex offenders is lower than for most other types of offenders.[104] Thus it appears that although a small sub-group of sexual offenders may present a risk to public safety, the majority may not. Increased reliance upon risk assessment techniques in recent years reflects acknowledgement that "the best opportunity for changing offending behaviour is properly supervised and supported reintegration into the community and that resources should follow risk — that most attention should be directed at the higher risk sex offenders."[105] Punishment of serious crimes is a crucial feature of the criminal justice system and is merited in light of the harm incurred by criminal activity, but it is not the only remit of the system. [8–34]

---

[102] Irish Prison Service, *supra* note 100.

[103] See Irish Prison Service, *The Integrated Treatment and Management of those Convicted of Sexual Violence*, available at http://www.irishprisons.ie/wp-content/uploads/documents_pdf/sex_offender_management_may2016.pdf ; Fitzgerald O'Reilly, "Post Release Supervision of Sex Offenders" (2013) 23(4) *Irish Criminal Law Journal* 108.

[104] O'Donnell, Baumer and Hughes, "Recidivism in the Republic of Ireland" (2008) *Criminology and Criminal Justice* 123- 146; Probation Service. *Recidivism Study 2007 – 2011* (The Probation Service, Dublin, 2012); Irish Prison Service. *Recidivism Study* (Irish Prison Service, Dublin, 2013).

[105] Department of Justice and Equality, "Ahern Examines Future Management of Convicted Sex Offenders" press release, 27 January 2009.

Social reintegration of offenders also serves a role in redressing criminal wrongdoing. Rehabilitative measures, both in prison and the community, are an important step in the process of reintegration of offenders, which, if successful can reduce, and perhaps even eliminate the risk of reoffending in the future.

Supporting Victims

[8–35] Another key feature of criminal justice systems has been an increased concern for the rights of those who have suffered sexual abuse. Victim-centred discourse has highlighted shortcomings in the criminal justice system's approach to assisting victims throughout the various processes of the system. Developments such as victim impact statements, compensation orders, and procedural amendments have been introduced in an effort to remedy some of these shortcomings and enhance victim's satisfaction in the criminal justice system.[106] It has been argued however that such developments have not gone far enough in terms of assisting victim recovery.[107] The rhetoric of victims' rights all too frequently results in the endorsement of conservative political policies aimed at punishing offenders more severely, rather than supporting victims. While conviction and punishment of offenders may be seen as the mark of justice and victim satisfaction by many, empirical research reveals that what ranks high on victims' overall priorities is information, compensation and procedural justice.[108] Recent internationally-led efforts endeavour to incorporate the voice of the victim into the criminal justice system with a view to establishing long term strategies for promoting victim satisfaction and recovery. Directive 2012/29/EU of the European Parliament and of the Council of 25 October 2012 establishing minimum standards on the rights, support and protection of victims of crime, entered into force on 15 November 2012 and aims to ensure that victims of crime are recognised, treated with respect and receive proper protection, support and access to justice. Ireland has recently taken the positive step of incorporating this Directive into law under the Criminal Justice (Victims of Crime) Act 2017.

[8–36] Sexual violence is not just a criminal justice issue, however. It is a social issue that significantly affects the lives of those touched by such wrongdoing. The reach of the criminal justice system in remedying the impact of sexual violence is obviously limited and thus a co-ordinated multi-agency

---

106 See also Kilcommins and Moffitt, "The Inclusion and Juridification of Victims on the Island of Ireland" in *Routledge Handbook of Irish Criminology* (Healy, Hamilton, Daly and Butler ed, Routledge, 2016).

107 See Dubber, *Victims in the War on Crime: The Use and Abuse of Victims' Rights* (New York University Press, 2006).

108 Simmonds, "What victims want! Victim support, an objective or relative approach to victims' needs" (2009) 3(2) *Social and Public Policy Review* 11.

approach premised upon education and support is essential in responding to and preventing sexual violence.[109] Addressing the harm caused by sexual offending requires identifying and implementing comprehensive strategies for bringing offenders to justice and helping victims to cope and recover in the long term.

[109] See COSC. *Domestic and Sexual Violence Services in Ireland: Service Provision and Co-ordination* (COSC, Dublin, 2011); COSC. *National Strategy on Domestic, Sexual and Gender-based Violence 2010 – 2014* (COSC, Dublin, 2010). See also Keenan and Joyce, *Restorative Justice and Sexual Violence: Ireland Joins the International Debate* (Working Paper Series WP34 UCD School of Applied Social Science, Dublin, 2013).

INDEX